Buddhist Women
on the Edge

Buddhist Women
on the Edge

Contemporary Perspectives
from the
Western Frontier

Edited by
Marianne Dresser

North Atlantic Books
Berkeley, California

Buddhist Women on the Edge:
Contemporary Perspectives from the Western Frontier

North Atlantic Books
P.O. Box 12327
Berkeley, California 94712

Distributed to the book trade by Publishers Group West

Cover image, *White Tara,* oil on linen, 24" x 24"
by Dechen Fitzhugh, Santa Fe, New Mexico

Cover and book design by Paula Morrison

This is issue #55 in the *Io* series.

Buddhist Women on the Edge is sponsored by the Society for the Study of Native Arts and Sciences, a nonprofit educational corporation whose goals are to develop an educational and crosscultural perspective linking various scientific, social, and artistic fields; to nurture a holistic view of the arts, sciences, humanities, and healing; and to publish and distribute literature on the relationship of mind, body, and nature.

Library of Congress Cataloging-in-Publication data
Buddhist women on the edge : contemporary perspectives from the
    western frontier / edited by Marianne Dresser
        p.   cm.
    Includes bibliographical references.
    ISBN 1-55643-203-8 (pbk.)
    1. Women (Buddhism)   2. Buddhist women.   3. Feminism—
Religious aspects—Buddhism.   4. Buddhism—Social aspects.
I. Dresser, Marianne.
BQ4570.W6B83   1996
294.3'082—dc20
                                                        96-25436
                                                        CIP

2   3   4   5   6   7   8   9 / 01   00   99   98   97

Acknowledgments

THIS BOOK could not have come about without the participation and help of many people, especially the guides and teachers—formal and informal—who have shown me the Way. A deep *gassho* to my root-teacher Daigyo Moriyama Roshi and my Dharma sister Joshin Bachoux Sensei; to Issan Dorsey Sensei, who helped me through the crucial first weeks and months of practice with a playful spirit and his gentle, deft illusion-smashing ways; to my dear friend and an incomparable exemplar of grace, humor, and quiet determination, Shinma Dhammadinna; to Jakusho Kwong Roshi and the folks at Sonoma Mountain Zen Center, with whom I shared many brief but wonderful retreats; to Thich Nhat Hanh, for his work and wisdom and the beautiful series of teachings he gave on the theme of "First Love" during the June 1992 retreat at Plum Village; to Chokyi Nyima Rinpoche, who eased my mind and threw fruit to me under the Bodhi tree.

My gratitude and affection to my sister Jannie Dresser, for her love and support and many long conversations about religion and poetry; to Andrew Harvey and Eryk Hanut, for their vast generosity of spirit and unfailing kindness; and to the many friends with whom I have practiced, discussed, and gnawed on the Dharma over the years.

My gratitude to Paul Rosenblum, for showing that practice really can be integrated into the workplace; and to all my colleagues at North Atlantic Books, whose support and encouragement has been essential to the development and completion of this project.

And to Zélie Pollon, who has been my greatest teacher in the reality of impermanence and the resiliency of love—thanks for all and everything.

Contents

Editor's Introduction
xi

Miranda Shaw
Wild, Wise, Passionate: Dakinis in America
3

Sallie Jiko Tisdale
Form, Emptiness; Emptiness, Form
13

Kate O'Neill
Sounds of Silence
19

Anne C. Klein
Persons and Possibilities
39

Jane Hirshfield
What Is the Emotional Life of a Buddha?
45

Anita Barrows
The Light of Outrage: Women, Anger, and Buddhist Practice
51

Kate Wheeler
Bowing, Not Scraping
57

Marilyn Senf
Unlearning Silence:
A Further Feminist Revaluation
of Buddhist Practice
69

Jan Willis
Buddhism and Race:
An African American
Baptist-Buddhist Perspective
81

Lori Pierce
Outside In:
Buddhism in America
93

Tsultrim Allione
The Feminine Principle in Tibetan Buddhism
105

Melody Ermachild Chavis
Walking a Few Steps Farther
117

Alta Brown
The Ruthlessness of the Practice of Compassion
125

Rita M. Gross
Community, Work, Relationship, and Family:
Renunciation and Balance in American Buddhist Practice
133

Judith Simmer-Brown
Romantic Vision, Everyday Disappointment
151

Celeste West
My Tantric Flip-Flop
159

Barbara Gates
Watering the Garden with My Eyes Closed
163

Maylie Scott
A Short History of Buddhists at The Tracks
171

Anne Teich
Frontier Buddhism
179

Sandy Boucher
Not To Injure Life:
A Visit with Ruth Denison
199

Shosan Victoria Austin
Suzuki Sensei's Zen Spirit
209

Nina Egert
Coming Home
217

Thubten Chodron
You're Becoming a What?
Living as a Western Buddhist Nun
223

Michele Benzamin-Masuda
Fertile Ground for a Warrior
235

Ji Ko Linda Ruth Cutts
The Dark Clue
243

Susan Moon
Wholeheartedness
257

Anne Waldman
Poetry as Siddhi
263

Erin Blackwell
The Province of the Saved
277

bell hooks
Contemplation and Transformation
287

Pema Chodron
No Right, No Wrong
293

Glossary
305

Selected Bibliography
309

About the Contributors
315

Editor's Introduction

THE FIRST BUDDHIST TEACHER I encountered was an American woman: Jiho, a nun at a small Zen temple in a Tokyo suburb I visited while on a "temple tour" of Japan in October 1986. Jiho had the task of guiding our group through a session of *zazen*, sitting meditation. As the sweet smell of *tatami* and sandalwood incense mingled in the quiet *zendo*, I sat with my breath and watched my mind grasp at any and all stimuli—my neighbor's uncomfortable shifting, the tiny rip in the rice paper screen in the line of my downcast gaze, my stomach's early-morning rumblings, the far-off sound of a garbage truck. The beginner's mind of the utter neophyte allowed me a glimpse into my own thought patterns, the constant activity of "monkey mind." I saw how a simple mental notation: "noise"—was soon followed by elaborations—"what is it?" "where is it coming from?" "wish it would stop!"—and how each successive thought built on the previous one until my mind had wandered very far from my actual immediate experience. Then I'd notice the gap, and, as Jiho had instructed, return to my breathing. The mental engine would begin to wind down as I attended to the movement of air and energy through my body.

When the bell rang, signaling the end of the sitting, I was astonished. The much-dreaded thirty minutes couldn't have passed already; it felt more like ten. Over tea, Jiho patiently answered our excited questions about meditation, the temple, Zen Buddhism, etc. Then someone voiced what we were all wondering: "How did you end up becoming a nun?" She laughed and proceeded to quite frankly sketch her life's path: an "average" middle-class American relocating to Japan with her husband, her growing dissatisfaction with a mediocre marriage and career. Finally she said, "I just decided I wanted my life to be about something meaningful."

Jiho's calm good humor and unsentimental self-appraisal made a tremendous impression. And that first experience of meditation hooked me. It revealed that you could turn the mind to study the mind, that awareness made staying present possible. It opened a crack in the psychic armor I'd spent years building and maintaining. It affirmed the possibility of freedom.

The next guide I met was also a Western woman, a French Zen nun living at Zuigakuin, a monastery in the pine-forested mountains southwest of Fujisan. Joshin was the main disciple of the temple's abbot, Daigyo Moriyama Roshi. With his fantastic Bodhidharma eyebrows, Roshi was to become my first "formal" teacher, and even though the group stayed only one day there, Zuigakuin was to become my first spiritual home. Zen had already claimed me.

One year later I returned to practice with Joshin and Roshi for a month at Zuigakuin. Joshin showed me the ropes and impeccably performed the time-honored monastic routine that I faithfully attempted to follow. Though he spoke little English and I spoke even less Japanese, Roshi taught me through the example of his relaxed, cheerful, and energetic presence. In November 1987, after three quietly intense weeks, I took the Ten Precepts *(Jukai)*, the Four Bodhisattva Vows, and received a Buddhist name.

In the year-long interim between these two visits to Japan, I searched out a place to practice meditation at home in San Francisco. Opening a copy of the lesbian/gay community newspaper, I found a listing for the Hartford Street Zen Center in the Castro district. I started sitting there a few times a week, then every day, then twice a day, attending both morning and evening sittings and services. In retrospect, I am amazed at how easily I stumbled onto such a place, where I could bring under the lens of practice the many facets of my identity: white, working-class, lesbian, feminist, adult-child-of-an-alcoholic, recovering addict, artist, intellectual, skeptic.

At Hartford Street, I met my next guide: Issan, the unpretentious, wickedly funny, gay Zen priest who had just become the center's first resident teacher. Issan's luminous presence transformed Hartford Street into a haven of sanity. He had the gift of making outwardly austere Zen practice joyful—even as we chanted through frequent memorial services for men who had died of AIDS, some of whom had spent their last days in the rooms upstairs from the basement zendo, in the care of residents and volunteers. Initiated by Issan in direct response to need, this practice of compassionate care for the dying, mostly homeless and destitute gay men, grew into Maitri Hospice, which became a model for the AIDS hospice movement in San Francisco.

After a long struggle, Issan himself succumbed to the disease in September 1990. I was never Issan's formal student, though our relationship was friendly and, in an unremarked-upon way, intimate. He remains a profound influence on my practice; I often recall the words he spoke during memorial services: "We have bonds with one another that go beyond life and death." Issan's example was a powerful teaching: Buddhist practice is not separate from the world of suffering *outside* the meditation hall—the relative world of politics and society, inequality, greed, cruelty, and exploitation. It is a profound means of cultivating compassion and love and effecting transformation on both an individual and global scale.

◇

The idea and impetus for *Buddhist Women on the Edge* grew out of my own meandering path to and through Buddhism. In most ways I am a "bad" Buddhist—I cannot claim a long, uninterrupted residency at a center or monastery, or intensive study with a particular teacher and *sangha;* my relationship to discipline, authority, and institutions has always been ambivalent. I have alternated periods of deep engagement in daily practice with months and years in which I never approached a *zafu* at all. Yet since my first exposure to Buddhism a decade ago, it has in both subtle and obvious ways informed my life.

As an American woman trying to forge an authentic spiritual life within an adopted Eastern religious tradition, here in the waning years of the twentieth century, I have had many sometimes conflicting experiences. Making sense of them has not always been easy or even possible. I have experienced what psychologists term cognitive dissonance in the conflux of acknowledging and honoring the perceptions that arise within notions of selfhood—variously gendered, marginalized, socially constructed and prescribed—and Buddhist ideals of nonduality and spacious acceptance.

For me, one of Buddhism's most compelling teachings is the Middle Way: neither fixating on what is commonly called "conventional" reality—*samsara,* the world of suffering and delusion, the perceived, mundane world we mostly abide in—nor clinging to an apprehension of "ultimate" reality, *nirvana.* Enlightenment is said to be the realization of ultimate reality, an opening into a realm beyond duality in which the distinctions and hierarchies inherent in the workings of the relative world fall away. But the key to this spiritual scheme is the necessity of abiding in the middle, which I interpret to mean as not to deny the real consequences to living beings of the suffering characteristic of the relative world, even as we practice to see through and beyond it—to recognize our interrelationship with *all* aspects of reality.

In my own case, Buddhist practice and philosophy have helped me to acknowledge and reflect on uncomfortable and discouraging experiences I have had with some institutions and individuals. For two and a half years of regular attendance at Hartford Street, I was the sole woman in the zendo. While Issan and most of the members were welcoming, the center nonetheless took on at times the aspect of a men's club to which I remained an outsider. When I once approached a professor of Buddhist philosophy, a gentle scholar and translator of Tibetan texts and a practitioner himself, with a project that involved examining the notion of renunciation and the history of the *bhikshuni sangha* from a feminist perspective, he was nonplussed, believing that feminism amounted to nothing more than "male-bashing."

I have heard racist, sexist, and homophobic comments made by Buddhist teachers and practitioners who seemed unaware of their harmful effect or even of their significance as such. And I have ben confronted by hostile remarks from some in "my" own community who question how a lesbian feminist can be involved in what is admittedly a patriarchal religious tradition.

Should any of this come as a surprise? No, of course not; these examples reveal human tendencies, and as we are all subject to the imprint of our particular cultural, social, and psychological conditioning, points of friction are inevitable. But I believe there is real danger in an unwillingness to look deeply at these conditioning fac-

tors, not only at the individual level but in the collective constructions of society and culture. And the very human tendency to silence
the dissenting—and disturbing—voice, as in any other social institution, exists in sometimes insidiously subtle forms in Buddhist institutions and among groups, organizations, and businesses claiming
a Buddhist disposition.

The idea of an anthology presenting some of the many voices of
American women who practice, study, and teach Buddhism arose
from my own experiences and the issues they revealed. What might
the potential be for women's full participation in the development
and transformation of Buddhism in the West? *Buddhist Women on
the Edge* is one forum for this discussion, but it is by no means a
final or definitive one. When I first began studying Buddhism, there
were a handful of books by or about women in the tradition. Now
that number has greatly increased, with important new scholarship
restoring vital components of Buddhist texts and history and excellent practical guides by women Dharma teachers and practitioners.
This is an encouraging trend, and I hope it portends many more
works to follow.

This book sets out to explore critical perspectives on the particular concerns of American women in Buddhist practice. Topics
addressed include issues of gender, race, class, and sexuality; the
accessibility of Buddhist institutions and frameworks of lineage, tradition, and authority; monastic and lay practice, family life, and
community; teacher-student relationships; psychological perspectives and the role of the emotions; crosscultural adaptation and
appropriation; and how spiritual practice informs creativity, personal relationships, and political/social activism. While certain common themes emerge in the contributors' discussions of these often
overlapping topics, there are as many varying perspectives and opinions. The reader will not come away with a monolithic image of
women in American Buddhism, simply because no single viewpoint
could express this rich diversity.

The term "critical" proved to be somewhat problematic. Some
writers were initially concerned that the call for a critical perspective meant only heated critiques of inequities in Buddhist traditions
and institutions, or vituperative exposés of individual teachers' flaws.

But as the essays in this book reveal, a critical perspective in the deepest sense is bringing a clear and mindful intelligence to bear on one's lived experience. I echo the sentiments of Dharma teacher Pema Chodron, who enjoys "a good lively debate" and maintains that it is not the ideas that are most important, but that "people are out there debating them." She also reminds us that "It would kill the spirit of Buddhism if it became uncomfortable or dangerous for people to hold opposing views."

What a Zen teacher once called the "Great Doubt" is part of an integrated spirituality, as necessary to the path as faith, trust, and commitment. A fundamental premise within the tradition itself is the Buddha's injunction to "see for ourselves"—not merely to accept the teachings at face value, but to verify their efficacy by putting them into practice and reflecting mindfully on them and their potential for transformation. This is what the contributors to *Buddhist Women on the Edge* have done, and they have graciously agreed to share the fruits of their explorations.

It was also my intention for this anthology to help open up the discussion of Buddhism in America to those whose voices have historically been marginalized or unheard. This applies generally to women, but also to sexual minorities, lesbians and bisexuals; more pointedly, it concerns people of color, the working class, and the working poor. Issan, himself a member of a social underclass, noted the rarity of people of color and working-class people involved in practice when he once remarked on the "white middle-class face" of American Buddhism.

A lack of racial and ethnic diversity is certainly reflected in the demographics of the majority of American Buddhist communities and organizations. But I suspect that there are in reality many African American, Latina, Asian American, and Native American women involved in Buddhist practice or sympathetic to Buddhist ideas. Their stories need to be heard, and I hope others will add their efforts to the ongoing task of making available more work by those who have not had adequate access to the forum. Ultimately, as Jan Willis notes, "the question of what Buddhism has to offer African Americans and other people of color may not be as important as what such people have to offer Buddhism in America."

Buddhist Women on the Edge represents a cross section of American women's experience, perspectives from the fertile margins of the dominant discourse. The view from the edge is panoramic, clear, less obstructed by received knowledge or codified notions of "correct" views. It takes courage to stand on the edge, and to speak. Miranda Shaw points out that "Collectively and individually, women's gendered identity is attacked, devalued, and pathologized in many ways in our culture, and many of the forms of devaluation have religious roots. Our shattered self-esteem must deliberately be restored." Shaw and the other contributors to *Buddhist Women on the Edge* suggest many ways that women can engage in and shape Buddhist practice to this end. The accomplishment of this work is the reclaiming of our rightful place at the very *heart* of Buddhism.

I believe this reclamation is already well underway, and I hope the essays and reflections in this book will inspire many other women on the path.

Marianne Dresser
San Francisco, California
June 1996

Buddhist Women
on the Edge

Miranda Shaw

Wild, Wise, Passionate:
Dakinis in America

VAJRAYANA BUDDHISM in America will be revolutionized as women assume the leadership roles that we have enjoyed throughout the long history of this tradition—as teachers, initiators, revealers, artists, writers, prophets, healers, ritual experts, innovators, systematizers, interpreters. These roles will not be new for women, but a continuation of a pattern that can be traced to the very origins of the movement. Tantra has an ancient past, with roots deep in India's prehistory. This primal religion—life-affirming, openly erotic, honoring of women—merged with Buddhism in about the seventh century C.E., resulting in what we now call Tantric Buddhism, or Vajrayana.

The earliest texts trace the origins of this movement to circles of women practicing together in the countryside. These intrepid women gathered in remote locations where they wouldn't be disturbed, such as forest clearings, cremation grounds, and circular yogini temples. The women assembled in nonhierarchical circles, feasted together, and shared their spiritual insights with one another. They made their own ritual regalia: crowns and garlands of flowers, implements of human bone, drinking vessels made from a human skull. The women taught one another meditation and yoga and inspired one another with sacred dance and ecstatic songs conveying their insights into ultimate reality. They empowered one another as women and as spiritual seekers.

Female Tantrics are generally called *yoginis* or *dakinis*. "Yogini" means a female practitioner of yoga, or spiritually advanced female. "Dakini" derives from a verb meaning "to fly," so it can be translated most literally as "a woman who flies." The flight of the dakini is a flight of freedom—freedom from social restraints and freedom that comes from knowing ultimate reality. Sometimes dakini is translated as "sky-dancer" or "woman who dances in space." Certain traits recur in the descriptions of actual and ideal female Tantrics. The literature presents women who are physically and mentally powerful, speak the truth fearlessly, anger easily, love to argue, never back down in an argument, undergo wide mood swings, and laugh and cry readily. They are described as proud and arrogant, aggressive and domineering, fearless and intoxicated by their ferocity. They are said not only to be untamed but to revel in their untamability.

When I studied the actions of female Tantrics in biographical literature, one of the first things I noticed is that there are no external authorities limiting their behavior or speech in any way. They absolutely speak their minds without restraint. They never encourage one another to develop qualities that would appeal to men or to seek the approval of men. On the contrary, the women impose explicit requirements of speech and behavior, ranging from respect to ritual worship, upon the men. Further, women freely act as self-appointed teachers and guides of men. Their main target is male self-complacency, and they often target the over-intellectualization that can alienate a person from life and stand in the way of intimacy and passionate relationships. The women's self-confidence is evident from the fact that they do not hesitate to instruct or rebuke men they have just met, as well as their male disciples.

Men recognized the wisdom of these wild women, so obviously free from conventional reality, and were eager to apprentice themselves to them. They wished to gain admittance to the circles of yoginis because if they deemed a man worthy to attend, the women would initiate him and teach him their Tantric lore. At times each woman would bring a male companion to join the circle, to feast and practice yoga together. A list of the men who attended these feasts is in essence a "who's who" of the reputed male founders of Tantric Buddhism. These men adopted the yoginis' teachings as their own.

The women in turn revolutionized Buddhism with dramatic new understandings of gender, the senses, and sexuality. Their teachings and practices form the core of Tibetan and Nepalese Buddhism as living traditions today.

Women's pioneering role and ongoing leadership in Vajrayana have recently begun to be documented by historical scholarship. Continuing that enlightening role in contemporary America will require a sense of entitlement and worthiness to bring forward our insights, religious creativity, and spiritual gifts. In Tantra, religious authority now, as then, stems primarily from meditative mastery, mystical attainment, and visionary inspiration. Women suffer no innate disqualification under these criteria. Therefore, any authority that women assume today will not be a dramatic new development made possible by Western feminism, but a reclamation of the precise dynamics that gave rise to this tradition.

Women have already begun to take the lead in Vajrayana circles and centers in America. We should encourage this trend if we are to replicate the conditions that made this tradition great. American men may at times protest female leadership, resisting a loss of gender privilege, but they can claim no doctrinal or historical basis for doing so.

In addition to serving as spiritual preceptors and initiating gurus, women can assume leadership in many concrete forms. For example, women might bring forward new deities that reveal themselves to us in deep meditation, or new liturgies for deities we already practice. We can offer oral and written commentaries on inherited teachings and practices, enhanced by the touch of our experience and wisdom. We might arrange classical ritual elements in our own ways or improvise with new ones to design meaningful and effective rituals. We should add our artistic creations to the treasury of Tantric poetry, paintings, and dances. It is time to commence writing our spiritual autobiographies, chronicling our struggles to encourage other women on the path, not letting false humility or pride stand in our way.

Some of us should master the scholarly tools—such as translation and historical study—that can enable us to do research on the accomplished women who have gone before us. We must translate the writings by and about women, retranslate texts whose English versions have been marred by an androcentric bias, and recover teachings relevant to our spiritual lives. Translating Tantric material is a process of inspiration and revelation as well as linguistic skill, and thus it is essential that advanced female practitioners take on this lofty challenge. We should take the lead in bringing the Dharma to bear upon secular disciplines we have mastered, such as psychotherapy, social work, medicine, computer science, and the natural sciences. In this way, we can transform society as we transform ourselves.

Women in American Vajrayana should perpetuate the practice of the yogini feast, or dakini feast. Gathering in a circle expresses our equality as sister seekers and recognizes that we all have insights and skills to share. We discover our own strengths as we honor one another. The basic features of the feast can be retained: creating the boundaries of the ritual circle, sacramental food and wine, invocation of deities, meditation, mantras, prayer, magic, recitation of inspiring songs and poems by ourselves or other Tantric yoginis, and sacred dance. Following our ancient sisters, we should begin our feasts at twilight, so that inner vision can take over as darkness falls. Intuition may prompt spontaneous contributions to the proceedings. Such feasts can be staged at the close of a retreat, timed with phases of the moon, or convened to celebrate a holy day or pilgrimage. The dakini days of the Tibetan lunar calendar are particularly auspicious for this activity. On selected occasions we can invite male aspirants to join us. These feasts offer a form of transcendent play—a way to refine awareness, heighten bliss, and open the portals of pure vision, the ability to gaze into the sacred depths of reality.

The founding mothers of Tantric Buddhism prized their femaleness as a source of precious insights. They did not seek to eradicate, repress, or deny their gender in favor of a nondual, androgynous, or purely transcendent ideal. Following the lead of our wise and wild sisters, American women must teach one another not only to affirm but to glory in our femaleness. It is crucial that we encourage one another to savor female embodiment—to recognize the female body as a unique, complex, intricately attuned instrument for experiencing and embodying ultimate truth. The female body affords us valuable insights, perspectives, and modes of relating to the world. Once we have recognized the value of female embodiment, we can share our discoveries with the men in our midst. The Tantric path requires close cooperation between men and women, so it is incumbent upon men to learn to honor the women with whom they would share this sublime journey.

Collectively and individually, women's gendered identity is attacked, devalued, and pathologized in many ways in our culture, and many of the forms of devaluation have religious roots. Our shattered self-esteem must deliberately be restored. In Buddhism, insecurity and self-doubt are ego distortions and obstacles to enlightenment just as surely as are vanity and conceit. The specific form of self-esteem that is sought on the Tantric path is known as "divine pride." This confidence, or self-respect, is qualitatively different from arrogance. It is not motivated by a sense of deficiency, self-hatred, or desire to be better than someone else or dominate others.

Rather, divine pride comes from discovering a sacred female essence within oneself—a source of liberating energy, wisdom, and power that emanates from the depths of one's own being. Divine pride gives a woman a solid, unshakable basis for self-esteem. The Sanskrit term specifies that this pride is indestructible. When this transcendent sense of confidence is attained, a woman does not need to seek outer sources of approval or give in to the discouragement or sense of inadequacy that must be eliminated if she is successfully to traverse the Tantric path. It is essential to have inner resources upon which to draw during periods of solitude, difficulty, and active opposition. Divine pride replaces dependence upon others for approval, emotional nourishment, and spiritual sustenance.

A powerful resource that can assist us in developing positive understandings of femaleness are the female deities of Vajrayana. These archetypal images have served women as powerful role models, sources of inspiration, and objects of meditation for centuries. They figure in a Tantric meditation known as deity yoga. In this practice, a woman develops a vivid mental image of a given deity and then imagines herself to have the appearance, ornaments, awareness, and liberating powers of that deity. She understands the deity to represent her own spiritual capacities and enlightened essence.

The deities include female Buddhas like Vajrayogini, Vajravarahi, and Nairatmya, as well as numerous female enlighteners known as dakinis and yoginis—labels they share with their human counterparts.

These divine females are beautiful, sensual, and erotically alive, as well as disciplined, spiritual, and in fact enlightened—qualities that have been sundered from each other in the Western worldview. We may not yet have grasped the empowering potential of these figures because they have come to us through a filter of male interpretation. The prevalent trend of interpretation was set by early Western interpreters—notably, missionaries and colonial administrators—who were appalled by the exuberant sensuality and absence of clothing and embarrassment of these female figures and judged them to be prostitutes, having no adequate interpretive frame in which to comprehend them. They did not understand that the apparent lack of constraint of these females is not lack of discipline, but a deliberate abandonment of all dualistic categories of conventional thought and life and a purposive integration of every aspect of being. These potent images carry an exhilarating message of women's capacity to integrate our sensuality, sexuality, and spirituality.

The female deities of Vajrayana communicate a unique vision of female wholeness and authenticity. The female Buddhas and dakinis sizzle with energy that bursts around them as waves of energy and rings of flame. They are physically vigorous, dynamic females who blaze with vitality, intensity, and passion. Some adopt dance poses that reveal the body in all its female glory, without shame or fear. Some assume yogic postures that demand strength, discipline, and flexibility. Others leap and soar beyond every form of bondage and illusion—psychological, social, religious. They openly rejoice in their femaleness and revel in freedom of every kind. To me, these images embody a woman's ability to appreciate her own body and celebrate its true purpose. It exists to serve her, as a vehicle of her pleasure, joy, knowledge, power, and spirituality.

The faces of the female Buddhas and dakinis communicate the quality of their awareness. Their eyes burn with passion, ecstasy, ferocious intensity. Their gaze is not averted or demurely downcast. They do not look away, offering themselves as passive objects of observation, evaluation, or even appreciation. Rather, they stare straight ahead with piercing one-pointedness, gripping the eyes of the viewer, challenging engagement. This wide-eyed, unwavering expression embodies the ability to face reality directly—never flinching, never turning away, never retreating in fear from the realities and mysteries of life. Some of the figures have the head of a wild cat, such as a lioness or tigress, symbolizing the cauldron of raw power they have tapped within their own being. A woman on the Tantric path will at times manifest a feline ferocity as she becomes untamable by the standards of conventional reality, or develops an uncompromising intolerance of anything that would detract her from her goal. A yogini can not let anything stand between her and her experience of ultimate reality.

These female images represent the divine potentiality of all women. In this worldview there is no clear-cut dividing line between the human and the divine. The goddesses represent the innate divinity of all women, while women who have realized their divinity and attained enlightenment are seen as living goddesses, or living female Buddhas. These enlightened prototypes provide women with an immediate and independent source of self-empowerment that is not mediated by any other human being, social construct, or institution.

Archetypal images of female wholeness are indispensable as a source of positive self-understanding that a woman can cultivate in any environment. They provide an antidote to the poisonously negative and destructive female imagery that pervades our culture, destroying our ability to nurture, appreciate, and value one another and ourselves. Meditating upon images like these can inspire a woman to reenliven her body and spirit, awaken her divine potentialities, and rekindle the passion that can be directed to her spiritual practice and the fulfillment of her life's purpose.

It is crucial that women receive initiation and instruction in female deities from women. This has always been the case. In an initiation ceremony, the guru embodies the deity into which he or she is conferring initiation, literally channeling the deity's energy to the initiates. The word that we translate into English as "initiation" is more literally translated as "empowerment." The purpose of initiation is to empower the initiate to do successful practice upon that deity and to awaken the enlightened qualities of the deity within herself. In the case of a female deity, it is deeply meaningful for women when the initiation comes from a woman. A female guru can provide what a male guru cannot—namely, the presence of a female deity manifesting in a female mind and body.

When a woman experiences that power emanating from another woman, she is encouraged to discover the same enlightened essence within herself. Further, when the energy of a female deity is transmitted through a woman, there is no implicit suggestion that a male must be present at any point to mediate, legitimate, or authenticate this process. An initiation received from a male teacher can be sublime, but the process takes on another dimension when it comes from a woman. It makes the extraordinarily empowering statement that women can tap directly into the ultimate source of power, energy, and truth in female form. It powerfully communicates the sufficiency of female embodiment as a vehicle of total freedom.

An ancient discipline that can serve us well as we seek to reclaim, appreciate, and cultivate our bodies on the Tantric path is the practice of sacred dance. Tantric dance traditions are preserved in both Tibet and Nepal, and several American women have begun to develop their own interpretations of these esoteric forms. One traditional form is to dance as a deity upon whom one is meditating, to enhance the process of visualizing oneself as the deity. It is possible to identify more fully with a deity if one puts one's entire body into the process.

My own experience with the dance tradition in Nepal introduced me to the power of dance as an imaginative tool and yoga of transformation. This was the form of dance that plays a role in deity yoga, or the yoga of transforming into deity. One of the dances I studied is that of Nairatmya, a female Buddha whose selfless essence is vast, spacious awareness—symbolized by the blue color of her body. Learning the dance made her bodily stance, gestures, implements, ornaments, and facial expressions vividly concrete for me. Rather than simply committing these details to mental memory, they became part of the kinesthetic heritage of my body.

As I studied the dance of Nairatmya, I ceased to regard her as a two-dimensional form on a flat surface and began to experience her as a living presence. I realized this when I sat on the roof of the retreat center where I was staying to enjoy the tranquility of day's end. As I gazed into the sky, as was my daily custom, spontaneously I began to envision Nairatmya dancing in the clouds above me, high above the mountains, her body the color of the sky, her bone ornaments glistening in the rays of the setting sun. Sometimes it was Nairatmya dancing, and sometimes it was me, sporting among the clouds, looking down upon the mountains and the birds flying far below.

No longer a static painted or sculpted image, Nairatmya became a living, moving, dancing presence. Between dance sessions, Nairatmya's spacious mode of being would at times replace my own. I would experience a glimmer of her imperturbability, her insubstantiality, her emptiness. The converging emptiness of Nairatmya, myself, and the world dissolved the seeming solidity of phenomenal reality into shimmering, translucent shells encasing empty space, casting no shadows, leaving no trace.

During the dance sessions, I would struggle to attain her absolute poise as she balances on one leg; the utter gracefulness, precision, and harmony of her sweeping movements; the equanimity and concentration of her gaze. It was clear that my obstacles were not physical, but emotional and mental—my own lack of balance, detachment, tranquility, gentleness, and one-pointedness—internal impediments that now had physical reference points. The undulating hip movements unlocked the energies frozen in this part of my body, generating streams of bliss that fueled the dawning realizations of emptiness. I realized that dance can be a powerful tool of transformation, helping to release the treasures of the female mind, heart, and body and enrich our sense of the sacredness of the world and of ourselves.

◇

Every generation faces the challenge of creating tradition afresh. Tantra has never been handed down as an unchangeable body of teachings and practices. One of the hallmarks of Tantra down through the ages is its ongoing revision and reformulation. There is a saying that "the disciple must surpass the master." This recognizes that each person will express enlightenment in a unique way. There is an understanding that enlightenment must be embodied anew in each generation, adapted to changing contexts and expressed in new aesthetic and intellectual forms in response to the infinite needs of sentient beings.

Progress toward enlightenment is understood to bring a divinely inspired creativity, an ever-increasing ability to develop new ways to alleviate suffering and increase happiness, well-being, and freedom—and this includes the ongoing creation of tradition. Tantric leaders have freely introduced new deities, practices, liturgies, doctrinal teachings, and institutional arrangements to suit the needs of their times and disciples. By virtue of the openness of Tantra to perpetual re-creation, women in contemporary America have the opportunity to shape the tradition in accordance with our vision, insights, and requirements. There are no arbitrary external limits on women's degree of participation. Women are limited only by our own degrees of realization.

We must listen to the voices of our ancient sisters and chart our own course. Our Tantric foremothers revolutionized Buddhism with a torrent of inspired poetry, literature, meditation practices, deities, doctrines, and rituals. They used their wisdom and compassion, bliss and freedom, to liberate one another and the men who joined them as peers and companions in the spiritual quest. American women should follow in their footsteps today. If we do, we will discover that their trail leads to a spacious realm of skylike freedom where we can soar as freer, more powerful, ultimately fearless women.

Women have transformed Buddhism innumerable times in the past and can do so again. We must assume our ancient, rightful, destined roles if Vajrayana Buddhism is to flourish on American soil and serve its true purpose: to relieve suffering, increase well-being, and liberate *all* sentient beings.

Sallie Jiko Tisdale

Form, Emptiness; Emptiness, Form

SEVERAL YEARS AGO, in the sangha in which I've practiced for a long time, there was a kind of silent disquiet, like a faint perfume. I remember conversations from that period, encounters brief but biting; I remember men and women, women and men, unable to explain themselves.

I remember a woman speaking up at a meeting. She was lonely, she said. Lonely here. A long silence followed. One man, and then another, said they didn't know what she meant; neither had felt that way. Someone added—and I don't remember if it was a man or a woman, because this tension seemed to fall confusedly on all of us— "Gender is a problem here, you guys. Gender makes a difference."

Another student disagreed. He is mild and kind; we have practiced together for years. I think of him as an ally—a brother. Now he looks at the woman speaking as though they had never met, and when I see the look on his face, he becomes a stranger to me again.

In the strained silence, I try to figure out how to explain my belief that yes, gender makes a difference here. That the basic principles of feminism can be useful tools for examining our own inherited beliefs. I didn't know how to explain the growing irritation I felt— irritation I turned to fantasy.

I imagined the men lost in a sea of female authority for a day. When we softened the masculine references in the scriptures, I found myself longing to harden them in a new way—to change every *he* and *him* to *she* and *her* for a while. I imagined chanting an ancestral line of women every day, a matrilineal transmission eighty-three names long, without a single male name, imagined my sangha brother catching on to how isolating that imbalance can be. I felt righteous and a little bitter at times, and for awhile just full of fear. It wasn't this hash of mild discontent, not our tangled paths. It's simply that sometimes we all seemed very far away from each other. Before I can speak myself, my ally, my friend, said, "And another thing. We talk *way* too much about feminism around here."

I heard a murmur of voices around me, high and low, male and female. "Here, we are not men or women." Nodding, comfortable. "Gender is just an illusion."

◇

We go on together, now. Men and women, getting older, welcoming new members, saying goodbye to old ones, becoming better friends. We are all softening, I think—certainly I am. Almost all my anger and fear have faded away, replaced by a kind of happiness in whatever surrounds me, in chaos and order alike, in the quotidian details of a community.

And yet.

I read stories by women in the Buddhist journals: stories on the cultivation of the feminine in Buddhism, stories about the experiences of women teachers, accounts of sexual abuse, examinations of ancient teachings which seem to imply women are inferior to men in the practice. I read letters to the editors in response, letters by men calling the stories "pseudo-Buddhist claptrap" and bad thinking.[1] I come across a one-page diatribe by a man who calls himself a "Roshi," with cruel puns made out of the Dharma names of female teachers whose words on gender are "puerile ramblings." He harshly insists that gender has no place in the practice, that gender roles are "conceptual contrivances to be overcome with practice."[2]

The world tells me gender is destiny, inescapable; my daily experiences tell me that gender has much to do with the conditions in which I train. Yet many men tell me that gender—and my experience of it—is only illusion.

Acceptance. Freedom. Joy in all conditions. Of course. There are no victims here, and no pity. Form is only empty, and all empty, and emptiness is form. In the absolute, the vast, the One, my concern—the concern of many women—that sexism is deeply harmful and must be addressed, is a chimera. A cage of our own making. And still, the relative will rear its head. I sit a little differently from the men who have for thousands of years written the texts on how to sit. My *rakusu* rides the small, uneven hill of my breasts. My center of gravity is different, my back aches with my menses, menopause turns my meditation upside-down; the body teaches, and this is part of the lesson.

I wanted to spend the night in the zendo, sleep near the altar. I was alone—I wanted to be alone. And I felt a terrible fright; I felt the demons of the human world surround me. Women have to take care at night, even in zendos; women learn to take care all the time, to withhold something, stay a little tense. Women learn to watch out for empty elevators and stairwells and parking garages and drive with the car doors locked, all the time. Women learn that anonymous laws tell us what we can and cannot do in private with our bodies. I hear the stories other women in other countries (in Buddhist countries) tell, about painful lessons, about lies, about terrible punishments. I hear the lamentations of women, their long ululations of loss amid oceans of tears—losses unique to women, and so often compelled by men. I see massive historical patterns that are not coincidental, not imagined.

In the face of it, another kind of joy: a chain of simple recognition, one woman to another. A community with a common language of the periodic, the tiny pulsing tides of the female body, the peculiar qualities of this gender. The peculiar binding of shared experience.

I'm told this is more illusion: a community of women as women implies that there is intrinsic female nature and male nature and the two are not the same. It is, I'm told, "un-Buddhist" of me to revel in female company, for its femaleness. Femaleness and maleness are simply social constructs, to be let go, to let go.

And I have let it go; sometimes this particular construct falls away entirely, and *we* are truly not *many*, we are truly bound, he is not *he* and I am not *she*, and we sit beside each other in intimate silence. Then my Dharma brother weeps beside me in the zendo and when I breathe in, I breathe in his outward-flowing breath, and when I let my breath go, he and I sigh together. We are unstirred by the relative, by the moving, evanescent world.

Then we stir again.

Stirring—not stirring—two, not two. Femaleness and maleness come into the world along with everything else, in a cycle of ignorance and movement and change, shaping the world and being shaped in return. We are born in a maze of body and mind, made into *men* and *women* by our culture. We make each other men and women by our experience. Practice, and acceptance, and real joy, is the dance between and beyond these distinctions. Beyond *and* between. One *and* many. Gender is not an illusion. Gender is karma.

"Make your mind as vast as the sky," writes the angry "Roshi," "Do not make man, do not make woman." That man and woman are already made, that each of us comes to the practice carrying them on our back, seems not to matter to him here. I want to tell him that it is just as contrived to refuse to attend to conditions as it is to live completely in them, but I doubt he would listen. That his anger seems personal and exaggerated he does not, I think, even know.

Personal responsibility for pain, gratitude simply for the ground beneath me, the spring of joy in every circumstance, the relinquishing of the past, the acceptance of all that has gone before—this is one side of a coin. Seeing clearly how the past appears in the present, seeing how each of us inherits cultural beliefs, is colored by historical circumstance, tends to perpetuate such circumstance, is the other side. And it is just one coin. In fact, this fine and troubling line is a central point of practice, endlessly subtle. We have to try not just to see each other, but to inhabit each other completely even as we let go. We have to accept, and act—not one, but both.

A letter writer says, "For a woman or a man to be free does not require doing anything about gender roles (although gender roles are ridiculous and deserve to be ignored). . . ."[3] Oh, I wholeheartedly agree. We need "do nothing" about conditions to be free. Gender roles *are* ridiculous. They are as ridiculous as racism, poverty, and ethnic wars. If it is ignorance to dwell too deeply in the harm they cause, what is it to pretend the harm does not exist?

Sometimes I cling to my illusory female self, cling because it feels so real. Again and again I hear men clinging to their view that it is illusory. If I love my illusion of the female, perhaps they love the illusion that they are not somehow male. Seeing illusion—*seeking* illusion—we can miss the subtle delusion within. My letter writer wants to live in his heresy of the Void, his dream of the undifferentiated; he wants me to take my illusions and my karma somewhere else, so he can imagine they are gone.

I know there is a place between, beyond, emptiness and form—a place of emptiness, form; form, emptiness. Nirvana, samsara; samsara, nirvana. That's where we are men and women, not men, not women, women and men, all at once. Where we are not two, and two. Know me by my illusions; this is one of the best ways we can know each other. Let me know you by yours. We are sacks of karma; let me know your karma, so I can know you. How else can we find each other? How else can we, together in a sangha, a community of human beings, find our way?

1. Letters: "Does Patriarchy Cause Suffering?," *Shambhala Sun,* Vol. 4, No. 3, January 1996, p. 7.

2. Zenshin Roshi, "Sex, Lies and American Buddhism," *CyberSangha,* Winter 1995, p. 28.

3. Letters: "Does Patriarchy Cause Suffering?," p. 8.

Kate O'Neill

Sounds of Silence

Silences. Not the silences between notes of music, or the silences of a sleeping animal, or the calm of a glassy surfaced river witnessing the outstretched wings of a heron. Not the silence of an emptied mind. But this other silence. That silence which can feel like a scream, in which there is no peace. The grim silence between two lovers who are quarreling. The painful silence of the one with tears in her eyes who will not cry. The cry of the child who knows she will not be heard. The silence of a whole people who have been massacred. Of a whole sex made mute, or not educated to speech. The silence of a mind afraid to admit the truth to itself. This is the silence the poet dreads.
—Susan Griffin[1]

"No eye, or ear, or nose, or tongue, or body, or mind. . . ."[2] These words from the *Heart Sutra* do not convey that things are truly empty, merely that they are empty of our ideas about them. To experience this is to stand in the truth of all life. This experiential ground of interconnectedness resonates throughout Buddhist teachings and practices. The table at which I write is made of wood; the wood came from a pine tree; the pine tree grew in the presence of intense sunshine and downpours of rain. There are key differences, however, in various kinds of emptiness, between what writer Susan Griffin describes as "the silence of an emptied mind" and "that silence which can feel like a scream, in which there is no peace."

The unacknowledged sexist bias inherent in many Buddhist teachings and forms has felt like a silent scream, a lack of peace for many women. Fortunately, some Buddhist writers and teachers have begun to address these issues.[3] Most of the stories told in Western culture, however, if not in fact told by and about men, are still imbued with patriarchal language, forms, and assumptions. Direct expressions of women's experiences have not entered most of Western culture intact, and this includes Buddhist practice in the West. The only record we have of the women who co-created Buddhism are the songs of enlightenment of the first Buddhist nuns. Then there is silence for hundreds of years.

My hope here is to share some observations from my personal experiences as a practitioner. I am *not* a Buddhist scholar or a Dharma teacher. Many of the ideas in this piece are new explorations for me, and I invite your openness and responsiveness. We are all more than the sum of our parts, but it may be helpful to know that my writing is informed by my experiences as an Irish-American, lesbian, feminist, Buddhist of mixed-class background and relative good health and ability. I am presently thirty-seven years old and I expect within the next year to complete a doctoral degree in human development and psychology at Harvard University in Cambridge, Massachusetts.

Since 1984, I have studied mostly in the vipassana and Zen traditions with both female and male teachers. Over the years, I have sat numerous one- to ten-day retreats, several two- and three-week retreats, and have taken several classes on various sutras. In 1992, I took the Fourteen Precepts of the Order of Interbeing with Vietnamese Zen teacher Thich Nhat Hanh. For many years I practiced weekly with a Buddhist sangha in Massachusetts, and now I practice weekly with a sangha in New Mexico.

I want to begin this exploration by sharing a few examples of the integration of politics and practice which have been particularly inspiring to me, and then explore from my perspective some specific ways in which gender, sexual orientation, and politics may weave together in Buddhist practice.

◇

In the early 1990s, in Boston, Massachusetts, I met on occasion with a Vietnamese Buddhist sangha. Their temple was near a large, beige-brick housing development, and what had once been a basketball court for the neighboring housing development was their parking lot. One day their offices were broken into, a computer was stolen, and their temple was vandalized. A leader of the Vietnamese sangha was interviewed on television. As he gazed steadily into the camera, he said simply, "I am trying to look more deeply, to understand why these people came and stole from us. Yes, I would like our computer back. But mostly, I wish to speak with the thieves, to see if there is something that we have done. Perhaps they want their basketball court back."

His compassionate attitude had an amazing ripple effect in the community. His looking deeply opened a way beyond crime and punishment, beyond violation and retribution. It was amazing to see him speaking like this on the evening news. This leader eventually did talk with the young men who broke into the Vietnamese temple, and the computer was returned. The community did not press criminal charges. Instead, they arranged for the young men to have access to their basketball court part of the time.

This urban center of Buddhist practice, like every other place of Buddhist practice, exists in a particular physical, social, and political environment. "Politics" comes from the Latin word *polis,* meaning "people." The essence of politics is people. The politics of Buddhism is the interconnection of all beings. This Vietnamese sangha leader gave our sangha, and the whole city, a powerful teaching on how to integrate practice and politics in a very poignant and concrete way.

As I remembered this event, I was reminded of something Thich Nhat Hanh once wrote. I was drawn to study with Thich Nhat Hanh because of the explicit political connection throughout his work, what he calls "socially engaged" Buddhism. Many years ago he addressed the distinction between religious ritual and the spiritual essence of Buddhist practice in one of his books. He described a conversation in which he was asked by an Israeli rabbi, "'What if Buddhism cannot survive in Vietnam? Will you accept that in order to have peace in Vietnam?' 'Yes,' he replied, 'I think if Vietnam has real peace—cooperation between North and South—and if it can ban war for a long time, I would be ready to sacrifice Buddhism.'"

Thich Nhat Hanh continued, "He was very shocked. But I thought it was quite plain that if you have to choose between Buddhism and peace, then you must choose peace. Because if you choose Buddhism you sacrifice peace and Buddhism does not accept that. Furthermore, Buddhism is in your heart. Even if you don't have any temple or any monks, you can still be a Buddhist in your heart and life."[4] This speaks to the pure root of Buddhist understanding, beyond forms of practice—rituals and chanting, sitting and walking meditation. This interpretation of Buddhism reflects the silence of an "emptied" mind: a mind beyond concepts.

What a radical notion—that we could drop the arbitrary boundaries of national borders, and even, in this case, the religious forms of spiritual practice. The attitude of the urban sangha leader and Thich Nhat Hanh's talk with the rabbi exemplify skillful means of integrating politics and practice: addressing the reality of political situations and feelings, without becoming solidified or polarized around political issues. A delicate balance, to be sure. No-thing is something in itself. Any-thing exists only in relationship with something else. From a place of deep understanding, differences are only differences to the point where they become different and yet the same. Everything, in its particular uniqueness, is interconnected. It is in this spirit that I wish to talk about political differences, not that they stand alone—or are somehow "true" in their seeming enormity, but simply that they effect and connect the psychological and material conditions of our lives.

Buddhism and feminism both require looking deeply into the nature of phenomena and experiences. Both facilitate receptivity and openness, which have traditionally been associated with a more feminine consciousness. Once we see the deeply ingrained oppression of women, and acknowledge that suffering, it opens our hearts and minds to a more compassionate awareness of women's experiences in the world. On an individual basis these issues of oppression can feel like the "silence of a mind afraid to admit the truth to itself." And yet, in connection with others, we can experience deep resonance. As psychologist Carol Gilligan has noted, "To have something to say is to be a person. But speaking depends on listening and being heard; it is an intensely relational act."[5] Buddhist practice asks of us that we sensitively and mindfully witness our own experiences, what we might call developing a "reflexive relationship" with ourselves. From witnessing, we move into the realm of pure intimacy with ourselves: simply *being* our experiences one by one. In addition, I think we also need affirming, responsive human relationships with others. I learned a lot about witnessing my own experiences in the presence of others when I first began to practice.

I began to meditate in early 1984, honoring a New Year's resolution. I went to a local spiritual bookstore and bought a basic guide to meditation. I set up a small corner of my living room, put a stuffed sofa pillow on the floor, and lit a stick of sandalwood incense. I chose a morning when I knew that I would have the house to myself. I sat down cross-legged, closely following the diagram in the book. I closed my eyes and slowly began to follow my breathing in and out, counting as I did. And that's about as far as I got—not because my mind wandered, but because I broke out in a sweat and started flinching. Almost from the minute I closed my eyes, I began experiencing what I later understood as body memories of trauma flooding my senses. At the time I had no language for what was happening to me; I just knew that I felt very anxious and vulnerable. I tried several remedies. I tried sitting with my back to a wall, hoping I wouldn't fear being assaulted from behind. I played quiet instrumental music, hoping to ease my tension. I tried sitting in a different room, a different time of day. Eventually, I gave up trying to meditate sitting alone.

I concluded that I needed to learn a form of self-defense, and decided on t'ai chi. The next week I signed up for a class at the adult education center. This proved to be very useful, although I almost dropped out of the class several times. I had been sexually assaulted by an Asian man ten years previously, and the t'ai chi class was taught by an Asian man. I promised myself I was going to hang in there. Four months later, I had finished the class and was able to sit and meditate without such strong physical reactions. I have heard from other women who have had similar traumatic experiences, and similar reactions to sitting still in meditation. I literally felt like a sitting duck. (I imagine some male trauma survivors may have similar experiences.)

I think t'ai chi class worked for me in a way sitting practice did not initially for several reasons. It was a form of self-defense, so I felt safer, and it was a more physically active form that allowed me to discharge some anxiety. Also, I could keep my eyes open, so I felt more protected. And, although I had more than one experience of trauma that may have been triggering my physical reactions, the consistent, time-limited exposure to what had for ten years been a trigger—namely the sight of an Asian man—gradually lessened. And finally, I was not sitting alone but was practicing with other people.

The practice and awareness of this kind of healing process, namely self-defense training, may be beneficial for others. It fits with trauma theorist Judy Herman's three-part model of recovery: getting safe—physically and emotionally; witnessing your experience—alone and with others; and reintegrating traumatic experience into everyday life.[6] Some women (and men) who have experienced trauma may find a way to engage in sitting practice without also exploring and practicing other forms. But when I recall the statistic that one in three women and one in six men are sexually abused before the age of eighteen, I feel there may be a more conscious need for an integration of a Western understanding of trauma and recovery along with Buddhist teachings of acceptance and practice.

◇

In the late 1980s, I attended a course at the Insight Mediation Center in Cambridge Massachusetts with a Tibetan teacher, Tara Tulku Rinpoche. During one talk, a participant asked Rinpoche about paying attention to her perceptions because she felt that this was particularly important as a woman. Robert Thurman translated Rinpoche's response: "Yes, women have been oppressed for centuries; you need to pay careful attention to your perceptions." I was stunned. For months I had been taking wonderful classes at this center and listening to inspiring Dharma talks. We were told to let go: let go of thoughts, let go of feelings, don't hold on to anything. Now here was this Tibetan Rinpoche telling us to pay careful attention to our perceptions—particularly as women! I was both grateful and shocked.

I sat in puzzled silence, letting his words sink deeply into my bones.

This feeling of amazement lasted for a few moments and then I gradually became annoyed. I realized that Rinpoche probably would not have made this incredibly important point if a woman in the class had not asked him about it explicitly. I appreciated his response, but I was also frustrated that his comments confirmed what I had already begun to suspect: that women had to calibrate the teachings to make them fit our experiences of life and practice. This was not a "one-size-fits-all" teaching. Even the Buddha said, in essence, "Do not believe in anything simply because you have heard it,"[7] implying that all of us need to pay attention to our own perceptions. I sat in the meditation hall thinking: We need to translate women's experiences into traditional Buddhist teachings, just as Robert Thurman is translating this Rinpoche's words from Tibetan into English.

I had been practicing meditation for a year or so at the time I heard this talk. Back then I kept wondering how I could give up "ego" when I was still struggling so hard, especially as a woman, to claim one in the first place. A phrase from a twelve-step program kept passing through my mind: "Take what you like and leave the rest." Each time this phrase floated through my mind, I noted the simultaneous emergence of guilt. This was not how Buddhist practice was "supposed" to be. As I understood it at the time, we were supposed to sit still, follow our breathing, follow the teachings. Whatever happened, we were not supposed to give in to the wandering, craving, aversive notions of the human mind in all of its clever complexity. If the mind wandered, you brought it back to the breath, just as you would take a wayward child by the hand and gently lead her away from oncoming traffic. We were encouraged to *forget* what we liked, not to distinguish it from the rest. No greed, no hatred, no delusion: no preferences.

Okay, I could buy that up to a point. But I kept feeling that as a woman, I needed more skillful means of transporting my psyche, such as it was, into more enlightened states. I kept struggling with my sense that the only way out is *through*, and the only way through is *intact*.[8] I kept sensing that women especially need to value our experiences, so that we have the possibility of seeing them more clearly, even if we then let them drop away. As Canadian writer and feminist theorist Nicole Brossard describes it, women, "through force of circumstance, will go so far as to have impressions of impressions, to the point where they have the impression that it is all in their head, made up, and that their perceptions are, after all, simply the fruit of their imagination."[9] This interpretation of imagination is different from the Buddhist notion of delusion, partly, I think, because this "gas-lighting" is a common experience based on gender, not simply an individual's misconception of the nature of reality. We need to acknowledge and accept our perceptions in order to "see through" them, to see through the delusion. Mindfulness cuts through delusion. Perhaps it is cultural delusion, but I wonder how it might be addressed as such, especially since a culture, per se, cannot meditate, only individuals can. Only a community that is mindful of oppression can work to eliminate it.

In a recent article on how women teachers are changing the practice of Buddhism in America, vipassana teacher Michele McDonald-Smith recalled:

> As a student, I didn't get much help from teachers in learning how to integrate the emotional work into practice, and that was very hard. Having certain traumas surface forced me to listen to myself, in my life as well as during retreats. I couldn't just sit and walk, sit and walk. I had to go off by myself and really open to my emotions before I could sit and walk again. There was no choice but to find my own way, because at the time there was no model for what I needed in Buddhism.[10]

There are now, however, women teachers (and more conscious male teachers) emerging who are acknowledging the particular experiences of women in practice. Although the Dharma is neither male nor female, most of us encounter very real differences in our daily lives based on gender. My experience is that there are many subtle differences between practicing with female and male teachers. I keep struggling to put into words this question of how to address these psychological, and perhaps even, dare I say, spiritual differences, without categorical language. It seems to me that one risk of practice without context may be an infinite regression into neutrality and relativity similar to the conundrum that I believe deconstructionism, with its multivariate analyses, leads us to.

There are several ways in which many women's experiences differ from men's. Making such broad claims about human beings who happen to be female risks a certain essentialism, as if these generalized differences are biologically determined. I believe, however, that these differences are in fact culturally prescribed and enforced rather than genetically imposed.

The first obvious difference has to do with female and male physical bodies: size, strength, endurance, abilities, sexuality, reproductive capacities, and experiences. All of these aspects of physical form exist in the context of cultural politics and political power surrounding these realities.

The second major difference has to do with violence against women. Statistical evidence makes a clear point: "95 percent of all violent domestic crime is perpetrated by men against women."[11] One in three women who go to hospital emergency rooms are there for injuries relating to ongoing domestic abuse.[12] According to the March of Dimes, the leading cause of birth defects in America is domestic violence. In addition to domestic violence, sexual assault is another grim reality.

The third aspect of experience shared by many women is economic oppression. Only 9 percent of working women in America make over $25,000 per year. Women are segregated in the lowest paying "pink collar" jobs—secretaries, waitresses, day care workers, and so on. Full-time women workers earn an average of seventy-six cents for every dollar earned by a man. Despite the horror stories of "welfare abuse" we hear, welfare comprises only 1 percent of the annual United States budget. A woman on AFDC with two children gets an average of less than $380 per month, which is still below the poverty line for a family of three in America.[13]

Besides these clear political reasons why women's experiences differ significantly from men's, I find the evidence for a different psychological development particularly compelling. According to the work of sociologist Nancy Chodorow,[14] girls develop with a psychological sense of connection and identification with their female primary caregivers (i.e., mothers); boys are thought to develop a psychological sense of separateness, based on their disidentification with their primary caregiver's gender (i.e., female). I would add that there is ample evidence from numerous psychological studies demonstrating that we treat boys and girls differently from the time they are conceived. Indeed, the first question we usually ask is: "Is it a boy or a girl?"

This seems to me to inform the emphasis in Buddhist practice, which has historically been based on male experience, of breaking down ego boundaries and separateness and focusing on interbeing and interconnectedness.[15] For women in practice, the emphasis may more appropriately be put on developing a clearer sense of perceptions and awareness. Especially during the earlier stages of practice, women may benefit more from learning to trust and acknowledge their own experience and perceptions.

The centrality of relationships in girls and women's development may also play a key factor in how many women experience themselves psychologically. The centrality of connectedness may be touched experientially by women more quickly in practice because of the relational nature and conditioning of girls and women. This has been my experience of the teachings so far. Obviously, attentiveness to both connectedness and perceptions are necessary for women *and* men.

Feminist psychological theorist Jean Baker Miller has come up with five phenomena associated with "growth-enhancing" relationships. I wonder how these aspects of relationship connect with Buddhist practice. Miller describes growth-enhancing relationships as those which include these criteria:

Each person feels a greater sense of zest (vitality, energy);

Each person feels more able to act and does act;

Each person has a more accurate picture of her/himself and the other person(s);

Each person feels a greater sense of self-worth;

Each person feels more connected to the other person(s) and greater motivation for connections with other people beyond those in the specific relationship.[16]

These five points seem compatible with much of Buddhist teaching and practice. In describing what is essential in a healthy human relationship, theorist Janet Surrey says "'Being with' means 'being seen' and 'feeling seen,' which is the experience of mutual empathy."[17] In Buddhism this is described as compassion (literally, "feeling with"), without getting caught or attached.

The relational needs of women are complex, both intrapsychically, i.e. how to balance "feeling with" self *and* others; and interpersonally, i.e. how to practice with children, family responsibilities, and often work outside the home. In addition, the centrality of relationships in women's development may mean adjusting Dharma teachings to include more interpersonal interaction between teachers and students, in sitting groups, and among sangha members. Given women's role as "the keepers of relationships," it may also, paradoxically, mean allowing women to be quiet, to not have to interact so much. The key point, I think, is to acknowledge and honor women's relational orientation in approaches to Buddhist practice.

One's relationship with oneself, especially for women, also needs to be an integral focus of practice. Intimacy with oneself is the deepest intimacy. Ultimately, it is intimacy with all beings, with everything. We all, teachers and practitioners alike, must take into account the importance of relationships in human development—especially for women, but also for men and children. By relationship I mean, ideally, a moment-by-moment present meeting with another being, especially other human beings. A relationship may happen instantaneously or develop over time. The critical element is the quality of the interaction, a kind of attentive back-and-forth, a kind of play, rather than a possession or usage of one being by the other. This is also true in our relationship with ourselves.

◇

In terms of practicing as a lesbian Buddhist, several issues have emerged for me. One is a desire to lessen or eliminate sexist, patriarchal language and heterosexist, homophobic language that assumes that everyone is heterosexual and partnered, and/or wants to be. The second is a wish to confront the fear of gay sexuality, lesbian sexuality, bisexuality, and the lack of willingness to openly discuss it. We live in the relative world as well as the absolute. The relative world is shaped by political and social constructs just as the absolute realm is empty of distinctions on the basis of gender, race, class, sexual orientation, able-bodiedness, and so on. Oppression is not simply a matter of bigotry, but rather of the institutional power to impose and enforce prejudice. Only those with power, status, and the economic means to do so can oppress others through institutional sexism, racism, classism, and homophobia.

Using gender-inclusive, non-heterosexist language and inclusive teaching stories are ways that all sangha members can feel more recognized within Buddhist traditions. Recognizing more women teachers, women and men teaching together, and openly lesbian, gay, and bisexual Dharma teachers are also ways to move toward greater inclusivity. As Thich Nhat Hanh once said, "The emptiness of delusion is the fullness of reality." Buddhists are just as capable of using silence as a cover-up, a form of delusion, as we are of making full contact with the diversity of our relative reality.

Instead of simply reacting to negative stereotypes, I also wonder what it would it be like to envision a world without sexism and homophobia. How might the "fullness of reality" be deepened by allowing these delusions to fall away? Here are some answers to this question generated by members of a social change workshop:

> Kids won't be called tomboys or sissies; they'll just be who they are, able to do what they wish.

> People will be able to love anyone, no matter what sex; the issue will simply be whether or not she/he is a good human being, compatible and loving.

> Affection will be opened up between women and men, women and women, men and men, and it won't be centered on sex; people won't fear being called names if they show affection to someone who isn't a mate or potential mate.

> If affection is opened up, then isolation will be broken down for all of us, especially for those who generally experience little physical affection, such as unmarried old people.

> There will be less violence if men do not feel they have to prove and assert their manhood. Their desire to dominate and control will not spill over from the personal to the level of national and

international politics and the use of bigger and better weapons to control other countries.

There will be no gender roles.[18]

A heterosexual male friend of mine, a student of Thich Nhat Hanh who was also very involved in the men's movement, remarked to me one day in a conversation that most American men would think that Thich Nhat Hanh was "a sissy or a faggot" because of his pacifist stance. Issues of gender and sexuality are more related to Buddhist practice than we usually allow ourselves to recognize.

My perceptions, and my experiences in practice, are influenced by my being a woman and also by my being a lesbian. I've experienced enough to know that my gender and sexual orientation will definitely close some doors and prejudice some minds. These are real experiences: prejudice and fear are real experiences on both the transmitting and the receiving end. We can settle on the breath, transcend all differences mentally, but there are certain aspects of our lives, in whatever forms they take, which are ours to deal with. These are experiences with which I deal, and bring to my individual practice and to my practice community. It was possible for me to take precepts with Thich Nhat Hanh, to make that level of commitment, because I felt welcomed by a supportive community of practice as a lesbian woman. In many places in which I've practiced these aspects of my experience haven't been overtly discouraged so much as they have simply been silenced.

Thich Nhat Hanh's teaching that nonviolence begins with ourselves has been a very helpful practice in dealing with my own internalized fear. Beyond this, I think lesbians offer Buddhism their understanding of oppression and also, along with all women, an understanding of the importance of relationships. Many lesbians, and others, are also involved with social change and have experience with alternative models of living and working together which can potentially be of benefit to Buddhist communities.

Lesbians and gay men are unlike other oppressed groups in that we have to recreate our communities anew each generation. We crack through the concrete of cultural stereotypes like unwanted weeds, and come through to our true selves only with great determination.

We learn intimately the nature of our suchness because we live in a world where we need to be consciously, and self-consciously, aware of who we are. We are required by our difference to choose between hiding ourselves or making our identities explicit in relation to family, community, and society at large. Because of fear and misunderstanding many of us have felt exiled from family, from other people, and from the larger society.

I actually think of myself, self-consciously, as a lesbian only a small fraction of the time. It is only a part of who I am. But there is a persistent voice in the back of my mind, necessitated by survival, which says: *Don't assume you're safe, don't assume you're understood, don't assume you're included, don't assume you'll be treated the same, one way or the other.* Someone once asked: What kind of a world is it where they give you medals for killing people, and condemn you for loving them? That world is the relative but real world of ignorance.

In Plum Village, Thich Nhat Hanh's community in France, a group of gay men, lesbians, and bisexuals met at the end of the June 1990 retreat to discuss the Dharma and our practice together. We composed and read the following *gatha,* or short verse, to the community as our gift to the sangha:

> *Having met as gays and lesbians*
> *and spoken together from the depths*
> *of our common pain and joy,*
> *we vow to acknowledge*
> *visible and invisible suffering*
> *from past, present, and future,*
> *and help alleviate it.*

Feminists have been saying for a very long time that the personal is political. Buddhist practice is also both personal and political. Religion, in fact, is more often about politics than about spirituality. We can try to wipe the glass clean, but we are still looking through the window of our experience. How else could it be? Especially when that experience is double- or triple-layered by gender, race, sexual orientation, and all the other experiences that require us to be aware of the values both of the dominant culture and our various subordinate cultures. Our survival has depended on learning to see things the way the dominant group or patriarchal traditions see them and teach them; our thriving has been in also understanding the world as *we* experience it. Buddhism teaches us that we are also, always, connected with all sentient beings.

I have practiced with teachers who embody the integration of traditional patriarchal teachings and a more inclusive feminist perspective in their teachings. One way they do this is by sharing teaching time, Dharma talks, interviews, and so on equally between female and male co-teachers. Another way they bring this awareness into teaching is explicitly to include the content of women's experience. A woman might explore how the experience of giving birth, or of being assaulted, relates to her Dharma practice; or she might mention her relational connections with other people, the importance of mother-child interactions, and so on. Many male teachers may be more comfortable talking about the lineage of Buddhist patriarchs than they are talking about screaming, crying infants. But together, such teachers can foreground the interplay of feminist and traditional teaching in good faith and with a good deal of humor. Western teachers, female and male, are evolving styles of teaching where they talk more directly about their lives as practice—revealing, yet again, that the personal is political *and* spiritual.

I am amazed at the absence of common references to women's experiences in most Buddhist discourse. There is a long history of perhaps unconscious, perhaps unintentional, patriarchal bias skewing the teachings toward men's experiences. Historically there have been many fewer women teachers. It is time these assumptions changed, and this kind of call-and-response teaching is but one way. I hope this dialogue continues to deepen and flourish.

◇

In September 1994, I went to Ireland, my ancestral homeland. Once I arrived, I traveled to a tiny crossroads on the western coast, where my great-grandparents lived: Maam, County Galway. My grandfather was born there in 1877. I looked around and took in the unrelenting, rounded marble mountains of Connemara, their hillsides dotted with long-haired sheep. I stood and stared at the gray, chalk cliffs, blinked at the cloud-spattered, sun-drenched day, and closed my eyes. This, I thought, *this* is what my face before I was born looked out upon.

I doubt the place has changed very much since my great-grandparents' day. A few cars, electricity, otherwise the valley is still remote and a bit desolate, full of the smell of peat fires in the tart, early-autumn air. The whole valley is called "Joyce Country." My great-grandmother's name was Mary Bridgette Joyce. The old Catholic Church records did not tell me anything else about her. As I question my connections with her I wonder about her life: Did Mary Bridgette Joyce know how to read and write? Did she ever write poetry? Did she have time? How old was she when my grandfather was an eight-year-old boy and they traveled to America? I suspect my questions have something to do with generations of women who were so busy cooking and cleaning and childrearing that they scarcely had time to think, much less to write. It has to do with generations of women who were never taught to read, with generations of women who wrote but were never published, or who had to be published under assumed names. It has to do with "a whole sex made mute or not educated to speech." I will probably never know the answers to these questions about my great-grandmother. But without her I would not be here. She is my connection with humanity, and yet I may never know the concrete details of her life. Like countless women, she will most likely remain silenced forever.

◇

I crave times of deep practice as a chance to sink like a smooth, solid pebble to the bottom of a rushing stream. I look to practice as a way to be totally present and to let go. I look to sitting as a safe haven, a way to come home to the present moment, to take refuge in the breath. I come to dwell in that refuge of the Dharma without respect to race, gender, sexual orientation, ability, and so on. The tricky part is that there is no place without politics. Human beings have a say about the planet, our lives, and how we interact with one another. This is true both on and off our zafus.

If I had not been born a woman, if I were not a lesbian, I may not have become as politically conscious. These realities have shaped my awareness in myriad ways through the ten thousand things of my everyday life. I cannot sit on my cushion and be indifferent to needless suffering. The added suffering caused by ignorance and prejudice can be lessened. An old meaning of the word courage was "to speak one's mind by telling all one's heart."[19] By speaking up about my experiences, I hope to play some small part in lessening ignorance.

I heard a talk in Plum Village several years ago given by a veteran, consumed with the pain of his past, who told of how many people, including children, he had killed during the Vietnam war. This man is now working with Bosnian refugees. I am inspired by witnessing the transformative effect on him, and on others who have been devastated by prior trauma who are healing through helping others in the present. This is at the heart of my understanding of Buddhist practice: the past and the future exist in the present. We can recognize our oppressive prejudices and heal them in the present. We can let go of old hurts. We can move toward a more inclusive, enlightened future, informed by our unique differences and shaped by our common commitment to create communities of refuge and courage.

I recently ended a job of two years working as a crisis counselor with rape survivors and women who have been battered and abused. The only way I was able do that work was with an awareness of the incredible interconnectedness of all humans and of all suffering. It felt healing for me, as well as helpful to others, to play a part in this work. It also felt humbling to see the interwoven patterns of pain and healing, and to acknowledge my experiences on both sides of these realities.

I have heard it said that when we close our eyes in meditation we are neither male nor female, neither black nor white, gay or straight. I understand and appreciate this experience of connecting with what makes us all most deeply human. But I also think that in order to continue to feel our human connectedness, we need to recognize our differences with open eyes. Not in order to engage in countless power struggles and hierarchies of oppression, but rather, as Thich Nhat Hanh has said, to "put eyes in our hands." We need to understand one another's experiences in order to know how to fashion community from a place of connection and understanding.

I want to focus on the breathing and on the heart-mind capable of transformation, which we all share, without expecting a "one-size-fits-all" Dharma. I want us to speak up about our differences from a place of deep compassion. I want us to replace that "silence the poet dreads" with the "silences between notes of music." The practices we enlighten may be our own. The Dharma we transform may be our lives. The silences we break may enrich our sanghas.

May talking about our lives allow all of us truer happiness, braver hearts, and stronger communities. We need one another. May all beings be happy. May all beings be free from suffering.

My heartfelt thanks to Susan Berman, Marianne Dresser, Trudy Goodman, Susan McCarthy, Ginger Mongiello, Marcia Rose, Larry Sargent, and Paul Zelizer for their detailed, mindful, and positive responses to previous versions of this work.

1. Susan Griffin, "Thoughts On Writing: A Diary," in *The Writer on Her Work,* edited by Janet Sternberg (New York: W. W. Norton and Company, 1980), p. 117.

2. See Thich Nhat Hanh, "The Heart of the Prajnaparamita," in *The Heart of Understanding: Commentaries on the Prajnaparamita Heart Sutra* (Berkeley, California: Parallax Press, 1988), p. 1.

3. A partial list of women authors who have written books about Buddhism from a feminist perspective in recent years includes Tsultrim Allione, *Women of Wisdom* (London: Routledge & Kegan Paul, 1984); Lenore Friedman, *Meetings with Remarkable Women: Buddhist Teachers in America* (Boston: Shambhala Publications, 1987); Sandy Boucher, *Turning the Wheel: American Women Creating the New Buddhism* (Boston: Beacon Press, 1993; revised edition); Christina Feldman, *Woman Awake: A Celebration of Women's Wisdom* (London: Penguin/Arkana, 1990); Rita Gross, *Buddhism After Patriarchy: A Feminist History, Analysis, and Reconstruction of Buddhism* (Albany, New York: State University of New York Press, 1992); Susan Murcott, *The First Buddhist Women: Translations and Commentaries on the Therigatha* (Berkeley, California: Parallax Press, 1992); Miranda Shaw, *Passionate Enlightenment: Women in Tantric Buddhism* (Princeton, New Jersey: Princeton University Press, 1994); and Anne Klein, *Meeting the Great Bliss Queen: Buddhists, Feminists, and the Art of the Self* (Boston: Beacon Press, 1995).

4. Thich Nhat Hanh and Daniel Berrigan, *The Raft is Not the Shore:*

Conversations Toward a Buddhist-Christian Awareness (Boston: Beacon Press, 1972), p. 20.

5. Carol Gilligan, *In A Different Voice* (Cambridge, Massachusetts: Harvard University Press, 1982, 1993), p. xvi.

6. Judith Herman, *Trauma and Recovery* (New York: Basic Books, 1992).

7. Quoted in Barbara Graham, "The Feminine Face of the Buddha," *Common Boundary,* Vol. 14, No. 2, March/April 1996, p. 35.

8. Marcia Rose, a vipassana teacher, recently pointed out another similar but qualitatively different way of understanding what I had once thought of as "You have to have something before you can let it go." She reframed this as "When one sees clearly the nature of phenomena, they drop away on their own."

9. Nicole Brossard, *The Aerial Letter,* translated by Marlene Wildeman (Toronto: The Women's Press, 1988), p. 75.

10. Quoted in Graham, "The Feminine Face of the Buddha," pp. 28–37.

11. According to *Crime in the United States: Uniform Crime Reports, 1986* (Washington: The Federal Bureau of Investigation, 1987).

12. Ann Jones, *Next Time She'll Be Dead: Battering and How to Stop It* (Boston: Beacon Press, 1994), p. 145.

13. These statistics on women's economic status are cited in *Ms. Magazine,* Vol. VI, No. 5, March/April 1996, pp. 36–37.

14. See Nancy Chodorow, *The Reproduction of Mothering* (Berkeley, California: University of California Press, 1978).

15. This assumes some crosscultural connection from Asian to Western cultures in terms of gender development, a complex topic beyond the scope of this essay.

16. Jean Baker Miller, *What Do We Mean By Relationship?* (Wellesley, Massachusetts: The Stone Center, 1986), p. 3.

17. Janet Surrey, "The 'Self-in-Relation': A Theory of Women's Development," in *Women's Growth in Connection: Writings from the Stone Center,* edited by Judith Jordan, Alexandra Kaplan, Jean Baker Miller, Irene Stiver, and Janet Surrey (New York: The Guilford Press), p. 55.

18. Suzanne Pharr, *Homophobia: A Weapon of Sexism* (Little Rock, Arkansas: Chardon Press, 1988), p. 7.

19. Annie Rogers, "Voice, Play, and a Practice of Ordinary Courage in Girls' and Women's Lives," *Harvard Educational Review,* Vol. 63, No. 3, August 1993, p. 271.

Anne C. Klein

Persons and Possibilities

IN THE CENTURIES after the historical Buddha's birth, Buddhist traditions carved out a special identity for themselves in India by vigorously denying the truth of the *atman,* or "self," doctrines of the Hindus. This is both ironic and a little bit prophetic. Today American women and men are all too likely to deny the truth of their own selves in establishing an identity as practitioners of Buddhism. At the same time, outside of Buddhist circles, women are beginning to understand their own identity as something distinct from male characterizations of selfhood.

What is this business of selfhood anyway, and why should Buddhists deny it? Don't we exist? Didn't the Buddha exist? Didn't he and all the other great masters of subsequent Buddhist traditions use words like "I" and "you," as well as teach attitudes to have toward oneself and others? Of course. How can one teaching preach both the wisdom which understands the lack of self, and the compassion which attends unendingly to the deepest needs of all selves?

My point, of course, is that the self which is denied in Buddhist theory and practice is *entirely different* from the self who receives compassion. It is also different from the kind of self we mostly worry about: too fat, too thin, embodied as a woman or a man with all the cultural and psychological baggage associated with that embodiment.

The further point is that the philosophical abstraction known as "selflessness," which many Buddhist traditions understand as synonymous with emptiness, can never replace the flesh-and-blood movements of real people. It's not supposed to. We must not confuse those aspects of selfhood denied in Buddhist philosophy—permanence, independence, or immunity from causes and conditions, for example—with the undeniable existence of persons who laugh, cry, and sometimes seek liberation. But how do we relate to ourselves, and to all that laughing and crying, in the process of seeking liberation from the illusion that these expressions, or anything associated with them, is permanent? If we can expand on this, we might well come to a different view of what laughing and crying is all about. A view we can sustain even as the tears flow and the eyes crinkle.

Some traditions of meditation emphasize that we are liberated already, some that we are not. This difference is often played out in philosophical debates among the various schools and sects of Buddhism. But it is more than that. Here are two profoundly different and yet beautifully complementary ways of describing how a practitioner might relate to herself or himself. And these two approaches may impact differently on women and men. After all, women and men are acculturated to different understandings of their minds, bodies, feelings, and purposes in the world.

Buddhist practices have often been presented in Western circles as a kind of super-accelerated self-improvement program. The ultimate psychotherapy, the deepest calming device, the royal road to various kinds of success. Certainly practices can be therapeutic as well as calming, but to leave it at that masks something which is just as relevant and just as true: Buddhist practices are not really addressing themselves to the kinds of mental aches and physical stresses which so centrally occupy our modern attention.

So even while we appreciate feeling a bit calmer after watching our breath for a few minutes, for example, we must not conclude that this is what Buddhist traditions are all about. Our understanding, as well as the potential benefit, will be severely limited if we relate to it as a style of personal enhancement. We might fail, for example, to honor the extent to which self-awareness and simple self-acceptance is the foundation of all practice. Buddhists call it mindfulness, and it involves among other things the ability to just see what is, without rushing in to criticize, enhance, or change. Just see. Just be.

The ability to just be is basic and healing. Whether we are in the process of discovering that we are liberated already or on our way to developing those qualities which will make us liberated, we have to start from where we are. And to do this we must accept that the person we are at this very moment, in all its unglory, is the perfect place for us to start from.

And how will we start? Toward a discovery that reveals the riches we've had all along, or toward a careful cultivation of famous qualities of enlightenment such as calm, compassion, and wisdom? Put another way: Will you become a sculptor or a gardener? A sculptor looks at a natural rock formation, a freshly mined slab of marble, a tree trunk, and sees the image that will reveal itself the moment certain strategically selected material is removed. Nothing is added to the rock, marble, or wood to create that image.

The revelation of discovery is fostered by being present, self-accepting, and relaxedly alert. This can be especially important in view of the enormous pressure women, and men as well, are under as to what we should look like, feel like, feel responsible for. No wonder we often dislike ourselves for failing to measure up.

The movement of development is fostered by being present and, at the same time, making focused effort on a specific purpose. Both self-acceptance and being present are grounding, another essential skill for women adrift in a sea of other people's opinions. Therefore, I want to strongly suggest that discovery and development are both valuable skills. The question is not which is better, but which is most appropriate to what purpose. In this way we can approach practice practically, rather than simply following along traditional lines of debate.

And being practical means different things for women and men, and different things for the same individual at different times, or in view of different purposes. When self-confidence is an issue, or when one feels too vulnerable to an impetus to behave in accordance with the expectations of another person, an emphasis on being present—grounded in body and centered in mind—and a willingness to simply be with whatever arises, can be enormously helpful. If there is a particular skill one wishes to develop, whether it is a more skillful way of breathing, a renewed attitude of kindness toward oneself and others, or becoming adept at cruising the Internet, focused intention and effort is crucial. Also crucial, however, is to the ability to make effort toward something without at the same time belittling ourselves because this has not yet been accomplished.

In other words, we take account of our personal, psychological, and cultural identity as we approach practice. Is there any other way? And yet sometimes in the name of "selflessness" we are tempted to discard such aspects of self and personhood as irrelevant. We easily fail to see the rich understanding of persons that lies at the heart of much of Buddhist philosophy and practice. This is an understanding which suggests persons are not *just* what they do, not *just* what they feel. The freedom not to be identified with whatever your awareness reveals about yourself is in fact crucial to the self-acceptance that characterizes mindfulness. It certainly does not mean there is no self. After all, without a self there is no basis for practice.

Buddhist tradition tells of a king and queen walking together one evening. "When I consider all the beings in the world," observes the king, "I realize no one is dearer to me than myself." "It is the same with me," responds the queen. This was not a romantic exchange — it was a moment of deep personal understanding. Disturbed by what they found in their own minds, the king and queen went to discuss this with the Buddha. "When I think of all the beings throughout the world," Gautama Buddha told them, "I realize none is dearer to me than myself." Is it surprising that the Buddha said that? But of course he did not stop there, he used this self-understanding as a means to understand others: "So too," he continued, "is everyone to himself or herself dear." Therefore, he concluded, it is appropriate to cherish all beings with love and compassion. In this context, selves and others definitely exist.

Indeed, in both Theravada and Mahayana Buddhism, the cultivation of compassion begins with a clear look at ourselves, at our own attitude toward ourselves, and reflection on how dearly we hold ourselves, or on the kindness we have received from others. Either way, the focus is on myself, in present time, and on my actual, not idealized, attitudes toward myself and others.

The loving self, the self that is loved, are nowhere denied in Buddhist traditions. That such a self can be permanent, unconditioned, autonomous, or causeless is vigorously denied. The middle way is finding a path, a way of being, that encompasses both these perspectives. It is also seeing that precisely *because* the loving self is neither permanent, conditioned, autonomous, or causeless, it can respond with love and compassion. A permanent mind could never grow, for only an impermanent (and, in this sense, "selfless") mind can move toward discovery or development. At the same time, the abstract possibility for change is always present. That possibility itself is eternal, unconditioned, and uncaused. And in that indestructible possibility lies everything. As Nagarjuna said, for one who understands emptiness, everything is possible.

Possibility, like emptiness, has neither shape, color, size, nor scent. It has no specificity at all. It is an open sphere, sometimes symbolized by the openness of the female body. But sheer possibility is nothing without movement, energy, and purpose manifested in living beings who, whether they know it or not, are continually bathed in that possibility.

It is said that the great scholar and practitioner Atisha, a major figure in the second transmission of Buddhism from India to Tibet in the eleventh century, used to see an old woman outside the cave where he was meditating. Sometimes she was laughing wildly, sometimes she was weeping hysterically. Atisha was concerned. "How is it with you mother," he said, "it seems you are deeply disturbed." "Oh no," she told him. "When I think of all the ways in which living beings create suffering for themselves, I weep and weep. But when I think that all they need to be free from suffering is to understand their own possibility, I laugh and I laugh."

She was no ordinary woman. She was a dakini, identifying for Atisha, and for us, the deep nature of possibility that animates all persons. Persons who know what it is to laugh and to cry.

Jane Hirshfield

What Is the Emotional Life of a Buddha?

> Within this tree
> another tree
> inhabits the same body;
> within this stone
> another stone rests,
> its many shades of grey
> the same,
> its identical
> surface and weight.
> And within my body,
> another body,
> whose history, waiting,
> sings: *there is no other body,*
> it sings,
> *there is no other world.*[1]

IN SOTO ZEN, though there is no formal *koan* study, practitioners are often encouraged to work with a question that arises out of their own experience. Some years ago I realized that a new one had emerged for me—"What is the emotional life of a Buddha?" The question

A version of this essay appeared under the title "Being Intimate with Demons" in *Tricycle: The Buddhist Review,* Vol. IV, No. 3, Spring 1995, pp. 56–57. Reprinted by permission of the author.

made visible certain preconceptions I had been holding about awakened being, and the fact that preconceptions on this matter quietly shape every Buddhist community and tradition. Yet both in the literature and, all too often, even in the ongoing conversation that is communal practice life, these ideas exist more as implicit assumptions than as the subject of direct examination. For me, it became important to bring this area of Dharma-life to the surface—to consider it, experience it, and question it more fully within the mind of practice. I wanted to sort through the subliminal ideas I was carrying about the emotions and awakened mind, to bring them up into the moment-by-moment experience of my own heart and mind and see what I found.

Let me begin at Tassajara, the Soto Zen monastery inland from Big Sur where I lived for three years in the mid-1970s. There, a stone Buddha of great beauty and concentration sits on the altar. From his lotus throne he radiates both serenity and acceptance, the traditional half-smile on his face greeting whatever is brought into the room. In many ways, I found this reminder of my own Buddhanature quite helpful. Without such equanimity, how could I sit without moving amid the many hours of thoughts, feelings, memories, physical pain, even the joys, that are an inevitable part of Zen practice? Without such equanimity, how could I learn that it's possible to feel strongly without necessarily acting upon those feelings, without reifying or identifying with them, fearing or desiring them?

And yet, my heart and mind continually failed to live up to this serene and imperturbable image. Some part of me believed that to experience the full range of emotions was a mark of ignorance and unripeness, and yet at some point I realized that a practice that required turning away from parts of my experience also didn't seem right. The fifteenth-century Zen master and poet Ikkyu once described literature as a path of intimacy with demons—this, I realized, was closer. To be intimate with demons, to hold passion and feeling as fully a part of the field of Buddha's robe, might be a path fraught with the possibility for error, but it is also a path of inclusion, not exclusion, and one that begins in the moment-by-moment experience of one's own life rather than some outer concept or goal.

Where had the idea of excluding the emotions come from? Surely not just from a statue. Some Buddhist teachings I encountered as a beginning student spoke of all thoughts and emotions as manifestations of Maya, the symbolic embodiment of illusion (and, no doubt not coincidentally, female). Others proposed the attitude "Offer your emotion a cup of tea, but you don't have to ask it to stay." Others suggested that thought-formations and sensory feelings be allowed to come and go as freely as the reflections of clouds in a lake. Still others used a language of self-control and will, of "uprooting" and "burning away" the impurities of anger, pride, sensuality. None of this was particularly well sorted-through in my mind, and the result was a number of clashing, coexistent prescriptions for dealing with the emotions. Also, within a mostly unarticulated community agreement, certain kinds of emotional behavior were valued as signs of mature practice, while others were regarded as lapses—X's temper vs. Y's evenness, A's emotionality vs. B's solidity.

Stories and poems on the subject of the emotions from various Buddhist traditions point in every direction. An interesting one, for many reasons, is the Chinese Zen tale of an old woman who has supported a monk for twenty years. One day, she sends a beautiful young girl to deliver his meal in her place—in some versions, her daughter. She instructs the girl to embrace the monk and see his response. He stands stock-still, and when asked afterward what it was like, replies, "Like a withered tree on a rock in winter, utterly without warmth." Furious, the woman throws him out and burns down his hut, exclaiming, "How could I have wasted all these years on such a fraud!"

Paul Reps, in his book *Zen Flesh, Zen Bones,* frames this story as a failure of compassion, a lack of loving-kindness on the part of the monk toward the girl.[2] Suzuki Roshi, the Soto Zen priest who founded Tassajara, mused in a lecture he gave at Reed College in 1971, "Maybe a true Zen master should not be like a wall or a tree or a stone; maybe he should be human even though he practices zazen." He then went on to add the opinion of the great thirteenth-century Japanese teacher Dogen, that all three showed good, steadfast practice: "The monk was great, the daughter was great, and the old lady was also great, they were all great teachers." While I have no example of a Tantric teacher's response, it seems to me one might say that the point of awakening is not the utter cessation of desire that the monk seems to show (or for that matter of anger, fear, or any other emotion), but that in awakened consciousness such arising energies are seen as transient and without self, but not without power or usefulness.

There are also more Western ways of looking at this story. One might be through the psychological theory of the "shadow," which says that if we cut ourselves off from our feelings through suppression, negation, or willed dissociation, they will come back to haunt us in increasingly destructive ways. The monk's words ring over-insistent, and we have seen enough recent examples of sexuality seemingly run amok in spiritual leaders both Eastern and Judeo-Christian to be aware of the dangers of a simplistic denial. If we attempt to exclude the emotions from spiritual practice, this reading says, they will reappear in a form demanding that we face them: we will be thrown out of the hut.

Another Western perspective is to look at the gender roles. The male monk is shown denying desire and the body; the old woman, as insisting on their inclusion—significantly, not in or for herself, but simply as a test of valid practice. Her response to his failure is no dried-out statement of practice philosophy but an immediate, vivid, and full-bodied application of the Bodhisattva Manjushri's sword of compassion. In this reading, the story can be seen as a call to include all aspects of life in Buddhist experience.

In Zen, there is no emotional life apart from the one that exists this moment. The question becomes not "What is the emotional life of a Buddha?" but "What is my own emotional life in its true nature?" In the moment of experiencing emptiness, what is my emotional life? What is it in the moment of experiencing loss? Is the spaciousness of awakened heart-mind a state of detachment or a state of non-attachment? Between those two words and concepts lie worlds of difference. One, detachment, says that the passions and emotions will either be cut off, or, in a slightly different description, will fall away of their own accord with increasing ripeness of practice. The other, non-attachment, says that so long as we dwell in this human realm, we will continue to feel anger, grief, joy, sensuality, passion, but that when these emotions exist free of a limited idea of self, we will neither suffer nor cause suffering in feeling them.

While it is not so simple a model to ponder as the unchanging figure on the altar, I have come to imagine a Buddha who feels the full range of emotions, yet feels them in a way not in the service of self but in the service of everything. Perhaps such a Buddha encounters each thing that arises—including limitless suffering, including the end of limitless suffering—as simply what is: not standing back from this moment's particular nature, but entering it more and more deeply, with awareness and compassionate intention. Compassion means to "feel with," after all; the name of the Bodhisattva Avalokiteshvara means, literally, "the one who hears the cries of the world and responds." If one looks only with the eyes of the Absolute, there is nothing and no one to be saved, nothing in which to take refuge, no eyes, no ears, no tongue, no body, no mind, no heart. But if one looks from the point of view where anything—the idea of compassion, the idea of a Buddha—is given entrance, all the rest comes flooding in.

The experience of practice itself teaches us that any conception or ideal of awakened being can only be a hindrance—neither practice nor awakening is about our ideas or images. And yet, however limited the finger pointing at the moon, still we point, we turn to one another for direction. So I have come to think that if the bodhisattva's task is to continue to practice until every pebble and blade of grass awakens, surely the passions, difficult or blissful, can also be included in that vow. And if awakening is also already present, inescapably and everywhere present from the beginning, how can the emotions not be part of that singing life of grasses and fish, oil tankers and subways, and cats in heat who wake us, furious or smiling, in the middle of the brief summer night?

1. "Within This Tree," from *The October Palace* (New York: Harper Collins, 1994). Reprinted by permission of the author.

2. "6. No Loving-Kindness," in *Zen Flesh, Zen Bones: A Collection of Zen and Pre-Zen Writings,* compiled by Paul Reps (Garden City, New York: Anchor Books, n.d.), p. 10.

Anita Barrows

The Light of Outrage:
Women, Anger, and Buddhist Practice

That light of outrage is the light of history
springing upon us when we're least prepared
—Adrienne Rich[1]

IN THE THERAVADIN TRADITION of Buddhism, part of one's practice consists of bringing the light of insight to bear on strong emotions. I have been concerned for some time that this process risks colliding with our Western acculturation of women, and may result in one more layer of disempowerment and disavowal of feeling. Anger, in particular, is considered negatively. It is considered to be akin to aversion—indeed, it is sometimes used interchangeably with aversion. Angry reactions to events—interpersonal, collective—are questioned: do they simply indulge the angered one's sense of injury?

As a psychologist working with women and children who have been abused, marginalized, and otherwise disempowered, I have found it essential to help them recognize and find means with which to express their anger. It has been critical to the people I work with that they begin making connections between their own experience of violation and the violation of the earth. Usually the earliest manifestation of this is a "free-floating" anger at the way things have gone, in their own personal lives and in the life of the planet. Anger has frequently been a "way in," after which fear, despair, and grief—

and ultimately some action or vision or reconstruction—may be reached. In my work with my clients I have frequently named the anger which so breaks open the heart "holy anger," as a means of distinguishing it from the kinds of anger we have all been taught to fear. Holy anger can be a searing flame, an energy which can cut through layers of deception and conditioning. Such anger, I believe, has great transformative potential.

As it has among feminist psychotherapists, a dialogue about anger has been arising among women Buddhists in this country for many years, since the flowering of women in Buddhist practice began during the 1970s. It is important to me to continue this dialogue, particularly at this moment in history, when we are perched on a very precarious ledge overlooking the possibility of the dying of our world. It feels important to me to search for ways in which the Dharma can help us find within ourselves the energy we need to transmute our pain into something we can use for the healing of our cities, our forests, our rivers, our brother and sister species, our psyches, our bodies. It feels especially important not to disavow the potential of anger in our lives as women, having endured for centuries the censure of patriarchal culture for anything we have done to stir things up, to sabotage the status quo. Such censure has manifested itself in various forms, from witch hunts to psychoanalysis. It has obscured for us the possibility that anger might not only be the warranted response to many situations, but that it need nor turn us into harpies—dry, "animus-ridden," nagging—or create irremediable ruptures in relationship.

I began thinking of the issue of anger and women and Buddhism during the Gulf War in 1991, when I heard many of my Buddhist women friends speak about their fear of the anger they or others were feeling, and their sense that they needed "to get beyond it." I was struck then by the discrepancy between my friends' clear perceptions of the injustice of the war and their muddledness about the emotional responses which accompanied their perceptions. Here we are again, I thought; now we are using Buddhism as a way to deprive ourselves of what we're feeling. What might liberate us is, in fact, adding to our confusion, to our self-denigration. How familiar it was, and how troubling.

It was obvious to me, of course, that anger could be destructive; but, as Jungian theory asserts (and this is certainly embodied in the Hindu goddess Kali and in the Jewish Shekinah), what is potentially destructive can also be enormously creative. The more I pondered this, the more it began to seem to me that what we needed to do was to develop skillful means in handling our anger, rather than purging it, boiling it down until we ceased to feel it.

In our culture we frequently confuse anger with violence. Half an hour in front of the television will convince us that violent action is, indeed, the only response to insult or injury, and our governments do no better in separating the two. We are conditioned by the very order of the society to expect little to intervene between our experience of anger (ours or anyone else's) and the impulse to act on it hurtfully. This happens in our streets and schoolyards and in our homes daily. As our society grows increasingly violent, and we worry that any minor altercation could lead to death, we feel more cause to be afraid of anger. But if we buy into a set of "corrective" values which results in our attempting to abdicate our anger, we lose touch with a deep wellspring of strength and a positive force for many kinds of change.

In working with my clients to discriminate between anger *qua* violence or aggression and "holy anger," I have found it useful to reflect on some connotations, some of the history of anger which we too often lose sight of:

Rage often summons for us the notion of something out of control. But rage can also be the power of a storm, sheer elemental force. Rage in the sense of outcry, rage in the face of the inevitable—suffering, old age, death. How can we reach acceptance without first going through rage? Rage in the sense of refusal, rage which can be set against the huge, the intransigent, the unassailable, precisely because it is not hampered by the conservative instinct which would enumerate to it all the ways in which it is doomed, mistaken, intemperate. Rage which knows it is doomed and goes on anyway, rage the intemperate, the untrammeled, the immoderate, the generous. Rage the abundant.

Outrage. With outrage, anger takes a leap into the arena of injustice. Outrage broadens the base: this is not only painful and humiliating—it's wrong! Outrage leads to resistance: we shall not be moved. Rosa Parks taking her seat at the front of the bus. The tree-huggers warding off the loggers. We have learned that the oppressor may be undermined by resistance: not by superior force, but by fortitude, faith, conviction, defiance of authority. Outrage is the *coniunctio* of rage and eros, where what informs rage is love and the absolute determination that what one loves shall be preserved. Without this energy of eros, rage may become brittle, strident, rigid; with it, it opens a space for tenderness—my outrage when my friend has been badly treated, my fervent desire to protect her. Outrage as a rush of passionate protectiveness: even (as the *Metta Sutta* says) as a mother loves her child, her only child—isn't she outraged when he is unjustly served? Are we able to love the world enough to be outraged at its destruction?

Rather than using our practice to boil down our anger, why can't we use it to explore it, to honor it, to give it amplitude, to restore to it its vitality, its usefulness, its freedom from destructiveness? Can we imagine that such anger, fully experienced, can initiate a process leading to the envisioning of possibility? Such anger would be replete with authority, grace, confidence. It would not be petty. It would embrace complexity and be channeled compassionately, but it would not resist the setting of limits, the standing firm, the necessary delineation of boundaries. Its aim would not be vengeance, punishment, humiliation, the suffering of the offender. It would take no delight in fantasies of the other's defeat; it would not be satisfied by these, because its aim would not be to continue the cycle of suffering, but rather to interrupt it and establish something new in its stead. It would not get stuck in victimization, bitterness, resentment, obsessive rumination on the wound. It would not be equated with aggression, which seeks power over the other. Because it would be expressed openly, wholesomely, it would not do its work by manipulation or deceit.

Why couldn't our Buddhist practice help us to develop these potentials of anger? There is a broader issue underlying this, which is the tendency of many interpretations of Buddhist practice to scale down emotion altogether. As Buddhism evolves in the West, and particularly as women practice and teach the Dharma, will there be a broader embrace of strong feeling? I am concerned that we might, rather, turn the Dharma into just another whitewashing brush, hoping that this, when nothing else has proved effective, will at last make us "good"—where "good" is identical with mildness, temperance, non-confrontationalism, serenity. Is our longing to be "good" greater than our longing to be whole? Women have been urged for centuries to squeeze the juice out of our feelings. Are we going to harness Buddhist practice to that end as well?

I am moved here to ask a number of questions regarding the ways in which Buddhist perspectives on anger have been expressed and interpreted. If we are told, for instance, as we have been by Thich Nhat Hanh (in *Present Moment Wonderful Moment),* that anger makes us ugly and contorted, and that we must transform it into understanding and forgiveness,[2] how does this echo for women the standard patriarchal line that "nice" women (and beautiful women) don't get angry? Elsewhere (in *Being Peace)* Thich Nhat Hanh asserts that "if we annihilate anger, we annihilate ourselves."[3] This feels more useful to me; but the stated aim, again, is transformation of the anger itself into "the energy of love."

It would be easy to read this—we are conditioned to read this by thousands of years of culture—as a Buddhist variant of "turn the other cheek." While I have no argument with the importance of bringing awareness to anger (otherwise we may, indeed, react with violence or aggression), I am concerned that conditioned resistance to seeing ourselves as angry ("I know that anger makes me ugly" is the first line of the gatha on anger in *Present Moment Wonderful Moment)* may cause women to flee too readily into introspection and self-blame, self-censorship, and denial. What do we do when our process of coming to awareness leads us to the recognition that a situation (a behavior, a pattern in relationship, a political act) is intolerable? If we leap too quickly into forgiveness and loving-kindness, don't we risk losing an opportunity to correct the imbalance, the injustice—to take right action? If we drain the energy from anger by neutralizing it too fast, don't we risk compromising our own vitality in ways which are only too familiar?

It is too easy, given our acculturation, for women to read "transformation" as "neutralization." It is too easy, given our history of oppression and dependence on the oppressor, for us to accept that any expression of anger may be dangerous—that it is our anger, and not what is oppressive to us, that destroys us. It is too easy for us to pull back from our anger, to imagine that it is excessive, disproportionate, overly intense. We have been told similar things about our passion, and we have learned to fear and suppress it in similar ways.

I am concerned that the Dharma may be interpreted as one more encouragement to cultivate in ourselves the docile, even-tempered "angel of the house" Virginia Woolf lamented in *A Room of One's Own.* In our culture, in which it has been customary to brush aside the source and content of women's anger and to focus instead on the inappropriateness of our expression of it (and, I may add, of other strong emotions), can we afford to let our Buddhist practice become one more means of repression?

How can we use our practice, instead, to transform our fear of our anger, our shame about our anger, our apologies, our trivialization, our distrust of our anger, so that we can use our anger and use it well? How can we use our practice to understand that anger is something we have been all too ready to cast aside, often at our peril, and mostly because of these painful reactions that arise in its wake, which drive it underground until it resurfaces as resentment, bitterness, withholding? If we can learn to be present to our anger, to know it and feel it, I think we will begin to see the ways in which it can open the heart rather than closing it. I think we will see the pathways of change it reveals to us, the ways in which anger is genuinely inextricable from love.

Can we allow our anger not to dissolve, not to lose itself, until we have found out what it is asking of us?

1. Adrienne Rich, from "Through Corralitos Under Rolls of Cloud, IV," in *An Atlas of the Difficult World* (New York: W. W. Norton & Co., 1991), p. 49.

2. Thich Nhat Hanh, "Smiling at your anger," *Present Moment Wonderful Moment* (Berkeley, California: Parallax Press, 1990), pp. 66–67.

3. Thich Nhat Hanh, "Feelings and Perceptions," *Being Peace* (Berkeley, California: Parallax Press, 1987), p. 44.

Kate Wheeler

Bowing, Not Scraping

WHY BE A BUDDHIST? After seventeen years of practice, I still some-times think I need my head examined. How did my Burmese teacher convince me, for four whole years starting in 1984, that I was going to hell? How many bows have I made to old, brown men on thrones? What about the little boys the men once were? I've bowed to them, too, tiny kids taken from their families at an early age, forced to wear huge crowns, bless multitudes, and sit weeping through ritu-als that even adults find tedious.

What *am* I doing in a religion whose formal expression is a highly defended, medieval, male, sexist hierarchy?

I can hardly discuss these thoughts with anyone. My secular-humanist friends pity me; the Buddhists tell me to go and meditate until I feel better. Buddhist logic says that if I'm mad and sad because I'm a woman, I'm also a woman because I'm mad and sad. It's karma. If I keep indulging negative thoughts, I'll be reborn as a woman again—or worse, since the lowest hell is reserved for those who crit-icize the Buddhist teachings.

This essay appeared in *Tricycle: The Buddhist Review*, Vol. III, No. 2, Win-ter 1993. Reprinted by permission of the author. The author would also like to acknowledge Susan Murcott's *The First Buddhist Women: Trans-lations and Commentary on the Therigatha* (Berkeley, California: Parallax Press, 1991) as an invaluable resource for information in this essay.

Personally, I'd be more than happy to stop fixating on the differences between women and men. This would be easier if our beloved tradition stopped doing it, too. But it's hard to stop behavior that one won't acknowledge. Even His Holiness the Dalai Lama, a most compassionate human being and nuns' advocate, said, after hearing Western women talk about sexism in the Buddhist tradition, "Some of these problems may be more imagined than real."

The historical Buddha abandoned his wife, and named his infant "Fetter": is this a model for how a spiritually motivated person should behave? Must I believe Pali texts' insistence that a fully enlightened Buddha must have "a penis with a sheath"? At Wat Suan Mokkh, in Thailand, there's a painting of a sexy lady, her miniskirt adorned with scary barbed hooks as she slyly displays a fishing rod: she's a warning of dangerous female intentions. Is it rude to suggest lust be cleansed from monks, rather than just projected onto women? Zen schools are like boot camp; where are the female roshis in Korea and Japan? The Tibetan word for *woman* means "lesser birth"; women serve tea to slake lamas' thirst while they chant the rituals that women can sponsor but are rarely qualified to conduct. The Pure Land of Great Bliss has no women, the scriptures recount. Why not? For this, there *is* an answer: because it's supposed to be pure and blissful!

If women must be excluded from purity and bliss, then the tradition betrays its own deepest truths of wisdom and compassion. No way around it: traditional Buddhism, like most religions, is dominated by men—in imagery, language, practices, hierarchical institutions, income, prestige, and perks. This is dangerous for women most visibly, for men more subtly. Does Buddhism's male bias flavor its practices, encouraging, for example, the discounting of ordinary human bonds? With what results? Certainly, if men dominate all meanings, abuse and corruption are guaranteed.

"It were better for you, foolish man, that your male organ should enter the mouth of a terrible and poisonous snake than that it should enter a woman," the Buddha said to a monk who slept with his ex-wife. The Buddha praised renunciate life as the best path to freedom, but he didn't want to ordain women. Only after his softhearted attendant begged three times on women's behalf did he relent. He required nuns to submit to Eight Special Rules explicitly subjugating them to monks (the nuns' leader at the time protested) and later added at least eighty-four additional precepts for nuns on top of the monks' 227, often stipulating worse penalties for similar infractions. Later, the Buddha sourly predicted that the nuns' ordination would halve the life span of the Dharma. (We've now surpassed his omniscience by several hundred years. Is Buddhism a dead science?)

Under no circumstances may a nun criticize a monk nor admonish him. A monk bows to any monk ordained before him, but the First Special Rule of nuns says that a nun "even of a hundred years' standing" shall bow down before a monk ordained "even a day." The strict seniority system, designed to eradicate caste in males, perpetuates subjugation—in pointed, nasty language—as soon as women appear.

Lots of people say that Buddha was using skillful means in restricting women's privileges. Some even bend their minds trying to discover meaning in the belief that it must continue thus; they remind me of Christians, not so very long ago, who found excellent justifications for the institution of slavery. More liberal thinkers say the Buddha had already rocked the boat enough by criticizing the upper classes: he was a reformer trying to get by in his Iron Age society. This is right, to some degree, since the Buddha often explained new restrictions by saying that laypeople would never gain faith in the Dharma if they saw, for example, pregnant nuns. However, as the German biographer H. W. Schumann suggests, it may be simplest to conclude from the records that the historical Buddha didn't respect women very much. This attitude can be considered secondary, if we feel entitled to form our own judgments about what's valuable in Buddhist teaching and what isn't. Just before his death the Buddha entrusted his monks to discard all minor rules, saying he knew they were able to discern the essence of Dharma. Over-cautious, the monks decided they couldn't decide, and kept all the rules. In effect, they denied the Buddha's last wish.

If we have to have a bowing order, could it not be reversed on alternate days, with men recognizing the strengths of women, elders the potentialities of youth? Wouldn't this equally express an important truth: that we all are trying to discover, and then expand upon, the seed of enlightenment all beings possess?

That's what I thought in 1977 when, as a college graduation present to myself, I went to my first vipassana retreat in the redwoods above Mendocino, California. The teachers gave us one utterly simple method: turn awareness toward each moment, no matter what is happening. Each breath, each step, was its own fulfillment. Sometimes there were cloudy or joyous emotions, sometimes the beauty of young deer feeding in the meadow at dawn. I entered my life for the first time.

In the vipassana tradition of Thailand and Burma, I lived slowly and simply. For a time in 1988, I wore nuns' robes at a monastery in Rangoon, Burma. A few years ago, I began practicing in the Tibetan Vajrayana tradition, learning the magnificence of the Dharma's full expression. I vowed to do 100,000 prostrations, a commitment whose magnitude is gradually making itself felt in the form of sore knees. Buddhism reminds me to wake up, let go, be myself in each moment: this vivid and centerless clarity that belongs to no one, not even me, not even the Buddha. Practice is my reason to be a Buddhist, still.

I shaved my head and wore robes at one of the biggest monasteries in Rangoon, but technically I wasn't a nun. The Buddha's original nuns' order, the *bhikkunis*, vanished a thousand years ago everywhere except China, where an authentic Mahayana nuns' transmission survives. A few monkly authorities support the spread of the Chinese lineage; women from many traditions now travel to Taiwan to receive full ordination and training. Yet the vast majority of devout women in Tibet, Burma, Thailand, and Sri Lanka still take fewer vows, and wear robes in a no man's land outside the "real" transmission, where they are neither fish nor fowl, ordained nor ordinary. Many say they like the freedom of indeterminacy; that's understandable, especially since it can be difficult to find monks and laypeople willing to provide the intensive support bhikkunis need in order to keep their vows.

It's not recorded why the bhikkunis vanished, but their cumbersome relation with the male order must have been a factor. *Bhikkus* (monks) had to support bhikkunis' retreats, ordination, and confessions. Meanwhile, both orders relied on the same lay community for food, shelter, and medicine. (Neither order works, nor handles money; a holy example is their offering to society. This system provides great feedback, since if monks and nuns don't seem holy enough to ordinary folk, they must eventually disrobe, or starve.) What must have happened during famines?

I've heard one monk claim it's ten times as meritorious to donate to a male as to a female; perhaps ancient monks said or implied the same, even though the rules forbid angling for donations. A thousand years later, the male order's resistance has not died out. One up-country Burmese master claimed he had found the only way to revive the bhikkuni transmission. Hermaphrodites ordain as monks, then as nuns; but hermaphrodites can't join the Buddha's order in the first place. Ha, ha, it's simply impossible! You see?

Still, when I was a Burmese *thilashin,* a "possessor of morality," I loved being one of a tradition of determined women. The robes were beautiful; like the Buddha's original nuns, I felt freed from unwelcome male advances, curiously freer to be fully womanly.

Nonetheless, I used to muse sometimes that if the Burmese army, which was murdering demonstrators outside the monastery walls, should burst through the gates in a fever of blood lust, I'd get raped, nun or not. The robes' protection wasn't absolute; I was still a woman underneath.

The monks and monastery officials knew it, too. On the day the monsoon retreat began, my preceptor called me to his cottage. This was a privilege; by his delighted welcome, I could see he expected me to be pleased.

In his audience room fifty monks sat on the floor waiting for presents. Traditionally, at the beginning of the Rains, each monk is given new robes; my privilege was to kneel before each monk and, careful not to touch him, offer the packet with both hands. My knees hurt for days afterward; toward my preceptor I felt a weird combination of tenderness and rage. Need I say that no new robes were offered to nuns entering the same retreat?

The monastery's secular treasurer kept calling on my fellow nun, a woman from California. He'd show her a photo of his nephew, a glowering young man who needed a U.S. green card. Would she marry him? If she'd been a monk, the treasurer wouldn't have dared. Burmese respect their monks, even half-baked Western ones.

I began to wonder whether I wanted to spend my life as a representative of inequity. I asked a junior abbot how a nun disrobed: if I went to the States and was unhappy, must I fly back to Burma and find my preceptor?

This big, handsome monk had charge of all Burmese women meditators, interviewing 400 each day. "You're not a nun. Anyone can shave their head, wear pink shirts, and not eat dinner, even a man. No monk is needed to disrobe you."

Shortly afterward, the translator monk made a nasty remark about one of the sponsors. "She's nothing but a woman," he sneered. Since she had no other apparent faults, and had helped us generously, we Western ladies went to the abbot.

"Why do monks disparage women?" we asked. Needless to say, the disparaging monk was translating; he showed no discomfort as he passed our words to the abbot.

The abbot replied that this did not occur, since monks perceive no men and women, only impersonal body elements and mind. Had we not experienced this in meditation, too? Oh, yes, we said. He went on in praise: more females lived in the divine realms, since women are more ethical than men. Women got enlightened more easily, because we suffer more, thus easily renouncing the world. We're better meditators, docile in following instructions.

"Then why are there no women teachers, if women are so enlightened?"

The abbot paused. "Women are lazy," he said, "and hate responsibility. Wives sit around at home until the husband hands over his wages, then they go shopping. In the same way, nuns and female meditators let monks support them spiritually. When Burmese peasants carry a heavy load of rice, they divide it into two sacks and tie one to each end of a long, strong bamboo. Two people shoulder the load, but if the person to the rear creeps forward, the person in front bears most of the weight. That's how women do." He looked so proud of this analogy that we hardly dared go on. But the translator was smirking, and I felt outraged. "Housewives pound rice and carry water, and never get paid or respected. Women do seventy percent of the world's labor, eat twenty percent of the food, and get ten percent of the pay." My numbers were inexact, but good enough for

Rangoon. The monk-translator didn't bother to pass this on, but answered me himself. "Who will pay these women? Men?"

We women could only bow and leave.

My Burmese teacher was right: I have not yet taken full responsibility for carrying the truth. For one thing, there's evidence that I'm not fully connected with wise, loving, authentic Buddhamind. Why else do I keep swallowing and then spitting out Buddhist-isms— the mere husks of truth?

I'm not saying it's easy. In traditional contexts, questions can bounce back as accusations. Sermons, admonitions, and gossip tell us what to think of doubters: they're full of greed, anger, ignorance, intent to harm, pride, and bad manners—Dharma Enemies bound for Vajra Hell. Most Asian teachers aren't interested in learning "worldly things" from us, the "red-faced barbarians" who come to them for wisdom. But is equality among beings "worldly"? The Greeks were inventing democracy around the same time as the Buddha sat down to rend the veils of illusion. Perhaps it's time now for the world's two greatest ideas fully to recognize their commonality.

◇

Three years ago, I first heard Tibetan Vajrayana teachings on the nature of mind. It was like falling in love with an old friend. I liked the tradition's *joie de vivre*, how lamas moved and laughed so much more flexibly than the tight-wrapped Theravadins. (Sometimes too flexibly, as when I learned some lamas are multiple seducers, a form of misbehavior quite rare in my previous tradition.) Finally, I was glad to hear that there are many female Buddhas, plus a tantric vow not to look down on women. But to whom is that vow addressed?

I vowed to do a *Ngondro*, or preliminary practice, which begins with 100,000 prostrations and refuge prayers. This combination is supposed to reunite me with the essence of my enlightened mind, purify all obscurations, and prepare me for Vajrayana practice. I certainly hope so! After 19,000 prostrations, the magnitude of the commitment has begun to dawn. My deltoids are burgeoning. My knees click. Any sane person would have doubts; mine take the form of wondering whether Ngondro is really good for me.

Here I am, a Western feminist, abasing myself physically in front of an odd Tibetan painting—of a man. Of all possible symbols of truth, is this the one for me? Yet in the refuge prayer that runs, half-garbled, through my mind, I also vow "to reach the level of the guru." Who is that guru? What's his level? Examining the *thangka* painting, I see the eighth-century Indian spiritual patriarch Padmasambhava on his lotus throne, that flying saucer on which he erupts from his idealized Himalayan background trailing sacred white scarves. Will I ever reach his level on all three tantric senses—outwardly, inwardly, secretly? Or must I be content with secretly and inwardly, while visible thrones are reserved for men? For an answer, at the bottom of the thangka sit Padmasambhava's two tiny consorts (he had five). The women arch gracefully toward the master, parabolic mirrors reflecting his glory. Meanwhile, Padmasambhava stares, frowning, straight out of the painting.

Like many other Western women practitioners, I mentally repaint the thangka to console myself. I add Tara, compassionate remover of obstacles; Kuan Yin, the all-encompassing; Sojourner Truth, liberator of slaves; and the Lion-headed Dakini, a wrathfully dancing female deity, to my Ngondro refuge tree. When I make my prostration's final slide toward Padmasambhava's outstretched boot, I often imagine Yeshe Tsogyal touching my head in blessing. I like Yeshe, whose name means wisdom. After her enlightenment became equal (almost) to Padmasambhava's, she went off on her own, raised a sixteen-year-old Nepali warrior from the dead, and took him to a cave for tantric practices.... Maybe I'd like to be some combination of Yeshe Tsogyal, Susan Sontag, and Sojourner Truth.

Did the boy act like a lama's wife, fetching tea while Yeshe rang her bell and muttered over her *pechas,* those long, skinny, unbound Tibetan prayer books? I wish I could think their relationship was equal, but then I'm the heiress of an expanded Greek democratic ideal, while Yeshe Tsogyal was not. When she acted as secretary, recording events at famous eighth-century tantric gatherings, she'd list the princes, lamas, and yogis present by name and lengthy title. At the end, she named herself most simply: "And I, the woman, Yeshe Tsogyal."

Woman would be title enough for me too, all other things being equal—which they're not. Raw experience bears no label: I learned from outside I'm a woman. Why do people fixate so strongly on the difference? If the Martians landed, they'd confuse all two-eyed beings with legs: cats, dogs, Chinese, butterflies, and dreamers.

I hope one day that all of our perceptions will shift to a more open, universal field. So far, alas, men still seem to be hanging on to a position at the center of the center-less universe. Examining other thangkas, I note that female Buddhas are rarely the principal figure. Rather, they're mostly faceless, sitting with their back to the viewer, necks painfully twisted sideways.

They're consorts, emanations of the male. His qualities, his light, his empty or material aspect. I appreciate men's efforts to connect with so-called feminine qualities, but this does seem a man's view of women. Texts say all women should be seen as dakinis, female emanations of enlightenment; but in practice, this word often seems to equate with "sexual object."

Yes, there's Tara, and Vajrayogini; dakinis, *khandros,* and one or two female rinpoches and *tulkus* (enlightened incarnations); so few they prove the rule. If wisdom's really nondual, why isn't the proportion fifty-fifty? Why are there no enlightened women on altars, on thrones, in books, pictures, or lineage prayers? "There's Sogyal Rinpoche's aunt—Jamyang Khyentse Chokyi Lodro's wife," one friend said. But what's her own name, I wonder; does anyone know it? Why hardly any women tulkus? "Bodhisattvas don't really make decisions," a scholar said smugly. "They just get reborn where there's a need, according to circumstances. Women can't accomplish anything, so they don't come back as women."

It would be a fine accomplishment, I think, to help all beings to perceive liberation in female form.

Right now, my male partner is closeted with our lama getting a special, secret teaching. I'm jealous, frankly. If I made 400,000 prostrations, learned Tibetan, and did all the other things he'd done, would I qualify for same? And if the tradition is so macho that I wouldn't, why should I bother? After her million-and-a-half prostrations, I am sure the lama's wife has not received this transmission—but also sure that she doesn't feel too deprived. I'm terrified to ask Rinpoche about this. He's blissfully undogmatic, but he's still an elderly Tibetan. What if he finds something to dislike in my intentions, actual or perceived?

I don't know if I can bear to be disappointed. I wouldn't want to shame his wife, who's always in his room, sitting on the floor at his feet.

Is this a cop-out? I gather courage and go in to ask my question. I prostrate to Rinpoche on his carpeted bed. The old lama is amused, even slightly interested in discussing men and women. "Is your mind shaped like this?" and he loops his fingers, forming a vagina. "Is my mind shaped like this?" He holds up his forefinger, a phallus.

"No!" We laugh together. His wife, sitting on the floor behind us, below us, laughs too.

◇

I know reality's transparent; nonetheless, it seems to have its effect on nearly everyone. All over this floating world, women fear to walk alone at night. According to the *Journal of the American Medical Association,* violence by male intimates is the leading cause of death for women in the United States between the ages of fifteen and fifty, surpassing auto accidents and disease. At least 25 percent of women are sexually abused in childhood; adults all endure seeing our bodies splayed across billboards, used to sell everything from tractors to iced tea—to celibacy, as in the painting at Wat Suan Mokkh. When the massive patriarchal system that tacitly encourages such crimes grinds on unquestioned—even is enshrined as holy—how can women not feel revulsion?

It's not my job to get my sixty-year-old lama and his wife to sit in chairs of equal height. My Asian teachers are trying to help me by passing on what's valuable; some younger ones ask questions about sex issues and eco-friendly housing. His Holiness the Dalai Lama has promised to convene a monks' council, and ask them to change the rules subordinating nuns. He says he can't be certain of his influence, but he will do his best.

Yes, the situation's changing. It's been difficult even for Western males to cross racial barriers and be empowered by Asian masters; but some have, and they tend to be more flexible and democratic than Asian teachers. Fewer women receive such recognition, but there are some. When Burmese villagers threw rocks at the Western nun Shinma Beyri, the late Ven. Taungpulu Sayadaw accompanied her on her alms round, an ascetic practice usually denied to mere thilashin nuns (they're supposed to eat the monks' leftovers). The villagers quit throwing rocks; eventually Shinma Beyri was able to gather alms independently. Returning after many years in the East, Beyri now lives in Colorado, where she works with disabled and dying people, a perfect field for her deep experience of practices that break the mind free from false images of the body. Another Asian teacher, the late Ven. Kalu Rinpoche, offered Western men the title of "Lama" after they did a three-year retreat. He offered women the lesser title "Ani," nun, for the same qualification; but somehow Lama Kalu's women disciples are slowly becoming "lamas" too. Changing a tradition isn't easy: even the Venerable Kalu was criticized for his liberal gestures.

But if we look a little more closely at the institutions, there's been little in the way of genuine change. Twenty-five hundred years ago, the Buddha's stepmother, Mahapajapati Gotami, who breastfed him after his mother died, became the head of the nuns' order. She said it would be good if men and women in his order could revere each other on a basis of equality. The Buddha's recorded reply was that if false teachers do not allow women equal status then how much less could he—the true teacher—allow them equal status. In the case of women, the Buddha was wrong—and we have to have the courage to say so.

Marilyn Senf

Unlearning Silence: A Further Feminist Revaluation of Buddhist Practice

*Humanity has been held to a limited and distorted view
of itself — from its interpretation of the most intimate of
personal emotions to its grandest vision of human possibilities — precisely by virtue of its subordination of women.
... As other perceptions arise — precisely those perceptions that men, because of their dominant position, could
not perceive—the total vision of human possibilities en-
larges and is transformed.*

—Jean Baker Miller[1]

By now American Dharma communities are becoming familiar,
though (one hopes) not entirely comfortable, with women's attempts
to grapple with their experiences of Buddhist teachings and meditation practice. The way that Buddhism's advent to the West has
co-arisen alongside the feminist cultural resurgence of the past three
decades seems a great piece of synchronicity to me, and has certainly provided an interesting ferment so far. But if their juxtaposition may truly be what the Tibetans call an "auspicious
coincidence," as Rita Gross suggested in her exploration of the possibilities for a post-patriarchal Buddhism,[2] then clearly there is the
need for ongoing inquiry, both personal and communal, into its
deeper implications.

Since I have never really been able to disentangle feminism from my experience of the Dharma, the struggles taking place within Buddhism feel to me like just the beginning, the hoped-for groundswell of a more profound feminine revaluation of the teachings that I believe may become an essential element in Buddhism's transformational journey to the West. For me there is simply is no way around the awareness that for all its wealth of wisdom and the mind-boggling, radical epistemology developed through its practice, Buddhism did develop in a patriarchal context and is still thoroughly permeated with androcentric values. This is no longer news, and has been acknowledged by a number of Western Dharma teachers. What is still less clearly recognized, I believe, is how this may have led to certain subtle internal contradictions in traditional Buddhist teaching. While this may sound sacrilegious to some, there is—or should be—nothing in Buddhism that merits, or needs, protection from feminist or any other earnest scrutiny in the light of our own experiences. Surely the Dharma can be trusted to withstand the most painstaking process of inquiry.

I must clarify, though, what I understand by the term *feminism*. Contrary to some preconceptions, for me it doesn't have much to do with ideology, or dualistic notions of how "bad" violent men colonized and tried to control helpless "good" women, their children, and even nature itself—though of course history *can* usefully be viewed through this, and other, lenses. I prefer Gross' terse, carefully worded definition: "the *radical practice* of the co-humanity of women and men."[3] At the core of this understanding of feminism is an array of personal experiences and apprehensions of the sort that occur when we introduce a different consciousness into our lives, and attend to how our perceptions are structured and conditioned by gendered assumptions. In my own life, these experiences have regularly dovetailed with the changes in awareness arising in meditation practice, and have had a parallel impact. Such a definition highlights the demand essential to the practice of both feminism and Buddhism: to look beyond conventions, prejudices and conditioned beliefs, and inquire into our own actual experience—to see for ourselves, in other words. At best, both feminism and Buddhist meditation are awareness practices, each with the power to illuminate how our conditioning and "deeply structured" assumptions keep us from discovering our true nature. While Buddhism focuses on helping us to see through the heroic fiction of the ego, feminism allows us to deconstruct the pervasive but largely unconscious mythology about gender, previously invisible because of its widespread cross-cultural prevalence.

The idea that feminism and Buddhism have much in common may still be rejected as near-heresy by some. A tendency certainly exists in many Dharma circles implicitly to value its "spiritual" insights as emanating from some other, "truer" plane than more socially or politically based consciousness. Though to a degree I share this bias, as a feminist I also mistrust hierarchies of truth, and question whether this perspective doesn't reflect a subtly dualistic and patriarchal privileging of "spirit" over "matter" (matrix/mother). In writing this I am reminded of how uncharacteristically nervous I feel when expressing such views, even in the liberal, less formal circles I sit with. Fears of displaying "lower" consciousness, of spoiling others' apparently happy communion, of being pathologized, marginalized, misunderstood, and so forth, seem tangible. I am also wary, and certainly weary, of the unflattering stereotypes that are regularly applied to women who speak out.

This dilemma, common to women in so many situations, seems particularly acute in Buddhism, which in its traditional interpretation has had considerable distaste for, even aversion to, the direct expression of "afflicting emotions," especially anything faintly resembling anger. But when we do acknowledge that "there is some anger" at the effects of 3,000 years of patriarchy on Buddhism, and, as often, at the ignoring of this reality—still, *it's just anger,* part of the unsurprising, inevitable baggage from a long, painful human journey. As such it is certainly no more to be feared or warded off than any other emotion. Rather like male guilt about those same events and consequences, it's all tied up in the same bundle with our love, fear, and pain, all simply more grist for our increased attention. With this realization, we create space for honest inquiry and allow for the development of illusion-piercing clarity. Then the real question becomes: Can we rise to the challenge implicit in the Dharma and really see how gendered dualities and divisions are structured into our consciousness and even into our practices, creating suffering in ourselves, in our lives, and in our institutions?

This is not as simple as it might seem. That Buddhist institutions, and even the Buddha himself, shared in the gendered assumptions common to patriarchal cultures testifies to the power of our unconscious conditioning around gender. Apparently such conditioning may persist in a given individual—a teacher, say—coexisting with a considerable amount of wisdom about the Dharma. Indeed, the suffering caused by a false division between humans and nature is more clearly recognized within traditional Buddhist wisdom than has been the far-reaching damage done by gendered dualisms and hierarchies of consciousness. It is interesting, to say the least, that it has usually been easier for many Buddhists to empathize with the suffering of ants or mosquitoes than with the plight of women! But for an amazingly long time, and even now, women have themselves been more easily inhibited than these creatures from impressing their human needs upon the sangha.

Nowadays, though, in a widening variety of disciplines—psychoanalysis, ecofeminism, anthropology, and the history and philosophy of science, to name a few—there is a growing awareness of the interrelationship of our sense of alienation or separation from the "natural" world with misogynistic fears and assumptions. A crosscultural, fear-based human tendency to equate women with nature has been discerned, and the effects of this on science, religion, and epistemological thought are now being probed. Of course women themselves have internalized the same deeply misogynistic values as men; whether "condemned to immanence," as Simone deBeauvoir described so well, or to samsara, as has commonly been the fate of women in Buddhist cultures, we co-participate in our plight.

Fortunately, nowadays many women practitioners are managing to write and speak out. But I also hear us uttering the usual disclaimers we feel are necessary to distinguish ourselves from others' possible projections—lest we be thought "shrill," "negative," or, heaven forbid, spiritually unevolved, and thus unentitled to speak. In the same vein we rationalize and apologize a good deal for some of the misogynistic elements common to monasticism, and even for some of the stranger statements and actions attributed to the Buddha. We often mince our words, and while this is not always such a bad thing, I am more concerned that we skew our perceptions and distort our understanding in the process. This cannot serve us well for long.

It is still early days for women as equal participants in Buddhism. Not surprisingly, the initial rumblings from women practitioners have often reflected the preoccupations of "first stage" feminism—that is, the wish to share access, power, and influence on equal terms with men within the hierarchical and often authoritarian power structures common to most traditional Buddhist institutions. I am not aware that these structures themselves are yet widely questioned.

Instead, there has been great concern about men's overt privilege and the related misuse of power and sexuality within Buddhist institutions and practice structures in the West, as sexual politics within many emerging Buddhist communities are regularly discovered to replicate those in the rest of the world. In recent years certain dramatic abuses—and, perhaps even more important, their anxious concealment by women and men—have featured dramatically in the ongoing discourse in our growing Western sangha-at-large. Frank scrutiny of these events, though inevitably painful and occurring in the face of resistance and denial, is surely crucial to Buddhism's healthy survival here. As the furor subsides, and after the most obvious reparative steps are taken, I hope we will find time to reflect upon—and speak openly about—the deeper questions such events raise, with the understanding that these issues may possibly reverberate to the core of Buddhism as we know it.

At this time, though, the treatment of feminist issues in the Dharma circles I frequent still tends to focus more on the old, obvious power imbalances. The usually unstated assumption is that "just adding women" will remove the most crucial impediments to women's equality within the Dharma. Then, supposedly, women will be free to develop their practices, becoming "just as good as men" at attaining freedom—"equal opportunity" Buddhism, in other words. The problems with this formula have been well described outside of Buddhism, in many different spheres, as women have struggled to participate equally in various existing power structures.[4]

But while the basic structures in Buddhism are still in place, there is evidence that some in the wider community are now beginning to glimpse beyond this stage. Recent Dharma talks by (still mostly male) vipassana teachers reflect both good intentions and a greater sensitivity to traditionally feminine concerns. While very glad of this, still I suspect it is more useful not to go overboard with the reflexive gratitude I am apt to feel when men take "women's issues" seriously. Though these shifts are cause for cautious optimism, complacency about the capacity of Buddhism and the willingness of its adherents to come to terms with the androcentric bias, even misogyny, interwoven into the Buddhist tradition still seem premature.

The subtle blend of understanding and unconsciousness that we sometimes now encounter in groping toward the next stage was well illustrated in a recent talk by a local teacher on the anniversary of women's suffrage in this country. Here again I notice the reflexive need to say how much I value his teaching, perhaps as a way to cushion my response to this talk. The mention of women made me sit up expectantly, and the talk began promisingly enough, citing Riane Eisler's work discussing the transition from matricentric to patriarchal cultures. *The Chalice and the Blade*[5] is a popular but fairly hefty feminist tome, well beyond "first stage" thinking, and I was pleased that the teacher knew it.

After a bit, though, he lapsed into a more familiar Dharmic mode: oft-told stories extolling those early exemplary nuns who sacrificed so much in order to be recognized as practitioners. But as well-intended as such tales may be, I confess they do not gladden my heart; on the contrary, I find them discouraging, even faintly condescending. Surely the idea that women can practice just as well as men hardly qualifies as a revelation these days. Instead, these tales reiterate for me how utterly normal it is, in spiritual practice as elsewhere, that to be taken seriously, women must be exceptional: if not martyred, like the Christian saints, then they must outdo men at classical male heroics. Most painfully, their sexuality must also be neutralized or mutilated.

As is customary, there was some time for questions and comments after the talk, and though several woman's comments had a skeptical feminist edge, most responses seemed placid and appreciative. In this atmosphere I was reluctant to give voice to my confused feelings, and left feeling vaguely troubled, but also just a bit *wrong,* somehow, for feeling this way. After years of practice and Dharma talks this has become such a familiar state for me that I scarcely noticed it at the time.

Later, though, when I began to write this article, I found myself musing about my discomfort with this talk. Even after placing these women's struggles in their historical context, I wondered why I could not more wholeheartedly admire their courage and ferocity. With this question in mind, I went to my women friends for refuge. Speaking with several of them quickly helped to clarify my confused perception of this dilemma in the context of spiritual practice. This enabled me to connect these stories with my own lifelong struggle for approval, recognition, and acceptance, often in male institutions and on male terms, and reminded me of how routinely I have discounted and betrayed my own understanding, often subtly harming myself in the process. This makes me cautious about the price I and other women are willing to pay for trying to "join the guys," in spiritual practice as elsewhere. All too often the price is the decreased visibility—to ourselves—of our own experience.

Writing about this has really underlined my sense of how much, throughout my experience of Buddhist practice, I have quite literally "sat on" recurrent feelings and irreverent perceptions, and the ambivalence, doubt, and questions they raise—often discounting them as opinions, judgments, or mere mental chatter, thus negligible in Buddhist terms. At times this has led me to envy the apparently simple faith of others. Though I remind myself how often I've heard other women voice similar doubts, feelings, and perceptions privately, formal practice structures make little public space for this.

Though in my own practice these phenomena sometimes seem to recede in importance, they do not go away. Their outlines can be perceived even in periods of the most intensive practice, and over the years I have watched and experienced them from different angles, some intensely personal and others apparently more archetypal and impersonal. Seldom, however, do they truly get exposed to light and air through the process of public expression. I have long wondered— silently—if there might be more skillful ways for me to work with and honor them, if we might begin to speak plainly within the larger sangha about such perceptions and the doubts they raise.

The truth is, I'm increasingly weary of choking back my own perceptions. This was certainly true at the end of a recent retreat—in most ways a powerful deepening experience. But on the last night we were shown a film about the current plight of Tibet. Again I saw the plazas full of monks, all men and boys, nary a woman in sight, and reexperienced familiar conflicts, confusion, and doubt. The women featured in this film were prematurely aged, gnarled from toil, long-suffering, contrasting starkly in my mind with images of serene and relatively healthy-looking Tibetan monks. The anguish of their current circumstances was apparent, as was their generosity of spirit and devotion to their religion, but for me this juxtaposition had a painful side. One teacher suggested that these women were very spiritually evolved. If there was truth to this statement, I could find no way to evaluate it. My own response to the whole film was far more ambiguous, and complicated, no doubt, by a sense that some kind of shared reverence was expected of us. With my heart pulsing away, and in the hypersensitive atmosphere of a retreat ending, I was quite speechless. But I mused privately that for centuries Tibet had been governed by a male-dominated theocracy—a form of government which most Buddhists I know would in other contexts regard with a more jaundiced eye. I then wondered if under more favorable circumstances all but the most exceptional women hadn't customarily found themselves in a similar, if less extreme, position in Tibetan culture. This has long been women's customary role in other patriarchal religions: *dana*-giving, devotional, self-sacrificing caretakers who are at once both essential and peripheral to the traditional structures. However great their spiritual attainments may be, this is not reflected in their veneration, let alone in their ability to make policy or theology, or to influence existing power structures, however benign these may be.

After the retreat ended, I shared the feelings generated by this film with several other women. I was surprised and fascinated to hear some of the different ways that their private perceptions diverged from the publicly expressed received view, often mirroring and even amplifying my own sensibilities and questions. Communication like this is vital to my feelings of inclusion in the sangha, and without it I'd probably have given up practice in this form long ago. But like much of women's communication, so often it occurs privately and personally, at the margins of official discourse.

Here again I encountered another of my old, private perceptions— of monastic Buddhism as yet another men's club—a kinder, gentler alternative to the army, to be sure, but still a world that is defined, perhaps more deeply than we know, by its exclusion of women. Though not without its appeal, from many angles this world seems alien to me as a woman. Its hierarchies and lineages are overwhelmingly male. The division and relative valuation of monastic and lay practice look absolutely loaded with gendered issues and assumptions to me. As a feminist, whenever I confront these familiar configurations, bells ring for me, and I experience a call to mindfulness of gender. I am then on watch for other associated phenomena—for starters, the attendant heroic attitude toward the body and the pleasures of the physical world, often coupled with fear and aversion toward women and sexuality. More subtle, though, and directly relevant to the situations I am describing here, is an anxious, even phobic stance toward emotional expressivity and difficulty in tolerating interpersonal conflict, with the resultant need to subsume it in false or enforced unity.

As (among other things) a feminist American psychologist with an agnostic/rationalist upbringing, I am keenly aware that my experience and perceptions of Buddhism are inevitably colored by my own cultural background, personal projections, fantasies, and so forth. I have no real way to know how Tibetan women—or women from other Buddhist cultures—have viewed their lives and their religion. It's easy enough for me to imagine that they were simply glad when their men weren't killing each other, but were instead making art and religion, dressing up, praying, singing, and leaving the women to get on with the rest of the business of life. Maybe—sensibly, enviably, and unlike me—most women were unambivalent in their faith, and did not experience a sense of exclusion. I can only speculate, though, and in a fundamental sense the answers to these questions wouldn't alter my own situation a bit.

But at this time it seems clear that for an abundance of reasons, I cannot approach Buddhism, or any other religion, naively, as received wisdom. At times this causes me conflict and pain, and I struggle to find an honest place for myself within this tradition. Sometimes this feels like an impossible task. But then always, underneath the trappings, there is that bare-bones phenomenology of the Dharma that I love so much, that beckoning to inquire, with its powerful feminist potential, and this makes leaving or sitting on the sidelines unacceptable alternatives.

Because of this, I seek a way to give voice to my experience. This is not because I believe that my views and feelings about all of this are solid, or "true." Experience has taught me, though, that the need to keep thoughts and feelings hidden or secret often has the effect of making them seem not only more solid, but also somehow more personal. My growing awareness is that they truly are *not*—that they arise and pass as elements of larger extra- and interpersonal processes that at this point we only dimly understand. I've come to feel that the search for larger truths is always compatible with simple honesty with one another about where we are now, in the present moment, expressed with respect, humility, humor—and the knowledge that this will always be changing.

This makes me feel the need to begin to develop more skillful means for exploring our experiences with others in our practice communities—in other words, to learn to inquire into our processes as a group, just as we each learn to do in the privacy of our own practice. I am not sure exactly what such a process might look like, though some simple models already exist that might be appropriate for adaptation into our practices. If we do this mindfully we have the potential to make the Dharma accessible to a greater diversity of people, and by no means just women. I have some faith that if the different experiences and perceptions that each of us brings to our practice and to the sangha are honored as contributions, they have great potential to broaden and deepen our appreciation of the Dharma, expanding our vision of human possibilities in ways that we cannot yet foresee, just as Miller suggested in the passage I quoted at the beginning of this essay. But while Buddhism will certainly wear new and unexpected faces in these encounters with Western institutions and values, the Dharma reminds us that our challenge is to remain as mindfully open to the changes to come as we can be. This will truly be a "radical practice," one which can allow our understanding of the Dharma to permeate more deeply into our daily lives and our relationship with the world. That's a feminist-enough agenda to suit me.

1. Jean Baker Miller, *Toward a New Psychology of Women* (New York: Beacon Press, 1976).

2. Rita M. Gross, *Buddhism After Patriarchy: A Feminist History, Analysis, and Reconstruction of Buddhism* (Albany, New York: State University of New York Press, 1992).

3. Gross, *Buddhism After Patriarchy*, p. 127. Emphasis added.

4. See Sandra Harding, "The instability of the analytical categories of feminist theory," in *Signs: Journal of Women and Culture*, Vol. 11, No. 4, 1986, pp. 645–664.

5. Riane Eisler, *The Chalice and the Blade: Our History, Our Future* (San Francisco: Harper and Row, 1987).

Jan Willis

Buddhism and Race: An African American Baptist-Buddhist Perspective

I'VE CALLED MYSELF a "Baptist-Buddhist" not because I intend to take up explicitly the subject of how these two faiths come together. Nor do I mean, necessarily, to contend with writers like Rodger Kamenetz, for example, who in his widely-selling book *The Jew in the Lotus*[1] bemoans the idea that so many young people of Jewish background seem to have "gone over" to Buddhism—though perhaps my particular heritage and background would form a sort of rebuttal to that idea.

I've headed my essay this way simply because it is *descriptive* of who I am. Actually, I think of myself as being more "an African American Buddhist" really; when I seek to make sense of things or to analyze a particular situation, I am more likely to draw on Buddhist principles than Baptist ones. But ... if it seems as though the plane I'm on might actually go down (and such has been, frighteningly, the case), I call on both traditions! It is a deep response.

I have often been asked over the years—by friends as well as colleagues—whether or not I feel a "gap," a kind of disjuncture, between what I do and who I am. By this, I take it that they mean a disjuncture between the facts that I am an African American who has studied and taught Tibetan Buddhism for many years. I admit that I may be somewhat of an anomaly. I don't myself know of another African American who teaches Tibetan Buddhism, or any Buddhism for that matter, at the university level. But it hasn't *seemed* anomalous to *me*; it is, after all, *my life*. It is me and it is what I do.

Only recently have I begun contemplating what particular benefit might come from my *making a point* of this "unusual" or "anomalous" combination of circumstances. But, a benefit for whom? One obvious answer, I have come to believe, is that my doing so might be of some benefit for other African Americans, and other people of color, generally. Moreover, in adding my voice to such discussions as those in this book, it might well be the case that there is some benefit for "American Buddhists" and for Western Buddhists more broadly.

◇

Over the years, it has certainly been the case that other persons of color have come up to me in various Buddhist gatherings and told me, "I was *so glad* to look around and see *you* here!" It is a way of validating their own choice to be there, a way of not being pulled under or dismissed by being "the other," a way of finding sanity in the scene. White Americans don't yet seem to get the point that, given the history of societally marginalized people in this country, whenever we find ourselves in spaces where we are clearly in the minority, we have a natural tendency to be fearful, guarded, and mistrusting.

Whether at Buddhist centers, at meditative retreats, or at large gatherings at which His Holiness the Dalai Lama is speaking, there are simply *not* many Blacks to be found. (When His Holiness spoke in Boston in September 1995 there were exactly *three* in a crowd of several hundred: a wonderful African American Buddhist monk, once known by the nickname "Yogi," but now called Venerable Jampa Kunchog; an African American woman named Loyse who'd just returned from India after journeying there following a car accident during which a vision and voice had told her to journey East (!); and myself.) Those "others" of us in the crowd always seem to find one another. I, too, notice the composition of the audiences. Most times, however, I am the only African American (and the only person of color) attending or teaching at a Buddhist retreat.

I should say that I am aware of a few other African Americans who have taken to the various traditions of Asian Buddhism. In the

San Francisco Bay Area, for example, there are not only groups of women Buddhist practitioners but also at least one separate group of African American Buddhists. One man wrote a letter, published in *Tricycle,* that said in part: "As an African American Buddhist practitioner, I am astounded at the number of seemingly well-meaning white Buddhists who simply 'do not get it.' Some assumptions that I am greeted with would be laughable, if they were not so hurtful. Many Asian practitioners that I know and love have suffered similar experiences. Here in the Bay Area a number of African American men have formed our own sangha to create a safe haven within which we may learn from the Dharma. The cultural dismissal that we have individually encountered in the Bay Area is sad, but we are collectively hopeful...."[2]

The African American monk, Reverend Suhita, according to another *Tricycle* piece, "prides himself on being 'the first Afro-American ordained in all three traditions of Buddhism'" (Theravada, Mahayana, and Vajrayana).[3] Rev. Suhita founded a small temple of his own, the Metta Vihara in Richmond, California. Rev. Suhita's center has become a haven for the homeless and for those infected with the HIV virus or already suffering from AIDS. His is "engaged Buddhism" in practice.

I know of at least three African Americans who are serious Buddhist students and practitioners living in Hawai'i: Lori Pierce is an African American woman completing her Ph.D. at the University of Hawai'i with a dissertation on American Buddhism. An African American monk-priest of Jodo Buddhism also resides there, as well as an African American woman, Leslie Robinson, currently on a three-year retreat. Readers familiar with Patricia Bell-Scott's anthology, *Life Notes,* will already have come to know about Faith Adiele, who became the first Black woman to live as a nun in the Thamtong Temple nunnery in northern Thailand.[4]

When I taught at the University of California, Santa Cruz in the mid-1970s I was somewhat surprised when a group of African American students taking my large lecture course "Introduction to Buddhism" asked if I would lead them once a week in "a meditation session that was just their own." Although we didn't form a group, we did meet throughout the quarter, separately. Some of these students still maintain an interest in and connection with Buddhist Dharma. Still, these folk only account for a smattering of the slightly more than 500,000 "American Buddhists" in this country.

That Buddhist centers in this country have not exactly had an "open-door policy" toward people of color is a fact so well known that it is almost taken for granted. Some people have been noting the absence of people of color for some years now. In 1988 Sandy Boucher put the matter quite bluntly when, in her *Turning the Wheel*, she characterized the number of North American-born people committed to Buddhism as being "overwhelmingly white and middle or upper middle class."[5] Yet, there seems to be little open discussion of why this is so or of how the situation might be changed.

Again, after noting that the only school of Buddhism in America able to boast comparatively large numbers of people of color is Nichiren Shoshu of America (NSA), Boucher stated:

> Many people in the world of American Buddhists are leery of Nichiren Shoshu, seeing it as a pseudoreligion in which people 'chant to get a Cadillac,' and they are repelled by Nichiren's aggressive recruiting tactics. It is also said that Nichiren is 'political' in some ill-defined but presumably sinister way.... People in Nichiren do chant to get a car, a house, a job, a better life. It is also true that the majority of people in this country practicing the other forms of Buddhism already have access to those things and so can comfortably choose to renounce them.[6]

I am neither a member of nor an advocate for NSA Buddhism. I do, however, think that their "success" in attracting people of color into their groups makes them worthy of study, and in some respects, perhaps even worthy models. NSA organizations have done two things in particular that impact upon their having a more diverse community of members: 1) NSA centers are located in large urban areas, and they draw a more diverse following; and 2) the ritual practices that are enjoined upon members are simple. Apart from the mandatory recitation of the *Nam-myoho-renge-kyo* mantra, the scriptures and prayers are recited in English.

More recently, the Korean Zen Master Samu Sunim remarked in an interview:

We Buddhist teachers—those of us who came from Asia—are like transplanted lotuses. Many of us are refugees. Here we find ourselves in the marketplace—as dharma peddlers, you might say. I am concerned with the Zen movement becoming more accessible to ordinary common people.

The Venerable Sunim went on to say:

It was largely the intellectuals who were attracted to Zen Buddhism in the beginning. Even today most Zen Buddhists are college-educated, liberal-minded—they're mostly white baby-boomers who couldn't make it back to their own childhood religions. We have failed to attract people from African-American communities. And we also have this attitude: if you cannot sit properly on the mat and cushion, then you cannot practice Zen meditation. That's not very inclusive.[7]

It is worth noting that, as far as I know, it has always been either women or "ethnic," that is, Asian, Buddhists who have noted the non-inclusiveness of the various Buddhisms in Western societies. Western men haven't seemed to notice. That, in itself, may say something. Whenever I've brought up the subject, I've been told: "But Buddhists don't proselytize! They never have." Historically, though, this isn't exactly true. Except for the three-month "rainy season," the earliest Buddhist mendicants were told to travel continuously and spread the faith.

◇

When certain people ask me whether I feel a "gap" between who I am and what I do, it seems to me that they are really asking, "What does Buddhism offer to *any* African American?" That is a legitimate question, and one that I feel is worthy of real consideration. To answer most simply, I believe that Buddhism offers us a methodology for enhancing our confidence. This is especially true of the various forms of tantric Buddhism, since tantric Buddhism aims at nothing less than the complete transformation of our ordinary and limited perception of who we are as human beings.

I was very fortunate to have been a close student of Lama Thubten Yeshe. We met in Nepal in fall 1969. Lama Yeshe kindly accepted me as his student and I was honored that he chose to call me his "daughter." When I look back on the fifteen years that Lama Yeshe was my teacher, I see *confidence* as his main teaching—not only to me but to countless others who over the years came to him for guidance. Indeed, when Lama Yeshe discussed the essential teachings of tantric Buddhism—as he did so simply, eloquently, and so profoundly in his *Introduction to Tantra*—he stated this idea quite explicitly. Here, I provide only a few examples:

> According to Buddhist tantra, we remain trapped within a circle of dissatisfaction because our view of reality is narrow and suffocating. We hold onto a very limited and limiting view of who we are and what we can become, with the result that our self-image remains oppressively low and negative, and we feel quite inadequate and hopeless. As long as our opinion of ourselves is so miserable, our life will remain meaningless. . . .[8]

> One of the essential practices at all levels of tantra is to dissolve our ordinary conceptions of ourselves and then, from the empty space into which these concepts have disappeared, arise in the glorious light body of a deity: a manifestation of the essential clarity of our deepest being. The more we train to see ourselves as such a meditational deity, the less bound we feel by life's ordinary disappointments and frustrations. This divine self-visualization empowers us to take control of our life and create for ourselves a pure environment in which our deepest nature can be expressed. . . . It is a simple truth that if we identify ourselves as being fundamentally pure, strong and capable we will actually develop these qualities, but if we continue to think of ourselves as dull and foolish, *that* is what we will become.[9]

> The health of body and mind is primarily a question of our self-image. Those people who think badly of themselves, for whatever reasons, become and then remain miserable, while those who can recognize and draw on their inner resources can overcome even the most difficult situations. Deity-yoga is one of the most profound ways of lifting our self-image, and that is why tantra is such a quick and powerful method for achieving the fulfilment of our tremendous potential.[10]

This is not just my interpretation of Lama Yeshe's view. Once, when Lama Yeshe was visiting California, I took him to hear a lecture given by Angela Davis. She spoke one afternoon in the quarry on the UCSC campus. Lama Yeshe was visibly excited to see and to listen to Davis speak. Several times during her talk, with clinched fist, he said aloud, "*This* is how one ought to be: strong and confident like this lady!"

Still, none of the great benefits that tantric meditative practice offers can be experienced and realized by "ordinary, common people" if those people don't hear about it and don't have a chance to try it for themselves—in short, if the teachings are not *accessible*. And as long as Buddhist practice is viewed and packaged as a commodity—like so many other commodities in the West—it will remain inaccessible to a great many people. And here, it seems clear that the question of accessibility is one of *class*, not—at least not *necessarily*—one of race. In order to study and to practice Buddhism in America, two requisites are absolutely essential: money and leisure time.

I met Tibetan lamas because I was able to travel to India (on a fully paid scholarship) for my junior year of college. I was part of that late 1960s phenomenon of Western students traveling to the mysterious East; part of the infamous 60s "counterculture." I would not have met the Tibetans had I not been able to travel East. Neither would I now be able to attend or to afford Buddhist meditation retreats were it not that I have the kind of job I do, both in terms of the financial security and the ample vacation time and break periods it affords.

The Tibetans took me in instantly and I saw in them a welcoming family of compassionate and skilled people who, as I viewed myself, were refugees. I soon learned that the Tibetans possessed the type of knowledge and wisdom I longed for—knowledge of methods for dealing with frustrations, disappointments, and anger, and of developing genuine compassion. Indeed, their very beings reflected this. They had suffered untold hardships, had even been forced to flee their country. We shared, it seemed to me, the experience of a profound historical trauma. Yet, they coped quite well, seeming to possess a sort of spiritual armor that I felt lacking in myself. Lama Yeshe's personal example inspired me and his compassion led him to entrust some of the tantric teachings to me. Having come personally to see the benefits of such teachings, I would like to see them disseminated much more widely than they are at present.

Once Lama Yeshe looked at me piercingly and then remarked, "Living with pride and humility in equal proportion is very difficult!" In that moment, it seemed to me, he had put his finger on one of the deepest issues confronting all African Americans: the great difficulty of having gone through the experience of 250 years of slavery during which one's very humanness was challenged and degraded at every turn, and yet through it all, to have maintained a strong sense of humanness and the desire to stand tall, with dignity and love of self, to count oneself a human being equal with all others.

It is the trauma of slavery that haunts African Americans in the deepest recesses of their souls. This is the chief issue for us. It needs to be dealt with, head-on—not denied, not forgotten, not suppressed. Indeed, its suppression and denial only hurts us more deeply, causing us to accept a limited, disparaging, and even repugnant view of ourselves. We cannot move forward until we have grappled in a serious way with all the negative effects of this trauma. Tantric Buddhism offers us some tools to help accomplish this task, since it shows us both how to get at those deep inner wounds and how to heal them.

But again, none of Buddhist tantra's benefits can be recognized if more African Americans and more people of color generally don't have access to it. So the question remains: How do we remedy this situation? As international Buddhist leaders and their American counterparts continue to mount extensive dialogues and conferences that focus on "Buddhism and Science," "Buddhism and Psychology," "Buddhism and Christianity," and so on, they would do well, it seems to me, to devote efforts toward trying to make Buddhism in all its forms more readily available and accessible to a wider cross-section of the American population. Indeed, such efforts would go a long way toward helping a truly "American" Buddhism to emerge.

◇

In the end, the question of what Buddhism has to offer African Americans and other people of color may not be as important as what such people have to offer Buddhism in America. For even when African Americans deny, out of shame and embarrassment, the horrors of slavery, they carry the deep knowledge of that experience in their very bones. Amiri Baraka, in his classic text on African American blues and jazz, *Blues People,* expressed this well, I think, when he wrote:

> The poor Negro always remembered himself as an ex-slave and used this as the basis of any dealings with the mainstream of American society. The middle class black man bases his whole existence on the hopeless hypothesis that no one is supposed to remember that for almost three hundred years there was slavery in America, that the white man was a master, the black man a slave. This knowledge, however, is at the root of the legitimate black culture of this country. It is this knowledge, with its attendant muses of self-division, self-hatred, stoicism, and finally quixotic optimism, that informs the most meaningful of Afro-American music.[11]

This deep knowledge of trying to hold on to humanness in a world firmly committed to destroying it adds a kind of spiritual reservoir of strength at the same time that it is so burdensome. The spiritual resilience of Black folk has something to offer us all.

The First Noble Truth of Buddhism asks us to "understand" the noble truth of suffering. Apart from the newness, exoticism, and aesthetic attractiveness of the various traditions of Buddhism now existent on American soil, in the end, it is the sobering and realistic recognition of our individual and collective suffering that marks the true beginning of the Buddhist path. The physical presence of more dark faces in Buddhist centers will serve both to focus the issue of what makes us *all* "Americans" and, hopefully, allow a freer American expression of Buddhism to emerge.

The atmosphere of a lot of Buddhist centers may be peaceful to most of their regular followers, but it is off-putting to some "outsiders" who find the sweetness and tender voices of the *pujas* and other ceremonies disingenuous. It's as though certain center members have just exchanged one pretense for another. I remember well the admonition from the great Kalu Rinpoche never to engage in such pretense. And I will never forget hearing Alice "Turiya" Coltrane at a birthday celebration for her teacher, the venerable Hindu guru Satchidananda. She began a hymn to Krishna by striking up her harmonium and singing, "*I said, ah,* Om Bhagawata . . ." with all the strength and power of an African American Baptist choir! My own heart rejoiced as I thought, *Now,* this *is truly the Dharma coming West!* There is clearly a sense in which more diverse membership in centers will stir changes in ritual and, perhaps, more straightforward and honest behavior.

I do not intend any of what I've discussed here either to glorify victimization or to vilify current Buddhist practitioners in America. My intention was to make needed suggestions about how changes might be begun. There is the perception that there is a disjuncture between what Buddhists in America preach and what they practice. One of these perceived disjunctures revolves around the issue of the non-inclusion of persons of color in the events and memberships of Buddhist organizations in this country. Clearly, if centers act as though people of color are anomalies within their precincts, then people of color will certainly become so. It would seem to me that changing such perceptions (and the actions that foster them) ought to lie at the heart of what genuine Buddhists are all about: in a word, "openness." In other words, equanimity and compassion toward all.

Just as Buddhism in America has begun to undergo transformations, to find its American identity—which is really a way of saying "finding itself" in this social and geographic space—to the extent that it has seen the disproportionately greater number of women teachers of the Dharma emerge here, so it will change for the better and become more itself when its overall audience is more representative of *all* Americans. That is, when the various forms of Buddhism are offered freely to Americans of all racial and economic backgrounds.

1. Rodger Kamenetz, *The Jew in the Lotus* (New York: HarperCollins, 1995).

2. Larry L. Saxon, "Nattier Storm Alert," Letters, *Tricycle: The Buddhist Review,* Vol. V, No. 2, Winter 1995, p. 8.

3. Quoted in Tensho David Schneider, "Accidents and Calculations: The Emergence of Three AIDS Hospices," *Tricycle: The Buddhist Review,* Vol. I, No. 3, Spring 1992, p. 81.

4. Faith Adiele, "Standing Alone with Myself," *Life Notes: Personal Writings by Contemporary Black Women,* edited by Patricia Bell-Scott (New York: W. W. Norton & Company, 1994), pp. 364–388.

5. Sandy Boucher, *Turning the Wheel: American Women Creating the New Buddhism* (San Francisco: Harper & Row, 1988), p. 306.

6. Boucher, *Turning the Wheel,* p. 311.

7. Quoted in Clark Strand, "Buddha in the Market: An Interview with Korean Zen Master Samu Sunim," *Tricycle: The Buddhist Review,* Vol. V, No. 2, Winter 1995, pp. 91–92.

8. Lama Yeshe, *Introduction to Tantra* (Boston: Wisdom Publications, 1987), p. 41.

9. Lama Yeshe, *Introduction to Tantra,* p. 42.

10. Lama Yeshe, *Introduction to Tantra,* p. 46.

11. Amiri Baraka, *Blues People* (New York: Morrow Quill, 1963), p. 136.

Lori Pierce

Outside In:
Buddhism in America

A BRIEF HISTORIOGRAPHIC SURVEY of Buddhism in America turns up very little meaningful critique or analysis of the development of Buddhism as a cultural event. That same survey will show that discussion of the history of Buddhism focuses either on Buddhism among North American or European converts[1] or on Buddhism among Asian immigrants.[2] It is telling that as these two communities of Buddhist adherents have been and largely remain segregated from one another, it is difficult to even discuss them in the same historical breath. Any discussion of non-Asian or non-Euroamerican adherents or sympathizers to Buddhism is nonexistent.

My own participation in this discussion is unexpected. Only recently in my graduate work in American Studies at the University of Hawai'i have I seriously entertained the notion that it might be possible to sustain a dissertation on Buddhism and racism. Though that remains to be seen, it is a happy coincidence that two areas of interest and research have begun to come together for me.

I trace my own interest in Buddhism back to the beginnings of my adolescent spiritual search for meaning. Because of, or perhaps in spite of, my upbringing in the Catholic Church, I developed an early fascination with spiritual practices. While my friends quickly became bored with the catechism lessons given almost by rote by the parish priest, religion class was never long enough for me. I was intrigued by the theological possibilities of a God who was both compassionate and vengeful. It wasn't the mechanics of Catholic life I found fascinating but the potential for meaning above and beyond mundane existence.

My two favorite books in junior high school were Chaim Potok's *The Chosen*, a novel about the friendship between two Jewish boys in New York, and *The Autobiography of Malcolm X*. These preferences now seem significant in light of my academic interests. What I remember most about Malcolm X's story was not his description of surviving and combating racism in the North, but his conversion(s) to Islam. It was clear to me that the most important questions and the most important decisions to be faced in life had nothing to do with career or family, but with how you chose to orient your spiritual self— and that it was possible to orient in more than one direction. God, it seems, did not live at St. Peter's in Rome, in Mecca, or in Jerusalem. God and/or a meaningful and purposeful life could be found at all of those places—or none. A truly religious life consisted of limitless possibilities, searching in any and all directions, if necessary. Some people may find this idea frightening; I found it exhilarating.

My college years led me out of the Catholic Church and onto a spiritual path that was both intellectual and emotional. Now, what is generally supposed to happen in a story like this is that after years of moving from group to group, teacher to teacher, I finally found happiness with Roshi X. Or, that as I'm writing this, I am still struggling with a practice of some kind—Zen, Vipassana, Tibetan, whatever. I squeeze an hour of sitting in between a hectic schedule of school, teaching, and raising a three-year-old, but I rarely do what I or anyone else expects. After years of spiritual searching, my path, for now, has become almost entirely intellectual.

When I moved to Oahu in 1991 with my husband so that he could study comparative philosophy at the University of Hawai'i, I had sworn off academic life forever. Two and a half years earning my Master's degree at Harvard Divinity School had, I thought, finished me. I was burned out, yet the pull was strong. I enrolled in American Studies at the university, ostensibly to study American culture and religion and to write my dissertation on Buddhism in America. But the program demanded that I broaden my scope and so, by default almost, I began to study African American history and culture and theories of race and ethnicity.

At this stage of my life I mark the moment of awakening with reading bell hooks' *Ain't I A Woman*.[3] Her passionate description of the struggles of African American women struck a chord in me I hardly knew existed. It was suddenly quite clear that would not be possible for me to pursue any path, spiritual or otherwise, unless and until I made sense of *all* of my selves. Being an African American woman was no longer just incidental to my identity—it was something that had to be incorporated into the deepest structures of my being.

I think of myself as a Buddhist sympathizer, but not necessarily a practitioner. For reasons I'm not yet able to evaluate or judge, practice itself is for me far less engaging than the intellectual tasks I've taken on. I don't necessarily see them as separate from each another, but it seems that I've left "practice," something that seems to be a way of working on oneself from the inside out, for intellectual training in order to be able to understand myself from the outside in. This essay, then, broaches a subject that is at work within me on a number of different levels. It is an attempt to weave together two strands of an intellectual endeavor which is also happens to be very personal.

A discussion about Buddhism and racism might go in two directions: We can begin to suggest how Buddhism can and should be used to dismantle discriminatory practices within American culture at large. We can also discuss how Buddhism as an institutional structure reflects and potentially perpetuates racism and other discriminatory practices. But before we can begin to address the possibilities of Buddhism and Buddhists as an ally in the struggle against racism, we should be clear about the nature of racism and the ways in which we talk about Buddhism in America.

Though Buddhism as a "live option" of religious choice for large numbers of the general public is a relatively recent phenomenon, the history of the knowledge and "public conversations" about Buddhism can be easily traced to the mid-nineteenth century. The first known English-language publication of a Buddhist sutra in America appeared in the Transcendentalist periodical *The Dial* in 1844. Though the translation is usually attributed to Henry David Thoreau, recent scholarship points to the journal's editor, Elizabeth Palmer Peabody, as the actual (anonymous) translator. The attribution to Thoreau was a mistake made by a journalist years later and was never corrected.[4]

According to Tom Tweed's study of Buddhism in Victorian America,[5] Buddhism proved to be extremely attractive to large groups of women, some of whom were already interested in other nontraditional religious and spiritual choices available at the time. That two of the most important and well-known adherents to Buddhism were women, Maria Canavarro and Madame Blavatsky, is a significant and under-investigated area of American Buddhist history. Tweed dispels the notion that an interest in Buddhism was the sole province of elite, upper-class, East Coast dilettantes with money to travel to the "Orient." He suggests that interest was much more widespread both geographically and culturally and he and Rick Fields proffer California as the meeting ground between Euroamericans and Asian immigrant adherents and Buddhist sympathizers.

To date, only Jan Nattier, in a recently published article called "Visible and Invisible: The Politics of Representation in Buddhist America,"[6] offers a model for understanding the development of Buddhism in America along a number of different trajectories. Her model, centering on the ways in which Buddhism has been transported and transplanted to America, creates a way of understanding and comparing the histories of the varieties of Buddhist practice in America, but also gives us insight into the ways in which racism, class bias, and other discriminatory practices created these separate Buddhist communities.

Nattier designates three different modes of transport for Buddhism to America: transmission via import, transmission via export, and transmission via "baggage." She labels imported Buddhism "elite" (not *elitist*), in that it was available to members of a specific class of people—Buddhist sympathizers who could afford to travel to Asian countries where they encountered Buddhism even if they had not gone there specifically to find Buddhism. Whether we are talking about nineteenth- or twentieth-century variations on this theme, "only a member of the elite level of society can start an Import Buddhist Group."[7] During the Victorian era the elite class of Buddhists were represented by people like Madame Blavatsky, who could and did travel extensively in India and Asia, bringing Buddhism back to America and Europe with them.

In the twentieth century these elite groups are founded by Euroamericans who encountered Asia directly during the war (Robert Aitken, Director of the Diamond Sangha in Honolulu, Hawai'i, is representative of this type) or those of the "Beat" generation who were among the first to go to Asia to experience monastic Zen Buddhism (the poet Gary Snyder is representative of this type.)[8] The category "elite Buddhism" calls attention to class status, race, and background, and how these necessarily effected and continue to effect the development of Buddhism as an institution in America.

Elite Buddhists have been largely responsible for the popularization of Buddhism by directly and indirectly importing Asian teachers and practices to America for a specific audience—other Euroamericans. Though there is some overlap, especially in the early post-World War II years, between Buddhism among Asian immigrants in California and these elite groups, it quickly dissipated. Shunryu Suzuki, for example, who came to America initially to minister to Japanese American Buddhists in San Francisco, was quickly "adopted" by young Euroamericans eager to learn Zen meditation practice.

Nattier designates Buddhism transported by export as "evangelical" Buddhism. These are the relatively rare Buddhist groups who missionize or actively (some would say aggressively) seek converts. Evangelical Buddhism is not directly sought, solicited, or underwritten by Americans. Soka Gakkai and Nichiren Shoshu are the representative groups of this type of Buddhism.[9]

What is distinctive about Nichiren Shoshu and Soka Gakkai for our present discussion is their appeal to urban working class and working poor Americans, which has meant greater participation by Latinos and African Americans, as well as more Euroamericans from lower class backgrounds. The very presence of Soka Gakkai and Nichiren Shoshu draws attention to the ethnic disparities between the three groups of American Buddhists.

Finally, there is Buddhism transported as cultural "baggage" with Asian American immigrants. This "ethnic" Buddhism is, of course, largely the province of Japanese, Chinese, and now increasingly Tibetan,

Vietnamese, and Laotian immigrants. Once again there is some overlap between ethnic Buddhist and Euroamerican Buddhist communities, especially among the largely middle-class structures of the Buddhist Churches of America, the oldest continuing Buddhist institution in America. Though the BCA's primary mission has been to the Japanese American community, it is a formidable presence in Buddhist higher education, especially on the West Coast and in Hawai'i.

Approaching Buddhism from this angle moves our attention away from an emphasis on practice and ideology and toward the institutional structures which frame practice and ideology. Most of the published material by, for, and about Buddhism in America is about Buddhism as a spiritual path and practice. Though this is certainly interesting and important (and necessary, if Buddhism is to be a tool in understanding and destroying discriminatory practices), this emphasis can distract us from questions concerning racism and sexism. Feminist scholars and female sangha members have vociferously critiqued Buddhism at the institutional level and examined how through hierarchical structures or adherence to unsuitable cultural forms, it has exacerbated problems between male and female teachers and students and other sangha members.[10]

We can use a similar mode of analysis to investigate racism in American culture and how that racism is replicated within Buddhist institutions. In examining the effects of sexism and sexist behavior on Buddhist institutions, we should be aware of the ways in which racist behavior can mirror or hide behind sexist behavior and tactics. The same practices which subtly exclude women from full participation in the sangha can and do exclude people of color, working class people, and the working poor. None of these behaviors are necessarily overt; sexist behavior is not always manifest in derogatory comments or openly discriminatory practices. Women have identified the inherent sexism in certain interpretations of the Buddhist canon and the historical lack of equal support given to Buddhist monks and nuns. The fact that full-scale ordination of women very nearly died out and has only recently been revived is evidence of not just the neglect of women's spiritual lives, but patently obvious discrimination based on gender and frequently justified by distorted interpretations of the Dharma.

Too great a stress on Buddhism as personal spiritual practice mirrors the common perception of racism among Euroamericans. Those who are not routinely the subject of discriminatory practices have a tendency to believe that racism and sexism are the problems of individuals and isolated interpersonal relationships. Because Buddhist practice focuses on the individual and the state of his or her own mind, it is a useful tool for examining the roots of racism and sexism in ignorance and fear. But racism and sexism also exist at the levels of institutions and cultural practices, and are linked to social and political power and authority. Our tendency to think that racism and other discriminatory practices will disappear when we all overcome our personal prejudices and thus abandon active discrimination is supported by Buddhist practices which stress the primacy of the individual.

Racism "creates or reproduces structures of domination based on essentialist categories of race,"[11] and as such it is not possible that all that is necessary to eliminate racism is that we all "change our minds." Individuals who harbor no personal prejudice or any wish to reproduce racism in society can and do participate in racism by tacit participation in racist institutions. A recent episode of 60 Minutes demonstrates the point admirably, in a story on tracking in an integrated school district in Georgia.[12] Lesley Stahl interviewed a group of white parents whose children were tracked, sometimes in spite of their test scores, in the college prep or upper tier of the schools. When asked if they thought it was strange that all the black students were tracked in the lower track and all the white students in the upper track, none of the white parents responded with much beyond a blank stare. Yet all decried prejudice and discrimination, and insisted that they could not be racist because they had black acquaintances or had lived with blacks all their lives. None of them felt any overt animosity toward blacks or any overwhelming desire to use the "n" word. They were not, they declared, racist. But it is clear from the story that they were participating in and supporting an overtly racist policy based on the unquestioned assumption that blacks were educationally inferior to whites. Public discourse that focuses on more obvious examples of racism—vituperative language or heinous hate crimes, on the Mark Fuhrmans and Randall

Weavers—obscures the ways in which racism is in fact an everyday reality for people of color.

In ferreting out racist practices in Buddhist institutional structures, we must turn first to the ways in which they mirror the racism inherent in other cultural and societal structures. Jan Nattier makes clear that the segregation of Buddhist groups is considered "natural" in a society where segregation between people of different ethnicities and class background is also seen as "natural." Rather than claiming how we would like to celebrate our diversity, it would be more useful for us to first understand our diversity and divisiveness as a manifestation of racism that inheres in our most basic institutional practices at all levels of society. To this end, we might look at the relationships or lack thereof between "elite," "ethnic," and "evangelical" Buddhist communities. Though there is increasing dialogue within individual communities, it is significant that American Buddhists have a more fruitful and longstanding dialogue with Christians than with other Buddhist groups in their own country.

Using race as an axis for analysis or an angle of vision might lead us to question the placement of practice centers in "affordable" neighborhoods and the lack of meaningful outreach to the surrounding community. Such an analysis will reveal the privilege inherent in "elite" Buddhist communities. Before asking "how might the sangha be more inclusive," we might ask how *this* practice, *this* sangha is exclusive. Does it require a car to get to your place of practice? Are sittings and teachings scheduled at hours convenient for working people? Though every religious commitment requires some sacrifice, do the sacrifices required to be truly committed to Buddhist practice force some to choose between economic survival and this spiritual path? Are members of your sangha active in the community, in schools, civic groups, and charitable projects? Are you a visible presence, a "live option" to those who would or could not have read or heard about Buddhism?

I don't mean to suggest that Buddhism is or should be an option for everyone, or that Buddhist groups should be out missionizing simply for the sake of being "inclusive." But Buddhists in America, especially those involved in "elite" groups, need to question themselves first. The question is not "Why are you not coming to us?"

but rather "Why and how have we not been available to you?"

This might lead us to investigate our own fascination with the East, if that is the avenue through which our interest in Buddhism came. Orientalism has a long history in the West.[13] Though cross-cultural exchange is usually couched in favorable and praiseworthy terms, we should question how blithely we "borrow" from other cultures and adopt their practices as our own. How much of this is mutual sharing and how much is appropriation—and where do we draw the line? We should be aware that not everyone is flattered when Westerners invade their country in order to "get in touch" with the roots of Buddhism. No matter how much money we contribute to an economy as tourists, there is still the potential element of exploitation that goes hand-in-hand with cultural "appreciation."

We might also question our culpability as Americans in the exploitation and economic degradation of "Third World" countries in which Buddhism is the primary religion of its inhabitants. The sangha is a global community, and we cannot and must not forget that American-style consumerism, economic domination, arms sales, and militarization directly contribute to the impoverished lifestyles of those in the Third World, including Asian Buddhist countries. Racism in the form of global imperialism has a direct impact on Buddhists, and for that we, as American Buddhists and Buddhist sympathizers, are responsible.

Finally, Buddhist practitioners who take seriously the necessity to dismantle discriminatory practices need to look deeply into their own lives and come to terms with how racism has affected their lives. For most white Americans of all classes, this will mean coming to an understanding of how simply being white, whether male or female, bestows unspoken privileges and rights in American culture. Racism is expressed as white supremacy in this culture, and by this I do not mean just the most egregious examples like the KKK or neo-Nazis, but the ways in which "white" or Euroamerican values, standards of beauty, standards of literacy, etc. are held up as the norm against which everything else is judged. White Americans are the benefactors of unseen and often unacknowledged privilege based on race, class, and gender, and seeing it work in our own lives is an essential first step toward dismantling racism and other discriminatory practices.

We need to be more fully aware of the depth and breadth of racism at an institutional level in American culture. In an era of conservative backlash against advances made by women and people of color in social, economic, and political arenas, it is easier now than before to excuse the perpetuation of discrimination under the guise of "being fair to everyone" or not wanting to grant "special privileges" to one group that are not available to all. In this atmosphere, our ability to focus on institutional manifestations of racism, sexism, and class bias are hampered by a prevailing mindset that suggests that focusing on these problems is somehow the problem itself. It is a perverse form of "blaming the victim" of discrimination to suggest that the continual struggle to claim fair treatment for all will somehow result in measurable amounts of reverse discrimination against the majority population.

More than ninety years ago at the dawn of this century, W. E. B. DuBois stated that the problem of the twentieth century would be the problem of the color line. It does not take any astute insight to see that this will remain a problem well into the twenty-first century. Perhaps the problem is not so much the barrier between groups of different races and ethnicities, but the widening gulf in which racial and ethnic diversity is exacerbated by economic disparity.

As future citizens of the twenty-first century, it is incumbent upon us to strategize ways in which structures of discrimination based on race, ethnicity, gender, and class can be dismantled. Buddhism is a powerful tool in this struggle, and is being used capably and admirably by well-known Buddhist figures such as the Dalai Lama and Thich Nhat Hanh. But Buddhism is not a religion known to focus on the authoritarian figurehead. The Buddha's final words to his followers on his deathbed empowered anyone who heard the Dharma even once to begin on a path that would lead eventually not just to spiritual achievement like the Buddha's but to actually *becoming* a Buddha, a "world savior."

The heart of Buddhist teaching in all its cultural manifestations focuses on the degree to which ignorance shapes our reality. Whether through meditation, chanting, or other ritual practices, all Buddhists strive to rid their lives of ignorance and fear and apply that powerful insight to helping others do the same.

1. Two popular accounts of this history are Rick Fields' *How the Swans Came to the Lake: The American Encounter with Buddhism* (Boston: Shambhala Publications, 1992); and Stephen Batchelor's *The Awakening of the West: The Encounter of Buddhism and Western Culture* (Berkeley, California: Parallax Press, 1994).

2. The only book-length publication to deal with Asian American Buddhism is Tetsuden Kashima's *Buddhism in America: The Social Organization of an Ethnic Religious Institution* (Westport, Connecticut: Greenwood Press, 1977). Most of the published material on Buddhism among Asian Americans is incorporated into works on Asian American history and culture.

3. bell hooks, *Ain't I A Woman? Black Women and Feminism* (Boston: South End Press, 1981).

4. See Wendell Piez, "Anonymous was a Woman—Again," in *Tricycle: The Buddhist Review,* Fall 1993, Vol. III, No. 1, pp. 10–11.

5. Tom Tweed, *The American Encounter with Buddhism 1844–1912: Victorian Culture and the Limits of Dissent* (Bloomington, Indiana: Indiana University Press, 1992).

6. Jan Nattier, "Visible and Invisible: The Politics of Representation in Buddhist America," in *Tricycle: The Buddhist Review,* Fall 1995, Vol. V, No. 1, pp. 42–49.

7. Nattier, "Visible and Invisible," p. 43.

8. See Carole Tonkinson, editor, *Big Sky Mind: Buddhism and the Beat Generation* (New York: Riverhead Books, 1995).

9. For a discussion of Soka Gakkai, see Sandy Macintosh, "As American As Apple Pie? An Insider's View of Nichiren Shoshu," in *Tricycle: The Buddhist Review,* Vol. II, No. 2, Winter 1992, pp. 18–25.

10. See Sandy Boucher, *Turning the Wheel: America Women Creating the New Buddhism* (New York: Beacon Press, 1993; revised edition); Jan Willis, editor, *Feminine Ground: Essays on Women and Tibet* (Ithaca, New York: Snow Lion Publications, 1989); Rita M. Gross, *Buddhism After Patriarchy: A Feminist History, Analysis, and Reconstruction of Buddhism* (Albany, New York: State University of New York Press, 1992); Miranda Shaw, *Passionate Enlightenment: Women in Tantric Buddhism* (Princeton, New Jersey: Princeton University Press, 1994); Anne Klein, *Meeting the Great Bliss Queen: Buddhists, Feminists, and the Art of the Self* (New York: Beacon Press, 1995); and Karma Lekshe Tsomo, editor, *Buddhism Through American Women's Eyes* (Boston: Shambhala Publications, 1995). Though widely divergent in form and purposes, these works draw our attention to the specific problems and concerns of women practicing in institutional structures traditionally dominated by men.

11. Michael Omi and Howard Winant, *Racial Formation in the United States* (New York: Routledge, 1994), p. 71.

12. "Racial Tracking," *60 Minutes,* CBS-TV, November 5, 1995.

13. See Edward Said, *Orientalism* (New York: Pantheon Books, 1978).

Tsultrim Allione

The Feminine Principle in Tibetan Buddhism

AS I SIT IN RETREAT high up on the rock ridge we call the Dragon's Back Ridge at Tara Mandala, surrounded by the southern San Juan mountains to the east and the La Plata range to the west, I reflect on what has happened over the last ten years since *Women of Wisdom* was published. It was the first book to address the gap between inclusive rhetoric on the one hand and a general absence of women in places of influence or respect in Tibetan Buddhist circles on the other. Tibetan Buddhism shares a unique heritage in that it is Tantric Buddhism. Tantra derives from cultures and times that had both powerful women teachers and matrifocal cosmologies, with the "Great Mother" or Yum Chenmo, at the core. However, the system in Tibet was highly patriarchal and hierarchical. So the combination of a tradition informed by female imagery and power and the cultural context of Tibet formed an unusual and often confusing context for the female practitioner.

Western practitioners coming into this situation have had the advantage of looking from the outside and being able to see the blind spots. From the absolute view the way is wide open for women, mind is nondual, the path is open to all, everyone has their obstacles—being a

This essay is adapted from the Introduction and the biography of Machig Lapdron in *Women of Wisdom* (London: Routledge & Kegan Paul, 1984; Reprint: New York: Penguin/Arkana, 1986). The preface was written by Tsultrim Allione in January 1996.

woman is just one of them. At the relative level, there have been precious few women teachers and the hierarchies have been almost exclusively male. In 1994, I went to Bodh Gaya, India when the Tibetans were having a prayer festival. There were 5,000 monks and lamas around the Bodhi tree. Where were the women? Then I saw the nuns around the outside circumambulation path. They were filling the "butter" lamps with some kind of toxic fuel, black smoke all around them, wearing flimsy masks that didn't offer any real protection. There were no women in the practice area around the Bodhi tree. No women on thrones, no women on the benches, no women at all. Maybe the mind is nondual, but there is someone defining nonduality!

At the same time I have found lamas like Namkhai Norbu Rinpoche, Dugu Choegyal Rinpoche, and others who are profoundly non-sexist and egalitarian. When the Dzog Chen Community first formed as an organization, Norbu Rinpoche was the one who said, "We must have equal numbers of men and women." These teachers make it possible for women to gain equally from the depth and power of all the wisdom Tibet has to offer. I have found the more egalitarian lamas often had yogini teachers, mothers, sisters, and grandmothers who inspired and instructed them.

At the time I wrote *Women of Wisdom,* my three children were all under the age of ten. Now they are grown up and I am in my first long retreat since my first daughter was born in 1974. I have recently founded a retreat center on a large and beautiful piece of land in Southern Colorado. The land has at its center a breast-shaped peak, an ample image of the bounty and generosity of the feminine principle. It is called Tara Mandala, the mandala being both center and fringe, the whole, and Tara, as the powerful goddess of compassion, imbues the mandala with her energy and warmth. After my retreat I will attend a conference for Western Buddhist teachers in Dharamsala with His Holiness the Dalai Lama. There will be some women representing different Buddhist lineages, and the question of women in Buddhism will be high on the agenda. After the conference I will lead a group of mostly women pilgrims to sacred sites of Mandarava, Long Life Dakini. We will be practicing her *sadhana* for recovery of lost or stolen protective life forces called the *"la."*

In some ways, all three of these events speak to what has happened for women in Buddhism in the last ten years. Retreat centers and Dharma centers serving as refuges and places of reinvigoration for women meditators have been established. Many women scholars and teachers have evolved in an atmosphere that welcomes and longs for them. Some of the most inspiring that I happen to know are Sylvia Boorstein, Pema Chodron, China Galland, Janet Gyatso, Anne Klein, Joanna Macy, Sharon Salzberg, Miranda Shaw, and Ani Tenzin Palmo. There is also the beginning of more crossover between goddess-loving women and Tantric Buddhism, with writers like Diane Di Prima, Hallie Iglehart Austen, Vicki Noble, and Alice Walker practicing Buddhism. These writers are the tip of the iceberg of meditators, mothers, yoginis, nuns, businesswomen, athletes, and so on, who carry in their hearts an honoring of the feminine and devotion to Buddhist practice. The male hierarchies have begun to open to the voices of nuns and women practitioners, and are concerned about creating a less sexist Sangha. The Mandarava practice that retrieves lost or stolen parts of our *la,* our protective life energies, symbolizes to me the recalling and reintegration of life forces by many female practitioners. It is also part of a body of teachings that have goddesses as central figures, not something new in Tibetan Buddhism, but something new in the West. Men and women are doing Tara, Vajra Yogini, Simhamukha, and Yeshe Tsogyal practices.

What I see is a great flowering of women practitioners. We have made a good start in the West. There are still disturbing notes, like translators who duplicate non-inclusive language in their translations, insisting that "he" means "we" and that "Buddha's sons" means all practitioners. There are still women being exploited sexually by teachers who use their power and mystique, imbued in them by their traditions, to seduce their students. There are still many ways nuns are not treated equally. There are also those who feel bringing these problems up is "dualistic." Mostly, though, such issues are being recognized as problems and are being addressed.

We must hold each other gently in this transition, and seek to provide support and facilitate the passage for those who follow. As first-generation translators and practitioners, we are setting precedence for the future. We have the teachings, we have the path. We have only to walk it, with our eyes open.

◇

Although many women in Tibet found ways to practice spirituality, they did so in a culture which gave them mixed messages. On the one hand they were subject to a religious and cultural negation of women as equal vehicles for spirituality. On the other hand they were supported by the notion of women being the essence of wisdom and the dakini principle. They had to prove themselves in ways that men and monks did not.

Western women are also conditioned by limited examples of truly spiritual women as role models within our patriarchal society. We must seek to recover from alienation from ourselves. We must articulate our experiences with very few resources from which we can draw inspiration, and in which we can recognize ourselves.

Even within the Tantric Buddhist tradition, which provides more or less egalitarian values for men and women practitioners, the male point of view is still emphasized, as Alex Wayman points out in *The Buddhist Tantras,* in his discussion of the Kalachakra (Wheel of Time) Tantra:

> When the yogin attains the Great Time his recessive female becomes actualized; when the yogini attains this time her recessive male becomes actualized. This casts a floodlight on the sexual symbolism of mystical visions. Almost all of the Buddhist scriptures were composed by men, as far as is known. Hence these works speak so much about attaining prajna, the void, the state of waking and light. Hence that large body of scriptures entitled Prajna paramita ("the perfection of insight") and the personification of the Prajnaparamita as the "Mother of the Buddhas."[1]

I would suggest that in order to make the Tibetan Tantric path more available to women, texts emphasizing the development of *upaya* and the finding and working with male consorts should be developed. Perhaps then the principle of the *daka* (male energy) would become as important as the dakini (female energy) principle.

Women need to become aware of what practices actually work for us, what practices are adapted to our energies and our life situations. We cannot be satisfied with just doing something because it is supposed to lead to enlightenment or blindly obeying the edicts

important differences between men & women in practice

of male teachers and administrators. We need to observe what actually works. Women need upaya (skillful means) as much as men need to balance their energies with *prajna* (profound knowing) and emptiness *(shunyata)*.

Perhaps women could begin writing about and researching upaya. Women tend to have a natural affiliation for the receptive states of meditation, intuitive knowing, and compassion, but have a harder time seeing clear ways of working with concrete problems and acting assertively and effectively in worldly situations. So perhaps women should at once take advantage of their natural affinity toward meditation and merging through practices such as those in the Dzog Chen tradition, and at the same time seek to develop their skillful means, and enter into new kinds of sexual relationships which would enhance both these aspects. In this way women within the Tantric Buddhist tradition can have a powerful and balanced spiritual path toward illumination, at which point these relative distinctions between men and women break down.

I have found that many Buddhists are anxious to leap to this absolute point of view and consider any discussion of possible differences in the spiritual paths of men and women as useless dualistic fixation caused by a lack of understanding of the true nature of the mind. But these people forget that *both* the absolute *and* the relative truth must be considered. It is often those who most adamantly insist that one should go beyond relative considerations about men and women who abuse and undervalue women practitioners the most.

Women also need a spiritual path that speaks to our sense of ourselves biologically. Unless we choose not to have children, a great deal of time and energy is absorbed by pregnancies and childrearing. Children cannot be intellectualized: when a child needs something we must drop everything and relate to that situation concretely—if we don't, sooner or later the situation will become even more demanding and unavoidable. The life of a mother is one of constant interruptions, day and night, when the child is small. I have tried to relate to this situation in a variety of different ways in order to integrate spirituality with diapers, noise, and delicate, forming hearts and minds.

One possibility is the "time out" approach. This means arranging time for personal retreats, be it for a few weeks or a weekend or even an hour in which I try to pick up the threads of a stable centered state and enter into meditation which goes deeper than the grocery list and telephone calls. This approach also includes time to go to hear teachings without bringing the children along (which I tried to do at first and which actually just disturbs and irritates oneself and everyone else). This approach provides a sense of islands of peace amid tempests, and I think it is actually necessary.

One might argue that women should have a spiritual path in which they do not have to remove themselves from their life rhythms in order to practice. I agree with this theoretically, and I would like to see more teachings given which really help in dealing with relationships and childrearing in a positive way. Such things as seeing motherhood as a constant attack on selfishness, an admirable ever-present testing of the Bodhisattva Vow to save all sentient beings before ourselves, provides ground for spiritual development. The arts of psychic and medicinal healing, a sacred sense of the home and preparation of food as a divine act, the one-value approach to diapers and a bouquet of roses, and so on, are all potential methods for spiritual paths for mothers.

The possibilities are endless, but I have never heard a male teacher discussing them, perhaps because these experiences do not generally fall upon men. I think it is the duty of women who are spiritually awake to make connections between their lives and the teachings. The path of a mother should be given its deserved value as a sacred and powerful spiritual path. It is infuriating to me when I hear, as I frequently do, a man saying that his wife or mother or someone else "does nothing." When I challenge them on this they say, "Of course I meant nothing in the outside world; they only cook, clean, shop, create atmosphere in the home, provide emotional support, etc." This is obviously a perfect example of a patriarchal value system which would give a secretary credit for doing "something" but not a wife.

These values have also infiltrated the spiritual path as well, and the tremendous spiritual potential of motherhood as a soteriological path has not been given enough appreciation and support. Someone commented to me when I had finished *Women of Wisdom* what a great accomplishment it was and what a lot of work it represented.

I replied that compared to the work, thought, and energy I have put into even one of my children, the book was easy.

I am still searching and seeking for practices and ideas that can be concretely applied to daily life situations. I think this is an integral part of spirituality for women. At the moment I use a combination of daily meditation without the children, occasional practice with them when they request it, occasional retreats, and trying to apply the equilibrium, humor, and sense of openness gained by these moments of quiet to the rest of my life. I must confess that I do have a longing to "get on with it" when they grow up, but I realize this is really missing the point, so I am trying to integrate spirituality with the rest of my life.

It may be that for the deeper states of spiritual development, unless one is already very advanced, extensive solitude or semi-solitude are necessary. We see in the biographies in *Women of Wisdom* that all the women chose this living situation. But I still feel that there is a vast untapped resource of female wisdom within so-called worldly life which could enrich our ideas about spirituality tremendously. Probably these resources have remained untapped because those who have defined the spiritual path for the last few thousand years have been men who associated spirituality with a separateness from nature and all that it represents, in terms of birth, death, children, and so on.

We must still struggle to find spiritual ways that are adapted to us as *women* and which validate and develop us as *women*—not as asexual entities who must deny their inherent nature in order to be acceptable on the spiritual path. When we do this we will certainly be of greater benefit to others than if we are trying to ape men, following traditions that were created by men for men.

Even though I believe that on the absolute level the true nature of the mind has no sexual characteristics, on the relative level the means to achieving illumination must be adapted to the individual. The differences between individuals must be appreciated and even celebrated. Women and men are different when we speak from a relative point of view, but how these differences are interpreted and whether these differences are seen positively or negatively is a matter of cultural and religious conditioning.

In order for women to find viable paths to liberation, we need the inspiration of other women who have succeeded in remaining true to their own energies without becoming fixated on their sexual gender and have, with this integrity, reached complete liberation. Hearing the biographies of real women, not mythological figures or divinities, can begin to fulfill this need.

We can also be inspired by the "Great Mother" principle at the core of Tantric Buddhism. This aspect of the feminine is mentioned several times in the biography of Machig Lapdron in *Women of Wisdom*.[2] She may be called "Yum Chenmo," "The Mother of the Buddhas," the "Womb of the Tathagatas," or "Prajna Paramita." This is the primordial feminine which is the basic ground. It is described as feminine because it has the power to give birth.

Trungpa Rinpoche explains the "Great Mother" in this way:

> In phenomenal experience, whether pleasure or pain, birth or death, sanity or insanity, good or bad, it is necessary to have a basic ground. This basic ground is known in Buddhist literature as the mother principle. Prajnaparamita (the perfection of wisdom) is called the mother-consort of all the Buddhas. ... As a principle of cosmic structure, the all-accommodating basic ground is neither male nor female. One might call it hermaphroditic, but due to its quality of fertility or potentiality, it is regarded as feminine.[3]

Starhawk in her book on witchcraft describes a very similar if not identical principle:

> In the beginning of the Goddess is the All, virgin, meaning complete within herself. Although She is called *Goddess,* She could just as well be called *God*—sex has not yet come into being. ... Yet the female nature of the ground of being is being stressed—because the process of creation that is about to occur is a *birth* process. The world is born, not made, and not commanded into being.[4]

The "Great Mother" is different from the Christian God, because it does not intend to produce a world and set down laws. The whole thing is spontaneous rather than intentional. God separates himself to create the world, but the feminine just gives birth spontaneously.

In Tantric Buddhism the symbolic manifestation of the "Great Mother" is the downward-pointing triangle called *Chos.'byung* (pronounced "chojung"), meaning "source of dharmas," the cosmic cervix, or the gate of all birth. It is three-dimensional and is white on the outside and red on the inside, but it is not something material. Trungpa Rinpoche explains it thus in his commentary on the Anuttara Tantra of Vajra Varahi in the Kagyu tradition:

> The source of dharmas arises out of emptiness and has three characteristics: it is unborn, non-dwelling and unceasing. Essentially it is absolute space with a boundary or frame. This represents the coemergent quality of wisdom and confusion arising from the emptiness of space. The source of dharmas is sometimes referred to as a channel for sunyata or as the cosmic cervix.... The shape of the triangle—sharp at the bottom and wide at the top—signifies that every aspect of space can be accommodated at once, microcosm and macrocosm, the most minute situations as well as the most vast.[5]

It is white on the outside because it is unconditioned and non-dwelling, and this is balanced and also activated by the blood-red interior, the transcendental ecstatic lust. Vajrayogini both stands on the triangular source of dharmas and has it in her "secret place," roughly the position of the human womb.

The Great Mother is described as "the void state of all the dharmas which we call the Mother of all Creation" in the biography of Machig Lapdron:

> When Machig was forty-one she entered the cave of Pugzang at the end of spring. While there, she received from Tara very rare teachings and initiations into the mandala of the Five Dhyani Buddhas yab-yum. Tara manifested as the consort of the Five Buddhas and they gave this prophecy to her:
>
> "You try to continue this teaching. It contains instructions of transforming the five passions, conquering the five Maras, entering into the five wisdoms, and achieving empowerment from the Five Dhyani Buddhas. This teaching has been manifested for all sentient beings so you, yogini, keep this rare teaching well. Make it the essence of your practice and enter into the stages of visualization and post-visualization with this mantra. Then, through your children, your lineage will continue like a string of pearls, one right after the other. After ten generations the lineage of your family will be interrupted. You will become the Vajra Demon Subduer Dakini, the chief of all

dakinis. You hold the secret consort, the Khatavanga, you hold the secret protection mantras and the lineage."

Then Machig praised the Five Dhyani Buddhas and Tara and said: "You have been very kind to me and have given me power. I am just a weak, stupid woman, but now I have become someone who can benefit others because of your grace."

Tara smiled and looked at the other dakinis and said: "Oh yogini, you have accomplished everything that you were supposed to accomplish of the teachings of Tripitaka [the Sutras (teachings), the Vinaya (monastic code), and the Abhidharma (Buddhist psychology), which constitute the Hinayana teachings] and Tantra. Now I am demonstrating to you that you are the incarnation of Prajna Paramita, Vajradhatu Consort, Source of all understanding of the Dharma. Do not be discouraged."

Then Machig said: "How can I know that we are not the same? Why am I the source of all understanding of the Dharma? Where is the Great Mother now?"

Tara said: "Listen, yogini, your past is cleared from your heart but I will explain it to you. The Great Mother is the void state of all the dharmas which we call Mother of all Creation. The Mother is the Mother of the Buddhas of the Three Times, the Dharmata of the Absolute State, beyond all obstructions, the pure essence of egoless voidness-Prajna. But accordingly, the Great Mother who is the object of offerings and accumulation of merit, by the energy of the prayers and invocations of sentient beings and by means of the luminosity of the voidness of the egolessness of things as they are, became a sphere *(Tig.le)* of yellow-red light which manifested as the Great Mother in a palace of pure vision, surrounded by Buddhas and Bodhisattvas of the Ten Directions. She had one face and four arms and was a golden color. She sat in the lotus position and in her heart was the orange letter MUM in a bead of light.

"She had all of the signs to perfection and lived in the Tushita heaven [a heavenly realm where the Buddha allegedly dwelt before his birth in Lumbini]. From my heart came a dark-green light which entered into the heart of the Great Mother and made her heart function. Rays of light spread out from her heart and accumulated the wisdom and blessings of the Buddhas and Bodhisattvas in all directions, and then this empowered light was reabsorbed back into the heart of the Great Mother. Then from there a dark-blue dakini with one face and four hands came forth. From her came the Vajradhatu dakini and infinite manifestations of the body, speech, and mind—

accomplishments which multiplied, and the essence of her mind became Dorje Dudulma, 'the Vajra Demon Subduer,' who has one face, two hands, and a pig's head coming out of the side of her head. She has power over all the dakinis, and the three worlds tremble under her. She activates all powerful beings and is the source of energy for all the dakinis. Dorje Dudulma incarnated many times to help sentient beings. She studied the Tripitaka and did much good for sentient beings. In the end she became you in Tibet!"[6]

In Buddhist philosophy all dharmas (which are fundamental factors or things out of which all experience is built) have no self-existing essence. A person or thing is the summation of its parts and has no self-essence, or soul, and is therefore void of self or ego. This essential emptiness is the primary matrix of existence and is therefore called the "Mother of Creation." It is the basic space that permeates everything and undermines the ego. Voidness is an expression of space. The Great Mother principle is the space that gives birth to the phenomenal world. This process of emptiness or space giving birth to phenomena goes on all the time. It is not a question of "once upon a time," but rather a fundamental process which goes on continually. So this permeating space and boundary, which is fundamental to all form, is the Great Mother, and her symbol is the downward-pointing triangle, the source of dharmas.

The Prajna Paramita, the perfection of profound cognition, is also a part of the feminine principle. It is said to be the "Womb of the Tathagatas" (the Buddhas, those who have gone beyond) or the "Mother of the Buddhas." The Prajna Paramita is the quality of sharp perception which comes with the relaxation of the ego. Meditation, because it slows down the confused grasping aspect of the mind, allows the natural luminous clarity of the mind, prajna, to come forth. This faculty of profound cognition is the source of or the womb for Buddhas to grow in and is therefore called "the womb of the Buddhas."

The combination of profound cognition, Prajna, the feminine, and skillful activity, Upaya, the masculine, is represented in male and female figures in sexual embrace in Tibetan Tantric art. This is called the union of *yum* (the feminine) and *yab* (the masculine). But when we speak of yab-yum we are no longer at the level of the primordial mother, because the Great Mother has no masculine counterpart, she (it) is basic space and emptiness. When we reach to the level of yab-yum we are talking about descendants of primordial space, energies which are working as polarities. The qualities of these energies are assigned by the culture which gives them labels. As we can see from the opposite attributes given to the masculine and feminine in Hindu and Buddhist Tantras, there is no absolute quality for the masculine or feminine. The Tibetans attribute the dynamic energy to the male, though the lunar energy was also considered masculine and the feminine is the wisdom aspect associated with the sun.

We can see, from the passage cited above from the biography of Machig Lapdron, the way the primordial feminine moves through the dimension of light and finally into female form. This human form might be called yogini or dakini, but Machig had to meet with her roots in the Great Mother before she could experientially move beyond the cultural prejudices that told her that she was weak, stupid, and not spiritually as capable as men. The sense of a noble lineage coming through the Great Mother, Tara, which Machig was shown, can also give a sense of spiritual heritage and inspiration to women. From this point of view we are not evil temptresses or unwelcome renunciants in a religion whose founder admitted women reluctantly, nor are we ignorant householders who might be able to renounce someday. Rather, we can connect with the lineage of the divine feminine, the primal matrix, imbued with compassion, actively wrathful and destructive where energy is blocked, ecstatic and playful, understanding the true nature of reality.

1. Alex Wayman, *The Buddhist Tantras* (New York: Samuel Weiser, 1973), p. 83.

2. *Women of Wisdom,* pp. 141–204.

3. Chogyam Trungpa, *Maitreya IV* (Berkeley, California: Shambhala Publications, 1973), pp. 23–24.

4. Starhawk, *The Spiral Dance* (New York: Harper & Row, 1979), p. 24.

5. Chogyam Trungpa, in "The Diamond Path and The Silk Route," exhibition catalogue, edited by D. Klimburg-Slater (Los Angeles: University of Southern California Arts Council), p. 236.

6. *Women of Wisdom,* pp. 176–177.

Melody Ermachild Chavis

Walking a Few Steps Farther

PINNED TO THE BULLETIN BOARD on the porch of the Berkeley Zen Center is a big chart of spidery lines with fine-print names spelled out in English and in Chinese characters. It is a chart of the Soto Zen lineage, the names of scores of Asian men, starting at the left side with Bodhidharma, who sailed from India to China in 532. The names of his heirs march all the way to the far right edge of the chart, ending with the founder of our temple, Shunryu Suzuki Roshi.

I stand on the porch regarding this patrilineage. *Every single one of them had a mother,* I think.

It's easier for me to identify with the life of his wife, left behind with her child, than with the young man going off to seek a spiritual life who was to become the Buddha. I was the oldest daughter of my family, and a young mother. Taking care of others has been a theme of my life. How could I choose a spiritual practice whose founder left his family, without a word in the middle of the night, to seek his way?

Yet in our sangha, several of the senior students are women, and they were there to welcome me when I came. Women frequently lecture in our zendo, and they often mention that when they first came to Buddhism they too, like me, worried that because of their gender they might be in the wrong place.

Sometimes the speakers repeat the story of Pajapati, Shakyamuni Buddha's aunt who raised him after his mother died, and how she led hundreds of women over many miles to ask the Buddha for teachings and for the right to become nuns. They had to ask three times before they were allowed to take vows. The nuns' order died out after a couple of hundred years. The women's tradition in Buddhism is only now being renewed. The name of one American woman, the late Maurine Stuart Roshi, has now been added to the lineage of the Diamond Sangha in Hawai'i.

Our temple sometimes has women's *sesshins,* and when we raise our voices to chant the ancient chants, I am always moved, thinking of the extra steps our women ancestors took, the extra times they had to ask. Hearing our voices, I like to think of that whole group of women walking together with Pajapati, instead of going one by one to hear the Buddha. I take comfort in the knowledge that I am not on my own, but one of many women who are practicing Buddhism together.

I picture the women walking so far with Pajapati, and I wonder about them. If they had no children, why not? Were their children grown up? Did they leave them behind? I picture them sometimes walking along helping each other, some of them with babies on their hips.

We must have women teachers—not because they understand the Dharma differently, but simply because women pull out from the whole body of Dharma what has spoken to them, benefiting everyone.

Maylie Scott, one of the women who teaches at Berkeley Zen Center, explained the meaning of the Full Moon Bodhisattva Ceremony, when we renew the four vows of the bodhisattva. The first vow is: "All my ancient twisted karma, from beginningless greed, hate, and delusion, I now fully avow."

Maylie explained the avowal of karma, one of the central teachings of Buddhism, in a way that made me able to understand its practice in my own life. She said she used to think that to avow meant to "discard," but that it actually means to "acknowledge." I, too, had thought at first that avowal meant something like "renounce," and when I repeated the vow, I would feel a little discouraged. Getting rid of all my ancient karma seemed an impossible task. Acknowledgment, though, sounds more possible.

Maylie gave a personal example. Her grown son had telephoned her. He was thirty, newly married, and his new wife had been called away by her job for a week and had no time for him. Maylie's son found himself awash in grief, missing his wife, and he associated his feelings with the time that Maylie had returned to work full time when he was two years old.

I could relate to this story. Several years ago my grown daughter invited me to lunch and told me what she and her therapist thought some of my mothering's ill effects on her had been. It was all I could do to listen without defending myself.

Maylie said one of the hardest things for her, too, is working with the effects of her years as a young and pressured mother. She told us how she and her son spent that long phone call avowing some karma, grieving their separation when he was two, and together letting some of it go. They hung up, she said, with full hearts.

At the end of Maylie's lecture, many people in the zendo had eyes full of tears.

In the question-and-answer period after the lecture, another mother in the hall raised her hand and asked, "What if your grown child doesn't call, and you don't have the chance to avow your karma with them?"

We practice, Maylie said. We still avow our "ancient twisted karma," sitting alone. If we're sitting by the phone holding onto our regrets, it might not ring. Our practice is to acknowledge karma and let it go, without anything extra, without shame or guilt, with no remorse.

It seems to me that being a mother necessarily includes feeling regret. I often ask myself what it means to be given human birth as a person who gives life to another. The karma of all mothers is as mysterious to me as the vast clouds of gas in outer space from which stars are born. I try to hold on to the mystery of my motherhood, but not to the mistakes that I've made. We avow our ancient karma first in the Full Moon Ceremony, and then we vow to "live and be lived for the benefit of all beings." The words "be lived" make sense to me as a mother. When I had young children I felt I was lived by them, and I still often feel as if my children and grandchildren are living me.

Of course, women have destinies beyond our lives as mothers. For years I've worked as a private investigator researching the appeals of death row inmates, conducting long interviews with murderers. I have spent a lot of time with people who live in hell realms of regret, spinning inside cyclones of unacknowledged karma.

Most people don't think that prisoners suffer the torment of remorse while they wait in prison to die. And not all prisoners do; some steadfastly deny their crimes in spite of crushing amounts of evidence, precisely because they are flailing about so far from avowal. These people cannot let themselves feel the emotions that would overwhelm them if they were to acknowledge that they had done such terrible acts.

Many, though, are impaled on the meat hook of "if only." "If only I'd gone to live with my dad...." "If only I'd stayed in the service...." "If only my mom loved me...."

Gene is one man I know who is twisting like this. He is a very young man who was convicted of killing several women after having sex with them. While I wait for the officers to bring Gene out of his cell for our meeting, I get a small offering ready for him: a drink from the vending machine. In the interview cell I'll be locked into with Gene, I set the can carefully on some paper towels as if they are a place mat. He comes in, a tall, heavyset man, and shakes my hand politely.

Gene loathes himself for what he's done, to the women and to his own life. He says he wants to die. He even says he hates himself for being too afraid to commit suicide, as some other death row inmates he has known have done, hanging themselves from their cell bars at night.

"I'm a moron," he says, slumped over, utterly downcast but not able to cry. "I'm an idiot."

He hangs his head. I gaze at his sandy hair, thinking about the karma passed on by his mother. She had failed to protect him when her father, his grandfather, raped him. She, too, had been molested by the man and was never able to hold or hug or kiss her own son during his whole childhood.

Investigating Gene's family story, I heard about belts used for whipping generations of children, belts with buckles that left marks. Gene has Native American ancestors in both his parents' families. He took the women to a remote mountain ravine, and shot them in a scene chillingly like a massacre, as if what had been done to his ancestors came down through the family, unhealed.

The pain of the families of the murdered women is also there in the cell with us.

Karma seems to me to twist down upon us as if it started far beyond our galaxy, light years above us, and is only now reaching us.

Tibetan Buddhists have a teaching that asks us to recognize every person as if he or she was our own mother. How can I see Gene this way? Certainly, he is a being who is living me, as I struggle to be with him.

Gene and I sit together at the eye of a storm of hatred. If you took a poll, most Americans would probably say they would like to see him dead. Many would say his suffering does not matter. His sentence, under our laws, is to live in this prison and perhaps to be put to death in the gas chamber, but no one has sentenced Gene to hate himself so much. Buddhism teaches me that if he could let go of some of his pain before he died, all beings would benefit.

I have seen that the smallest moments of avowal are precious windows of enlightenment through which people can step out of themselves—even in a prison—to offer help to others, perhaps another inmate, or a guard, sometimes even to make amends to the families of their victims. No one knows how far kindness may travel. No one knows when the work of a life may begin.

But how can I console Gene? Reaching out to touch him would be completely inappropriate where we are. When Gene hangs his head, another inmate peers, interested, from the next cell. This is not a safe place to look at pain.

I understand regret. I lived the middle part of my life, twenty-four years, wanting to start over again and do something differently. I wanted not to have given up my son for adoption. Even in the moment when I signed the papers, I wished I could stop my hand from writing. And from the moment I walked out of the adoption agency I wanted to run back and take back the decision my eigh-teen-year-old self had made, take the other path. But it was too late. Over and over I pictured myself saying "No!" and walking out with my tiny baby in my arms, even though I wouldn't have had any idea where we were going. Ideas about sin and retribution, repentance and punishment, did not help me bear my remorse.

My son gave me the chance to acknowledge what had happened by seeking me out when he was twenty-four years old. We did the best we could to open our hearts to our reunion. But for the first few years, we twisted in the bitter wind of "what if. . . ." When he looked at the photos in our family albums of his sisters wearing the Halloween costumes I sewed for them, he asked, "Where was I?"

It was wonderful for me to meet and love this young man who looks so much like his sisters and like me, but nothing could bring back the baby, the little boy I had lost. All those precious years were utterly gone.

I first came to Buddhism right after I had met my son, and the first few years of practicing I sat with my regrets. Buddhist teachings showed me the practice of being with what is. Gradually, I explored the shadows in my ancient twisted karma that had brought me to the moment when I signed those papers. Gradually, I found compassion for myself.

Now I picture my infant son flying to take human form inside my body. I birthed him and then sent him to his other mother to be raised, all of us doing the best we could. After years of sorting out together the effects of his adoption on both of our lives, he has found his place in our family. I have regained my son.

Although it is hard to accept, I tell myself that each baby somehow comes to exactly the right mother, even if she isn't able to raise him, or even to give birth to him, even if terrible things happen. It just is, and we go on. And still we try our best to save children from terrible conditions.

When I look at Gene, a big man collapsed in his remorse, I see the downcast five-year-old child he must have been, slumped alone somewhere after one of his grandfather's attacks.

"I don't think you're an idiot," I venture awkwardly. He lifts his head and struggles on with the interview, trying, for now, to stay in this life, to cooperate with his appeal, to make himself vulnerable in a completely unsafe situation.

Talking about his grandfather one day, Gene picked up one of the rough brown paper towels and pressed it to his eyes. A tiny bit of acknowledgment of what had happened seeped out of them.

In avowal is liberation. My own struggle to understand and live the Bodhisattva Vows has become central to my life. These are the vows I imagine the women with Pajapati walked so far to receive, to be given an opportunity to practice. When I regard the lineage that preserved the teaching of avowal, and transmitted it through the centuries so that I could hear and learn it, one of my feelings is a deep sense of gratitude.

I want all of us, men and women together, to acknowledge the patriarchal history of the transmission of the Dharma, to avow it and go on, practicing together with this knowledge, this avowal, so that the names of women will be added to the lineage chart on the porch outside the zendo.

Alta Brown

The Ruthlessness of the Practice
of Compassion

MY PRINCIPLE TEACHER, Chogyam Trungpa Rinpoche, laughed when
he told the members of his sangha that he had tricked us into taking
Bodhisattva Vows. We were delighted. He had confounded us again.
I was delighted, until I discovered that this promise was not like a
wedding vow, that there was no possibility of divorce. Of course,
those of us who have taken these vows are usually only embryonic
bodhisattvas. Nonetheless, we are faced with the necessity of learning to practice compassion in a cultural context entirely different
than that from which the Mahayana Buddhist tradition emerged.

As Americans in the Tibetan Buddhist sangha have begun to establish forms of practice which are directly related to our respective pro-
fessions, we have discovered the larger interfaith communities. My
part of this discussion is an attempt to engage in a praxis-oriented mul-
tilogue with those from other religious traditions who practice compassion out of different epistemological and soteriological locations.

At this time, and in this particular society, physical and mental

A version of this essay originally appeared in the April 1995 issue of the
newsletter published by The Center for Women and Religion of The Graduate Theological Union in Berkeley, California. It was one part of a three-
way interreligious discussion of compassion which included articles by a
woman rabbi and a woman Catholic pastor.

violence is escalating exponentially. For this reason, it is particularly important that those of us for whom the practice of compassion is a principle ethical mandate learn to work together in such a fashion that our practice enriches one another and contributes to the alleviation of the suffering which has become one of the distinctive features of the American cultural landscape. My teachers have encouraged me to do this, and the vows, which seem to have taken on a life of their own, have left me no choice.

◇

The central ethical mandate of the Mahayana Buddhist path is the practice of compassion, and this practice is ruthless—as ruthlessly compelling as the last stages of labor and as adamantine as the transition into death. When aspiring bodhisattvas, the ethical heroes of the Mahayana path, take the vows that commit them to the practice of compassion on behalf of every form of sentience, there is no escape clause. For as many lifetimes as are required, in fact, until all of the "six realms of samsara" are emptied, the bodhisattva's vow extends beyond both their ego boundaries and the dictates of convention.

If a particular situation requires some form of intervention which directly contravenes the most strongly held ethical prohibitions of the Buddhist code, bodhisattvas will nonetheless have no choice but to do exactly what the situation demands. Even killing a human being, the most strictly proscribed of all acts, is permitted in some circumstances, such as "[t]aking the life of someone about to commit an act entailing immediate retribution *(anantarya-karma)* in order to prevent them suffering the evil consequences of that act."[1]

Admittedly, such latitude is potentially quite dangerous, and suggests the possibility of real abuse. However, the ethical mandates of the Mahayana path are based upon the assumption that bodhisattvas will continuously involve themselves in meditative and post-meditative disciplines which are calculated to decisively undercut ego-protective states of mind, which according to this tradition are the source of any potential abuse. The practice of compassion can be ruthless precisely because it is founded on such disciplines.

Webster's Ninth New Collegiate Dictionary defines "ruthlessness" as a lack of mercy. For this reason, it may seem peculiar if not self-contradictory to characterize the practice of compassion as ruthless. If any quality is definitively associated with compassion, that quality is mercy. In fact, mercy is defined in terms of compassion, as "1. a: Compassion or forbearance shown esp. to an offender or to one subject to one's power."[2]

How can we understand the ruthless quality of compassion? In answering this question, we might formulate another question: To whom is compassion merciless? The answer to the latter question could not be more traditionally Buddhist: the offender to whom no mercy can be extended is the limited notion of a separate, autonomous "self." Within the Mahayana tradition, the attitude which cherishes the interests of self above those of every other being is considered to be the locus of every form of ethical enormity. For this reason, self-cherishing must be ruthlessly eliminated.

As Anne Klein has explained in *Meeting the Great Bliss Queen*, the self that is denied when a selfless attitude is recommended is "neither the modern psychological self nor the unique individual of common Western understanding. It is a self described in terms of its structure rather than its story."[3] The Dalai Lama describes this most common concept of self in the following manner:

> There are many different ways in which the person or I appears to our minds. In one way the I appears to be permanent, unitary, and under its own power; in this mode of appearance the I seems to be a separate entity from mind and body with the person as the user or enjoyer and the mind and body as what is used or enjoyed.[4]

According to the Buddhist tradition, this perception is profoundly mistaken. Buddhist teachers contend that the self is an idea, a conceptual construct, which is no more a "real" entity than is a philosophical concept such as poststructuralism or phenomenology. In *The Concept of Mind*,[5] the Western philosopher Gilbert Ryle explains a similar mistake in the attempt to "find" the university by inspecting the buildings, examining university publications, and interviewing faculty. The university is a conceptual construct which is both more and less than all of the entities which are understood to be included when the term is used. It is less, in that it has no physical existence; the buildings and properties which are now part of a particular university can easily become something else if the property is sold. It is more, in that the university is not exclusively identified with either any individual entity, or all of the entities which any university is said to include.

Self, in the context of Buddhist doctrine and practice, is understood as a conceptual construct, in that it is constructed by the mind. It is an idea of identity which is defended by certain reflexive strategies such angry rejection, passionate appropriation, and self-enclosed denial. Even though this construct is essentially nothing more than a conceptual shorthand for a series of structural dynamics such as feeling and perception, its experiential status is so compelling that any perceived threat is experienced as a survival crisis: defensive strategies are marshaled and the boundaries between self and other are strengthened. In this way, the series of conceptual structures which function together as the idea of a substantial, independent identity act as the basis not only for our own suffering but the suffering experienced by every other form of sentience.

The ruthless precision that cuts cleanly through all self-cherishing is traditionally called "the wisdom which sees emptiness." It is understood as the ability to identify the "self" as inherently insubstantial. With this understanding we can experience others directly, out from behind the screen of ideas through which our ordinary perception is organized. The metaphor of vision is employed because this conceptualizing process operates like a kind of blindness, selectively isolating certain aspects of any experiential situation, contorting others, and forming an interpretation on the basis of these operations. The focus around which the interpretation is organized is the notion of "I," "me," and "my" projects, possessions, and relationships. Interpretation becomes particularly obstructive when any significant threat to the organizing principle—the self—presents itself. Seeing the emptiness of selfhood—its lack of independent, inherent existence—renders these machinations transparent.

In the Tibetan tradition, "the wisdom which sees emptiness" is symbolically represented as an exceedingly sharp two-edged sword. The sword of wisdom is said to cut both the concept of substantial identity and the screen of self-protective mechanisms that obscure any given set of relationships.

Without this incisive wisdom, with which the bodhisattva can correctly and completely assess a problematic situation, the practice of compassion will in all probability degenerate into clumsy intrusion. Trungpa Rinpoche describes this form of intervention as a form of vandalism:

> The idea of helping each other is more subtle than we might think. Generally, when we try to help other people, we make a nuisance of ourselves, make demands upon them. . . . We want to make a big deal of ourselves, no matter if the other person wants to accept us or not. We do not really want to expose our basic character, but we want to dominate the situation around us.[6]

According to Trungpa, it is this desire to dominate which creates the conditions for personal vandalism:

> We just push ourselves into the other person's territory, like a tank going through a wall. We are not only committing vandalism to someone else's territory, but we are disrupting our own territory as well—it is inward vandalism too.[7]

The ruthless precision of wisdom is said to cut through cherished conceptions of self that disguise a hidden agenda, such as domination, while at the same time revealing the contours of a particular relational situation which either requires or prohibits intervention. This "wisdom which sees emptiness" is ruthless because it respects no agenda. It cuts decisively through any and all conceptual constructions, regardless of how much privilege—social, political, spiritual—any particular notion has accrued. It penetrates to the core of the most complex confluence of events.

"The wisdom which sees emptiness" is the partner of compassion, one of the "two wings" of enlightenment in the Mahayana tradition. Without wisdom, compassion is blind. It may become another vehicle by which the "I" expresses, defends, and aggrandizes itself. For this reason, the practice of compassion must necessarily include a continuing, merciless scrutiny of every mechanism which supports the idea of inherent identity.

It is interesting to note that in the general context of Western culture, the warmth and nurturing qualities associated with motherhood are also closely associated with compassion. Unfortunately, this form of compassion is often characterized as openhearted but also somewhat softheaded, the province of women, especially mothers, which is free of the male constraints of incisive, deliberative precision. However, in the context of Mahayana Buddhist doctrine and practice, it is the "wisdom which sees emptiness" that is associated with motherhood. Tsultrim Allione describes this most fundamental form of feminine energy as "the luminous clarity of the mind," which is the birthplace of enlightenment, or "the 'Mother of the Buddhas.'"[8]

The primordial wisdom which reveals the transparency of conceptualization is traditionally called the "perfection of wisdom," and it is:

> ... said to be the sacred mother because it is the mother of, i.e. that which gives rise to, the sacred ones, namely the Buddhas. It is through developing an understanding of voidness in one's own mind that one is enabled finally to realize the state of Buddhahood.
>
> Just as a child cannot be born without a mother, likewise, a Buddha cannot be born without relying on the "mother" of the perfection of wisdom.[9]

According to this account, feminine energy is of the nature of primordial, nonconceptual wisdom; as such, it is the womb of enlightenment, the mother of Buddhahood. It is, then, both the condition for enlightenment and, also, as we have seen, the necessary condition for the skillful practice of compassion.

It is not so difficult to understand why this should be the case. The series of conceptual constructions which create and structure the self are the locus of suffering and the specific occasion for the production of all samsaric states of mind. When these formulations are cut through, enlightened mind is revealed and with it the all-encompassing warmth and skill of compassion which is the heart of the Mahayana path.

The mother of the Buddhas wields the sword of wisdom, and she is ruthless.

Feminist scholar Sara Ruddick claims that an accurate, more complete Western characterization of maternal warmth and care does not exclude this quality of ruthless precision. In fact, according to Ruddick, "It is an ongoing task within maternal practice and the morality of love to see and speak truly while conceptualizing a truth that is caring."[10] Such care cannot always be conventionally kind, she argues, for while maternal love "is said to be gentle and unconditional," it is actually "erotic, inseparable from anger, fierce and fraught with ambivalence."[11]

This is so, she claims, because mothers must not only protect their children from each other and the dangers represented by individual adults and adult institutions, but from the frustration and confusion of mothers themselves:

> Children are vulnerable creatures and the vulnerable generally tend to elicit either aggression or care. Recalcitrance and anger tend to provoke aggression, and children are provocative.[12]

The real practice of maternal care must necessarily include the ruthlessly precise examination of both the specifics of any given situation and the set of attitudes and emotional states which the mothering person brings into that context. Whoever it is that mothers, in whatever capacity, she or he must, in order to protect the object of her or his compassionate concern, practice at least some version of the mercilessly critical assessment Buddhists call "the wisdom which sees emptiness"—the emptiness of self.

Ruddick maintains that truth is often unpalatable, but the person who mothers with genuine care must be able to see, speak, and act upon the truth. Mahayana Buddhist teachers would agree, but they would also hasten to insist that compassion and wisdom must always be paired. This tradition teaches that the merciless, incisive perception which sees the transparency of conceptual formulations, particularly the notion of self, never excludes the warmth and gentleness of compassion, but rather that the genuine warmth of Buddhanature is supported and revealed by that precision. The logic of the Mahayana path requires both compassion and wisdom simply because they are two linked aspects of the same practice.

The mother of the Buddhas wields the sword of wisdom, and she is ruthless in the service of compassion.

1. Damien Keown, *The Nature of Buddhist Ethics* (New York: St. Martin's Press, 1992), p. 143.

2. *Webster's Ninth New Collegiate Dictionary* (Springfield, Massachusetts: Merriam Webster, Inc. Publishers, 1988), p. 743.

3. Anne Carolyn Klein, *Meeting the Great Bliss Queen: Buddhists, Feminists, and the Art of The Self* (Boston: Beacon Press, 1995), p. 124.

4. Quoted in Klein, *Meeting the Great Bliss Queen,* p. 124.

5. Gilbert Ryle, *The Concept of Mind* (New York: Barnes & Noble Books, 1949, 1969).

6. Chogyam Trungpa, *The Myth of Freedom* (Berkeley, California: Shambhala Publications, 1976), p. 90.

7. Trungpa, *The Myth of Freedom,* p. 90.

8. Tsultrim Allione, *Women of Wisdom* (London: Routledge & Kegan Paul, 1984), p. 23.

9. Geshe Rabten, *Echoes of Voidness,* translated and edited by Stephen Batchelor (London: Wisdom Publications, 1983), p. 24.

10. Sara Ruddick, "Remarks on the Sexual Politics of Reason," in *Women and Moral Theory,* edited by Eva Feder Kittay and Diana T. Meyers (New Jersey: Bowman & Littlefield, 1987), p. 246.

11. Ruddick, "Remarks on the Sexual Politics of Reason," p. 246.

12. Ruddick, "Remarks on the Sexual Politics of Reason," p. 249.

Rita M. Gross

Community, Work, Relationship, and Family: Renunciation and Balance in American Buddhist Practice

ONE OF THE BASIC perennial Buddhist questions concerns what kind of lifestyle actually promotes "enlightenment," whatever that might be. While for many of us, enlightenment may seem to be something we can't define adequately, I think most of us hope to become more sane, gentle, grounded, helpful people through our involvement with Buddhist practice. For me, that constitutes the beginnings of an enlightened quality in my life, and fuller experiences of enlightenment will have to grow out of those qualities. But what lifestyles actually promote those qualities of gentleness and sanity? If the question of appropriate lifestyle is resolved, then we need to question what attitudes are to be cultivated as we go about our lives, since observing the external formalities associated with a specific lifestyle is not guaranteed to result in gentleness and sanity.

In early Buddhism, which has often been regarded by Westerners as the definitive form of Buddhism, the answer was obvious: renunciation of the conventional lifestyle involving career and reproduction in favor of a monastic lifestyle that bypasses both was thought to be more conducive to enlightenment for most people because it was more conducive to an attitude of detachment. But for some forms of Buddhism, especially those belonging to later developments in Buddhism lumped together as "Mahayana

Buddhism," the distinction between monastics and laypeople is not so clear-cut. The *attitude* of renunciation is thought to be more important than any particular lifestyle and not necessarily linked with any specific lifestyle. Nevertheless, except for Pure Land Buddhism and, to a lesser extent, other Japanese forms of Buddhism, most forms of Mahayana Buddhism still continue to honor monastics over householders in some way. Therefore, for me, doing my practices in the Tibetan tradition, in which there is a clear distinction between monastics and householders and in which monastics are highly valued, this distinction is perhaps more decisive than it is for other Western Buddhists, whose training is in one of the less monastic Japanese forms of Buddhism. On the other hand, Tibetan Buddhism also honors non-monastic lifestyles that encourage intensive Buddhist practice, which means that the monastic-lay distinction is not as decisive as in early Buddhism, which equated serious Buddhist practice with the monastic lifestyle.

Obviously, in a certain sense, for most Western Buddhists, the question of choice of lifestyle has already been made. In terms of the formal, traditional distinction between monastic and lay Buddhists, most Western Buddhists are lay practitioners, in that we have not taken vows that imply celibacy and renunciation of family and occupation. However, that affiliation as lay Buddhist practitioners does not have the simplicity and finality for us American lay Buddhists as it does for most classical Asian patterns of Buddhism, nor does it limit us to the same peripheral role of supporting monastics as it does in most forms of Asian Buddhism. Most of us see ourselves as trying to engage in full-fledged Buddhist practice as laypeople who also have some involvement in family and some responsibility for livelihood—an ideal that would have seemed preposterous in many forms of Asian Buddhism. Therefore, for us, questions of the interface between "enlightenment" and community, work, relationship, and family are nowhere nearly so clear-cut as they probably were for many lay Buddhists. We are in many ways without map or model, trying to find our way and to create new pathways.

Renunciation and Community: The Basic Tools

In my path-seeking here,[1] I want to use two torchlights from traditional Buddhism to light my way and guide my contemplations. One of them comes from the lineage supplication chant of my tradition, the Karma Kagyu sect of Tibetan Vajrayana Buddhism.[2] It consists of a single line from that chant: "renunciation is the foot of meditation." This line, of course, brings up an obvious question: "What is renunciation?" My other source of inspiration is the life story of the Buddha, read in a midrashic[3] style. In my midrash, I will counterpoise the Buddha's renunciation of conventional family and livelihood with his founding of a countercultural community that replaced them, asking what message we lay meditators can read from these choices. In these two traditional beacons, I think we may find some clues about how to deal with community, relationship, family, and work in the context of American Buddhism as a Buddhism of lay practitioners who fully engage the traditional Buddhist practices usually taken on only by monastics.

The term "renunciation" needs to be discussed at some length, since the traditional formal renunciation of family and livelihood is not what is meant by renunciation in the lifestyle of the lay practitioner. Nevertheless, the more I am involved in Buddhism, the more clearly I see that renunciation is indeed foundational to Buddhist outlook and practice and the more I am drawn to its mood. Perhaps the fact that my refuge name[4] includes the word "renunciation" has added some intensity to my contemplations of renunciation in the context of lay meditation. However, it should be noted that in Vajrayana tradition, renunciation may not look like many peoples' image of renunciation as asceticism. I also want to discuss what I mean by "community" and by "relationship." I contend that in the lifestyle of the lay meditator, they are "the matrix of enlightenment," by which I mean that they are at least as essential to developing sanity and gentleness as are study and practice, which are traditionally stressed as the matrix of enlightenment. I have dealt extensively with this thesis in previous works, especially in my book *Buddhism After Patriarchy*,[5] in which I devoted a major portion of my last chapter to developing this point.

Building upon these definitions, in this contemplation I will explore two intertwining and interlocking theses. It is my contention that in contemporary America, including American Buddhism, people spend far too much time and energy on work and family, and far too little time and energy on relationship and community, for a sane lifestyle ever to develop. Secondly, it is my contention that proper limitation of work and family is essential to a viable American lay Buddhism and that without such limitation, lay Buddhism simply dribbles off into conventional worldly, distracted, non-aware living. Such proper limitations of work and family are among the most essential meanings of renunciation in the lifestyle of the lay Buddhist meditator.

"Renunciation is the foot of meditation." To assert that renunciation is foundational to spiritual life is not an easy or attractive message to proclaim today. Renunciation is decidedly unpopular in American culture and when the topic of renunciation is broached, the kind of religious asceticism associated with some aspects of Christianity justifiably comes in for its share of criticism, from feminists among others. It has become commonplace to point out how some ascetical styles of renunciation, emphasizing anti-body, anti-sexual, and other-worldly attitudes, have promoted guilt, repression, and sexism. For obvious reasons, many Buddhists would prefer to distance themselves from such culturally familiar versions of renunciation.

Nevertheless, the longer I am involved with Buddhism, the more clearly I experience that Buddhist practice is fundamentally about renunciation. The lineage chant, with its proclamation that without renunciation there is no Buddhist practice, is not outdated. The fact that renunciation was central to the life story of the Buddha and to the development of the early community is not a superficial, culturally discardable aspect of the main storyline. The critical question, however, concerns what is the renunciation that is the foot of meditation? I do not believe that the *content* or *form* of renunciation remains constant in all Buddhist contexts. Rather, it is the *mindset* of renunciation that cannot be discarded in Buddhist practice. Not only can it not be discarded; renunciation is central to Buddhist discipline and vision at all stages of the Buddhist path.

The form that renunciation took in early Buddhism, i.e. celibacy and homelessness, was not an end in itself. It was the method used to promote a certain psychological and spiritual transformation, the experience of "cooling," the experience of the freedom, detachment, and tranquility known in shorthand as "enlightenment." To experience that state of being, certain things which go against the grain of ego, against the conventional hopes and dreams that are so deep-seated in ordinary humans, are required. We have to give up, to surrender, to recognize that we will not have our way in the world of impermanence. This is what is meant by the renunciation that is the foot of meditation, and where renunciation fits into the Buddhist path. At the most basic level, what must be renounced are the hopes and dreams for permanence, ease, and security that drive conventional lifestyles. Renunciation is a matter of finding the right tools to promote that transformation.

This kind of renunciation is ongoing, moment-by-moment renunciation, beginning with the first moment of agreeing in meditation practice to do the technique we have been given and to renounce our habitual wildness of mind, our conventional tendency to let our minds go as they please into whatever fantasy or fixation seizes us at any given time. What happens then? In a recent retreat, I was overwhelmed by the clarity of the demand to renounce triviality, superficiality, glibness, distractibility, and smugness. To renounce superficiality is to see deeply into things as they are, always central to Buddhism. In classic Buddhist language, with proper renunciation, one no longer mistakes the relative for the absolute, which is clearly being done when petty goals and issues dominate one's consciousness and dispel detachment and tranquility. Or to put it more colloquially, if we properly, fully renounce, we no longer mistake the molehill for the mountain.

Clearly, no lifestyle can guarantee renunciation of fixation and triviality, which is why some forms of Buddhism are less insistent that monasticism is necessary for renunciation. As American lay Buddhists, we participate in these less monastic forms of Buddhism without giving up our zest for renunciation. Since we practice not only for the accumulation of merit but also for the accumulation of wisdom,[6] renunciation is integral to our practice. We cannot simply do what we want to do anyway and call it "meditation in action"[7] without the proper attitudinal foundation of renunciation, which is perhaps the greatest threat to the integrity and genuineness of non-monastic forms of renunciation.

What does this fundamental renunciation have to do with community, relationship, family, and work? The Buddha clearly renounced family and work and set up an alternative community to take their place. Lay Buddhist practitioners do not renounce work and family in the same formal definitive way, but try to regard them as a realm of practice, as an extension of the meditation cushion and the meditation hall. That is to say, work and family become the arena for meditation in action.

Nevertheless, I would contend that there are definite limits to this practice, to the amount of work and family responsibilities we can take on without simply falling into merely conventional distraction and attachment. Getting too immersed in work or family will definitely preclude the mind of detachment and renunciation that is central to the Buddhist vision and to Buddhist suggestions about how to solve the unsatisfactoriness of conventional existence. I offer a subtle distinction of connotation: in the Mahayana vision, we do not necessarily need to renounce the householder lifestyle to achieve genuine renunciation, but we definitely do need to renounce *domesticity*. The ideal of settling into a comfortable, predictable existence characterized by nesting and self-perpetuation is not compatible with renunciation. Rather, vision replaces conventionality and comfort-seeking. Therefore, there is a definite quality of being "on the razor's edge" when one attempts to bring work or family into full-fledged Buddhist practice. Such a method of Buddhist practice requires proper renunciation, in the form of *properly limiting* work and family.

On the other hand, community or relationship is the "matrix of enlightenment." Buddhist tradition itself affirms that the companionship and feedback of our fellow travelers on this non-theistic path is so basic and so central that it is called a "Refuge," one of the very few that we have.[8] Though renunciation is an important theme in the life of the Buddha and of the early community, he established a *community* for his renunciants; he did not send them off individually to pursue enlightenment. This model is not to be ignored or taken lightly. In earlier work, I have emphasized the meaning of the fact that the sangha is, in fact, the third of the Three Refuges. But I also suggest that this fact has been overlooked and its significance ignored in Buddhism, as the sangha comes in a poor third to the

Buddha and the Dharma as a priority for American Buddhists and Buddhism.[9]

However, it is critical that "community" be understood as the sangha or community that is the third of the Three Jewels, not as some kind of club or in-group. Equally important, by community I do not mean merely a collection of individuals having the same institutional affiliation nor a group of people indifferent to each other but focused on some common purpose. If domesticity and nesting are inappropriate ways to integrate family and work into the lifestyle of lay Buddhist mediators, they are equally inappropriate understandings of the task of human community in Buddhist vision. As one of the three refuges, the purpose of sangha is to midwife enlightenment by providing feedback and companionship on the path, not to provide the security of a group ego or a safe social environment. By "sangha," I mean a group of people who in their pursuit of the common purpose of enlightenment are acutely attentive to the need for friendship, for psychological comfort and emotional nurturing as part of the spiritual journey, and who, therefore, care for and take care of each other, without falling into unhealthy codependence.

An important extension or deepening of the definition of sangha or community as a matrix of enlightenment includes, in my view, special relationships of spiritual or Dharmic partnership. By "Dharmic consortship" I mean non-domestic, often non-reproductive pairing whose major purpose is to promote the spiritual development of both partners.[10] Modeled on some materials found in Tibetan Buddhism,[11] Dharmic consortship is even less recognized and less well-understood than is the reality of sangha as the matrix of enlightenment.

In pre-feminist Buddhism, awareness that sangha as a community of caring friends is an essential matrix of enlightenment has been minimal. It will take feminist consciousness in Buddhism to fully appreciate the profundity of community as "matrix of enlightenment." Under patriarchal gender constructions, women are far more likely than men to notice the absolutely critical importance of relationships to spiritual well-being. In fact, in my view it is no exaggeration to suggest that relationship and community are as fundamental to spiritual well-being as are study of basic Buddhist teachings and the practice of meditation, which are so emphasized in Buddhist tradition. That is why the Buddha organized his followers into a community and declared community to be the third of the Three Refuges. This awareness needs to be integrated into Buddhism far more consciously, more deliberately, and more fully than has ever been done in the past. I also believe that this message is sorely needed in Western Buddhism, in which the Western myth of individualism, especially its American version of the "lonesome cowboy hero," seems to justify the highly individualistic interpretation of Buddhism typical of many American Buddhists.

Renunciation, Work, and Family in the Practice of Lay Meditators

Therefore, as lay Buddhist practitioners, we need to work out our pursuit of career and our practice of family life within the context of these core Buddhist values of renunciation and community. These classic Buddhist concerns, especially as seen through the lens of feminist interpretation, will provide some checks and balances for determining an appropriate level of involvement in work and family for lay Buddhist meditators. Having asserted that, in general, American Buddhists invest too much time and energy in work and family and too little in relationship and community, I would like to explore renunciation and community as values against which to measure how much is too much work or family for a sane and grounded lifestyle as a Buddhist lay meditator.

It is not difficult to make the case that the typical American lifestyle is far too workaholic, at least among the educated and professional types most commonly attracted to and involved in lay Buddhist practice. The demands on time and energy of most professional and business careers are becoming ever more extreme, with little discussion of how to reverse the trend. The impact of such demands on both family life and community, to say nothing of their impact on the requirements for serious Buddhist meditation practice, is devastating. Certainly the feminist vision and demand that women participate in the satisfactions of meaningful work did not seek a situation in which everyone, including both partners in an ongoing relationship, work sixty-hour workweeks, to the detriment of ongoing community life in which no one now has time to participate.

Rather, part of the feminist agenda was to share the burdens of earning a livelihood, so that both partners could experience the satisfaction of meaningful work while neither would be burdened with unreasonable and counterproductive demands to spend all or most of one's energies on work. This feminist vision has not been realized—a serious problem for both women and men, particularly if they are also serious lay Buddhist practitioners heavily involved in the time-consuming disciplines of study and meditation practice. In *Buddhism After Patriarchy,* I suggested that properly limiting one's livelihood and avoiding workaholism is an important contemporary interpretation of the precept of "Right Livelihood," the fifth component of the Eight-fold Noble Path, Buddhism's Fourth Noble Truth.

However, that too much energy and time go into family, especially in comparison to the time and energy that are put into community, may not be so intuitively obvious. Many people feel that families and family time are being neglected, not overindulged, in an age of dual career families. And if the contest is between excessive demands from the fast-track workplace and the needs of family life, I definitely would agree. But I am concerned about an imbalance between energy being devoted to *community* and to *family,* not about an imbalance between energy devoted to work and to family or community, which is a different issue and one largely unaddressed in most contemporary discourse. I am suggesting that community, friendships, and Dharmic partnerships are unlikely to be given the priority, energy, and involvement that would be appropriate for Buddhist lay meditators because people choose or feel compelled to give that energy to family instead, especially to the notion of family as a reproductive unit. Furthermore, I am suggesting that this imbalance is a problem for Buddhist lay meditators because community is more likely than the typical family environment to foster sanity and tranquility. The conventional family is often conflict-ridden and riddled with suffering and frustration, not due to ill will or problems that can be fixed, but due to the inherent nature of family life.

Because of the potential unpopularity of my message, let me make some qualifications clear. First of all, my skepticism is not directed at "family" in an extended sense, which is somewhat akin to what I mean by "community," but primarily at the so-called "nuclear family" cut off from the community, isolated unto itself, which fosters expectations of great emotional fulfillment and even spiritual meaning within its narrow confines. Furthermore, I do not claim that family life, even in its more narrow definition, cannot be an arena of Buddhist practice and a manifestation of sacred outlook. I am suggesting that conventional approaches to and expectations for family life are inappropriate in a Buddhist context because proper and necessary limits are not observed; or, to put the matter in Buddhist terms, the Middle Way is not observed. The result is that conventional family life is not often a matrix of sanity, tranquility, happiness, or fulfillment, but more commonly of frustration, suffering, and full-scale, unabashed samsara, particularly in the case of intergenerational relationships. The expectations are too high, the attachments too great, and the needs too overwhelming for any other results. As the most basic Buddhist teachings affirm, such needs and attachments cannot produce anything but suffering. And, as early Buddhism analyzed, family life easily produces intense needs and attachments.

Family life is *inherently* difficult, in my view, because we are introduced to the inevitable limitations, frustrations, sorrow, and unsatisfactoriness of samsara in our families. Some of the outburst of anger that we as children feel against our parents is, I think, nothing more than frustration with the inevitable limits of human life, its finitude and, in some cases, its unsatisfactoriness—which our parents were compelled to teach us. (This is not meant to deny that there is real abuse above and beyond the inevitabilities of samsara.) From the other side, I often watch parents frantically trying all the latest tricks of parenting, as if by being good enough parents, they could protect their children from ever encountering samsara. This initial encounter with samsara occurs in a context in which attachment and ego are very likely to be enhanced rather than diminished. Even meditators have a difficult time achieving any detachment vis-à-vis their own families, whether their parents or their children. Is it any wonder that family life so often involves so much struggle and frustration, so little tranquility or sanity?

Nor do I think that such assessments of family relationships are recent or confined to the supposedly degenerate West. Some contemporary Western Buddhist teachers and practitioners claim that the needs of Western meditators are quite different from those of Asian Buddhists because Asians come from healthy family environments, whereas many Western Buddhists do not and therefore need therapy in addition to meditation. While I do not dispute that many Western families are dysfunctional and that, therefore, therapy may be useful for some meditators, I disagree that Asian Buddhists come from necessarily healthier family environments. First and foremost, Asian Buddhists grow up in intensely patriarchal family environments, which simply cannot be sane and psychologically healthy environments. Nor do I believe that the flood of literature detailing family woes from incest to psychological abuse that is so obvious in our time and place actually represents a new level or experience of samsara. I believe that for various reasons, we are more willing to acknowledge that particular variety of samsara now than in the past.

The sad part, however, is not that family life is often so difficult. Why should we expect anything else, if we understand Buddhist teachings? The sad part is that people try so desperately to deny these realities and to replace them with the nonexistent mythically happy family. They neglect their communities, sending more energy into family, trying to fix the relationships, to achieve tranquility and happiness. Sometimes I liken it to sending good money after bad, when there are better investments readily available. However, when we concede the reality of inevitable unsatisfactoriness in family relationships, some of the bitterness of that reality is diminished, just as there is immediate relief when we concede the First Noble Truth of suffering. Simply recognizing the likely limits of satisfaction and sanity in family relationships frees us not to expect or pursue more and encourages us to devote appropriate energy to other dimensions of life, such as community and work. Paradoxically, relaxing our grip on the satisfactions sought in family life may well improve family relations. Focusing our attention outward into the community and loosening the bonds of the nuclear family, ironically, probably make family life more satisfying than any other medicine.

Thus, practicing renunciation regarding family as a lay Buddhist meditator means, first and foremost, fostering more realistic expectations regarding family life, which promotes more appropriate balance in the energy devoted to family and to community. But unless certain practical limits are honored, such balance is difficult to achieve, no matter how clear our understanding and intentions may be.

Of primary importance among practical guidelines to renunciation is the need to limit reproduction, for many reasons, not the least of which is simply that our time and energy are also limited and desperately needed for other concerns. As Mahayana Buddhists, our primary commandment is not to "be fruitful and multiply" but to "save all sentient beings." There is no dearth of sentient beings already needing our concern and care, and our commandment is to work with sentient beings, not especially to produce more. It should be obvious why, from a Buddhist point of view, only children who can be well cared for should be conceived. With so much misery already present in the world, we should not add to it by producing children who cannot be properly cared for, both physically and psychologically. There is no particular Buddhist rationale for having our own biological children at all and we should not feel pressured into parenthood by conventional demands. Unless we are particularly gifted and apt at parenting, it may be more appropriate and compassionate to forego the experience.

In particular, Buddhists should be wary of reproduction due to lack of mindfulness or motivated by ego. Apart from birth control failure, it is difficult to reconcile accidental conceptions with long-term training in mindfulness practice. More serious, reproduction as an extension or aspect of ego is extremely inappropriate for lay Buddhist meditators. To reproduce one's self and to perpetuate the family lineage are extremely common conventional reasons to have children. Another version of the same motivation occurs when people become parents in order to fill a void in their own lives or to find something to do with their lives.

When reproduction is an aspect or extension of ego, the child is, in fact, conceived to fill some obsessive fixation or need on the part of the parents, which is rather hard on the child. Such motivations for reproduction lead to styles of parenting that involve undue and unhealthy enmeshment in families. Detached parenting is impossible; the parents are too personally invested in who their children become or how they turn out. In other words, the parents' egos are excessively wrapped up in their children, which, of course, puts tremendous pressure on children. In many scenarios, which I fear are not all that rare, the parents, in effect, try to live their children's lives for them or become excessively emotionally dependent on them. Such psychological incest is, in fact, almost as devastating as its physical counterpart. And it is unavoidable unless parents limit their investment in family properly, balancing that investment with investment in community, work, and spiritual discipline.

The tragedy is that such emotional incest, such undue family enmeshment was and is still thought inevitable and appropriate in conventional samsaric logic, including the logic by which many Asian families operate. I believe that one of the areas where Buddhists could have the most to contribute to sane family patterns is in thinking through detached parenting, in bringing the Buddhist understanding of the virtues of detachment and renunciation to the arena of parenting and family life. Obviously, this vital addition to Buddhist understanding must come from lay Buddhists rather than monastics.

Buddhist leaders and communities must not romanticize and idealize nuclear families, but investigate more thoroughly the limits, both quantitatively or qualitatively, appropriate for lay Buddhist meditators for whom childrearing and nuclear families are viable lifestyle choices. Even more important, Buddhist leaders and communities should investigate and encourage other modes of bonding and of structuring primary relationships within the community. Lay meditators for whom nuclear families are not appropriate lifestyle choices should be supported rather than discouraged. For at least some American Buddhist communities, including my own Vajradhatu community, taking these suggestions seriously would mean far less pressure to form nuclear families and to have children, and far more attention to alternatives.

Community as Priority: Some Suggestions

Taking time and energy for friendships and community seems to be the lowest priority, to be fitted in after work and family needs are satisfied, if any time is left. Currently, my own local Buddhist community has almost ceased a meaningful level of community activity because too many members feel that they can only attend or participate in a few community programs per year, after they have discharged their work and family responsibilities. I suggest that the priorities be reversed among lay Buddhist meditators, if the vision of lay life as an expression of meditation in action is to have any validity. Giving higher priority to community is important because it is a central part of the matrix of enlightenment. The lack of sufficient community, of genuine friendship, psychological comfort, and emotional nurturing within the sangha is one of the most pressing and vital issues facing contemporary American Buddhists. Along with developing forms of hierarchy and authority that acknowledge achievement without becoming oppressive, developing a theory and praxis of community as the matrix of enlightenment is a primary agenda for Western lay Buddhist meditators.

But how can such an enormous agenda even be contemplated, especially given the highly alienated and individualized context of American culture? The most important requirement is simply the *recognition* that community is so basic to Buddhist life. In some ways, this is a radically new insight for Buddhists, and in other ways, it is not, given that sangha is the third of Three Jewels. Not only did the Buddha declare the sangha to be the Third Jewel; he and the Buddhist community throughout history have devoted considerable attention to detailed suggestions for how to make the *monastic* community work. It was recognized in the monastic context that community is not only important to each monastic's spiritual development and discipline, but that community does not happen without detailed attention to what is required if a group of individuals is to cohere as a spiritual community. But such insights regarding communities of lay meditators seem not to have occurred or be part of the Buddhist tradition, probably because this institutional form is relatively underdeveloped in Buddhism.

What in fact is required is a something comparable to the monastic *vinaya,* or rules of discipline, for lay meditators which details what is required if the sangha of lay meditators is to function as a genuine third refuge, a matrix of practice, and a matrix of enlightenment. If we concede that it is indeed important for lay Buddhist communities to function in such a manner, what can we say about guidelines for such Buddhist communities?

Perhaps only a single guideline will suffice. Proper balance between the energies devoted to community and relationship, on the one hand, and the energy devoted to family and work, on the other hand, is sorely needed. Nurturing and comforting other people, our sangha members, should be a very high priority in a functioning and functional sangha. Instead, we often find that many people are so absorbed in their nuclear families and their jobs that they claim they do not have the time or energy to be a friend, to comfort and nurture sangha members. From my own experience, I will offer several examples of what seem to me to be a severe lack of such balance. Unfortunately, based on my observations, I do not think such experiences are isolated and infrequent.

Several years ago, while I was grieving the death of my partner, most of my friends abandoned me. Having no family, they were my only source of comfort, but they all kept their distance. It seemed that unless I had some direct link to someone as a family member, I could rely on no one to care or comfort. It struck me then as highly inappropriate that in a Buddhist context, I had to have that level of legal, formal attachment to someone to receive attention and comfort. Now, some years later, after having learned as much from that grieving as from anything else I have ever experienced, I still feel that such abandonment was inappropriate. In a Buddhist environment, of all places, we should not have to have possessive legal or blood ties with people to receive appropriate humane and human concern and attention. In a functioning community, human bonds and humane emotional support would not be dependent on legal or biological ties. People would not so overvalue such legal or biological ties and so undervalue friendship that friends always get the leftovers of attention and love.

The more favored rationale for ignoring friends and community does not require extreme circumstances, such as grief, to be invoked. Many people act as if it is appropriate for anyone, anywhere, anytime to say, "I'm too busy, my job is too demanding," with the expectation that ties of friendship can go unattended and community responsibilities shunted off onto other "less busy" people. Asking such people what are their priorities or giving feedback that priorities seem to be skewed often arouses their hostility. The neglected friend or community is expected to accept such priorities without question and without complaint. Recently, a long-term valued friend suddenly came up with this rationale, week after week, for not maintaining our usual level of interaction. He expected me to understand that, of course, spending time with me was a low priority compared to work demands and also expected me not to mind being neglected, even not to interpret his actions as neglect. When I responded that I could not but regard it as neglect and as giving our friendship low priority because one always finds time for the things that are really important, my feedback only brought more defensiveness and alienation. Finally, I became frustrated enough to make a wish for him: "May your life experiences teach you the value of friends."

To rectify this situation, in which community is undervalued but absolutely essential to detached, sane well-being, I believe certain steps will be required. In my view, we need to take on the discipline of being a sangha member in the same formal and serious way we take on the disciplines of meditation practice and study of Buddhist texts and doctrines. The discipline of being a community member needs to be regarded with the same seriousness that is accorded to meditation and study and should be equally at the center of Buddhist methods of working with our lives. When we go for refuge to the Buddha and the Dharma, the first two of the Three Refuges, we expect, indeed vow, to take seriously the example of the Buddha's meditation practice and to use his Dharma teachings as guideposts to our life. In the same way, when we go to the sangha for refuge, this should be understood as a vow to do what needs to be done to foster community, including the boring and backbreaking work required to maintain a schedule of programs and maintain a center. That Third Refuge should also be understood as a vow to attempt to provide appropriate and necessary feedback and comfort to our fellow travelers.

For this to occur, of course, there first need to be specific and definite practices to foster our ability to be a sangha member, just as there are definite and specific methods of meditation and study. Developing such practices and priorities has been neglected outside the monastic sangha. This may be one of the important historical tasks for American Buddhists. We need to think very seriously about how to develop such techniques and practices so that the lay meditators' sangha is as genuine a matrix of enlightenment as the monastic sangha. To do so, we need to discover and develop techniques of group process and individual contemplation that enhance our sensitivity to others and our ability to listen, befriend, and nurture, as well as our ability to defuse our own projections and aggressions rather than turning them loose. We need to develop these skills and abilities to be able to focus on the priority of community as a matrix of enlightenment.

1. This essay was first presented at the San Francisco Zen Center in April 1993 in a series of talks on American Buddhism. It has been significantly revised and updated for publication.

2. A lineage chant invokes the generations of Buddhist teachers through whom one's own specific traditions and practices have been passed down, at least mythically, throughout the generations, from the Buddha to one's own teacher. In my liturgical tradition, the lineage supplication is part of the morning liturgy.

3. Midrash is the Hebrew term for the extended, contemporary, and fanciful interpretations of the Bible that have characterized Jewish ways of working with traditional texts for almost two millennia. The literal meaning of the text is put on hold to mine it for a reading of its contemporary significance.

4. In my tradition, a refuge name is given to a newcomer to Buddhism when one receives the Triple Refuge, otherwise known as the Refuge Vows, from one's preceptor and formally becomes a Buddhist. It is said to highlight one's style of working with oneself.

5. *Buddhism After Patriarchy: A Feminist History, Analysis, and Reconstruction of Buddhism* (Albany, New York: State University of New York Press, 1992).

6. Traditional Buddhism encourages practice of the "two accumulations," the "accumulation of merit" and the "accumulation of wisdom." Without the accumulation of wisdom, enlightenment is impossible, as the accumulation of merit brings only good karma and fortunate rebirth. The traditional division of labor between lay and monastic practitioners encouraged laypeople to practice the accumulation of merit by supporting monastics. In some future rebirth this accumulation of merit would lead to a life in which the accumulation of wisdom could be approached more directly by practicing a monastic lifestyle.

7. The phrase "meditation in action" was popularized by Chogyam

Trungpa, whose first book bore that title (Boulder, Colorado: Shambhala Publications, 1969). The phrase is used to refer to the fruitional practice of maintaining ongoing mindfulness, awareness, and tranquility in the midst of the ordinary daily activities we participate in after periods of formal meditation. Such meditation in action is far more basic to the Buddhist vision than is formal meditation practice, but, as is often said, "Without meditation, there can be no meditation in action."

8. Buddhism is a non-theistic religion that declares that its adherents may find refuge in three things: the Buddha as example; the Dharma, or teachings, as trustworthy guidance; and the Sangha, or community, as source of psychological comfort and feedback.

9. For more extended discussion see *Buddhism After Patriarchy,* pp. 257–269.

10. The subject of Dharmic partnership is broader than the scope of this essay and deserves its own fully developed discussion.

11. Miranda Shaw's *Passionate Enlightenment: Women in Tantric Buddhism* (Princeton, New Jersey: Princeton University Press, 1994) is to date the most detailed account of such relationships, as they are recorded in Indian Vajrayana texts.

Judith Simmer-Brown

Romantic Vision, Everyday Disappointment

> *Bitter, bitter my distress must be,*
> *And never, never must my heart give up*
> *Its great and overwhelming grief for her,*
> *Nor I be granted e'en a passing hope*
> *Of joy however, sweet, however good.*
> *Great joy could acts of prowess bring to me.*
> *I'll do none; all I know to want is SHE.*
> —Peire de Rogiers

ROMANTIC LOVE, no matter how delicious, is the primary symptom of cultural malaise, the central neurosis of Western civilization. By romantic love, I mean that which focuses upon the loved one as an object of passion, devotion, and fixation. The loved one becomes the answer to all of life's problems, the source of all our happiness, and potentially, the source of all of our woes. But, if we are honest with ourselves, we can see that romantic love is deeply unhappy love, addicted to misery and suffering, cloaked in fantasy and separation. It is the essence of "setting sun" world, in the tradition of Shambhala, the nonviolent warrior tradition of Tibet.[1]

A version of this essay appeared under the title "Romantic Love Versus Everyday Disappointment," in *Shambhala Sun*, Vol. 3, No. 3, January 1993, pp. 30–33. Reprinted by permission of the author.

Romantic love has become a kind of religion in Western culture. In his landmark book, *Love in the Western World*,[2] Denis de Rougemont traced the development of romantic love in the courtly tradition of the Middle Ages, describing it as a Christian heresy. He described how Christian nobles transferred their devotion from the unattainable god to the unattainable lover, imbuing her with ideal traits beyond any mortal woman. He argued that such a view of romantic love survives today; even now, one of the most pervasive and unacknowledged forms of theism is our romantic life. We have made the lover into a god, and we are in love with love rather than with the lover. The lover is cast in a specific role in order for him or her to remain a god.

What are the qualities of romantic relationships? First of all, romantic love thrives on separation. The unattainable love is the most attractive one—someone who is married to someone else, living in a distant city, or in a nexus of the forbidden. The girl or boy next door is not a good candidate for romantic fantasy, and neither is one's spouse. Separation makes the heart grow fonder, passion-wise, because with separation the fantasy of the lover can be kept alive. The reality of the person cannot threaten the fantasy. For this reason, many newlyweds become quickly disillusioned over the mundane realities of married life. The courtship was so exciting, but marriage is too real, too ordinary.

Because romance thrives on separation, it is sexy but never sexually fulfilled. If one were truly satiated sexually, then the romance would be threatened. Often, the lover chooses the mystical option of desire, giving up the living, breathing sexual partner for the fantasy of the unattainable lover. Illicit love affairs are hot, but are rarely resolved in marriage.

Secondly, romantic love is frightfully impersonal. We are looking for our "type"—an intellectual, a jock, an ethereal blonde. Our typecasting can become very subtle, including our lover's taste in clothes or way of walking. But we are in love with a fantasy; the person of the lover is absent. It actually helps not to have the person around too much, because they might destroy the fantasy. We have a terror that love may become too real.

Making the lover into a god, we foster a sense of poverty in ourselves. This is a lack of completion which manifests as insatiable desire. We feel inadequate and helpless without a lover. When we have made the lover into a god, we can never join our lover. We are stuck in a situation of desperate longing, of neediness and insecurity. This is why de Rougemont called romantic love a Christian heresy; passion means suffering, and we have misplaced our devotion onto a fantasy which has trapped us forever in unhappiness.

There is a death wish at the heart of romantic love. In classical myths and literature, one possesses the lover completely only in death—and we see this played out in newspaper accounts of domestic disputes daily. The desire for union with the lover is desire for oblivion. Anything more pedestrian interferes with the fantasy.

And this is the most difficult trait to acknowledge: romantic love glorifies unhappiness. The pain of romantic passion is something we find delicious. This is clear in our entertainments—films, novels, television, ballet, opera, and plays. We entertain ourselves with the scrumptious pain of a romantic story, and that pain makes us feel so alive, so real, and so convinced of the meaningfulness of romantic love.

When we examine this carefully, we sense the unhealthiness of a cult which glorifies unhappiness. The Shambhala tradition speaks of setting-sun vision, which elevates the most degraded aspects of human nature and which glorifies death. Setting-sun vision fixates on misery and ignores human dignity; it feeds on tragedy and snubs ordinary heart. The Shambhala tradition points out that the setting-sun approach is an unnecessary and inappropriate focus for human life. It undercuts our basic intelligence and wholesomeness and deprives us of living our lives fully. Romantic love is the epitome of setting-sun vision in our culture.

So, what choice do we have? We realize how unhappy romantic love is, but what else is there? All of us have experienced the way the bubble pops in romantic relationships, and the ensuing disappointment and disillusionment. We say we have fallen out of love. We begin to feel the pointlessness of the fantasy, and we begin to view the lover as a stranger or even an enemy. We feel so lonely and hurt.

But disappointment is simply the flip side of romantic love; in both cases, we are so totally wrapped up with our own fantasy that we never really see the other person. We don't see the person we're in love with; we don't see the person we're breaking up with. Both situations are impersonal. The poet Marge Piercy describes it this way:

> *When we are going toward someone we say*
> *you are just like me*
> *your thoughts are my brothers*
> *word matches word*
> *how easy to be together.*

> *When we are leaving someone we say*
> *how strange you are*
> *we cannot communicate*
> *we can never agree*
> *how hard, hard and weary to be together.*

> *We are not different or alike*
> *but each strange in his leather body*
> *sealed in skin and reaching out clumsy hands*
> *and loving is an act*
> *that cannot outlive*
> *the open hand*
> *the open eye*
> *the door in the chest standing open.*[3]

Disappointment is the more fruitful side of the coin because it occurs when our ambition and fantasy about the relationship become bankrupt. Disappointment could be the beginning of a true relationship. There is a kind of loss of innocence in disappointment which can lead to the appreciation of the lover for who he or she truly is—beyond fantasy.

Staying with disappointment requires a certain amount of bravery, for we find ourselves alone. Often it has been our fear of loneliness which caused us to so earnestly seek out a relationship; we need someone, anyone, to make us feel secure, solid, alive. And here we are again, alone and desolate.

Because this is such a familiar feeling, we begin to see that no one can take away our fear of loneliness. Our aloneness will always come up; even the best relationships end, through death or change. When we treasure our aloneness, it becomes so refreshing. When we feel it and acknowledge it as the basis of all our relationships, there is tremendous freedom. Of course, this guarantees nothing about the relationship itself.

When aloneness and disappointment dawn for us, the relationship might have the space to begin. There is tremendous groundlessness, for we really don't know where the relationship is going. There may be good times, there may be bad times. What happens, though, is that we begin to have a relationship with a *person*. We can begin to see the lover as someone separate from us, and we feel aloneness in relationship. Previously, the romance filled up the space in our lives and kept us company. We felt full because our fantasy filled in all our needs, or so we imagined.

But when we begin to really have a relationship with someone, there are gaps, there are needs not met. This is the ground for the relationship. When there is that quality of separateness and sanity, a very magical chemistry can emerge between people. It is unpredictable and unknown, and it does not follow the mythic guidelines for romantic love.

When we begin to see the other person, there is a new opportunity for romance in a sane sense. The lover's very otherness can attract us. It is fascinating what makes my husband furious, what makes him laugh. He really *likes* to garden, he really *hates* to shop. Continual fascination can bloom, because the other person is beyond your boundaries of expectation and conceptualization. That fascination can include moments of depression, discouragement, and resignation. It also includes moment of humor, delight, and wonder. But all of it is tangible and vivid. Even while we are intoxicated with the continual emergence of the other person, we are haunted and enveloped by our own aloneness.

And, perhaps surprisingly, there is an opportunity for boundless passion when you are not trying to fit someone into a role. This can be happy passion, because you are not trying to manipulate the lover into filling your needs; it is passion which can include sexuality without fear of intimacy. It is also the vertigo of high-altitude passion, because your own aloneness remains and the situation is so inescapable.

When you look at relationship beyond disappointment, you can begin to relate to the vivid phenomenal world. Your mate can become a symbol or representative of the entire cosmos. When he or she says "no" and is furious with you, you are actually getting a message from your world; when strain or difficulty occurs, it is very tangible and must be worked with. So everything that takes place in your relationship can become a message from the world at large.

It seems so much safer to stay romantically involved, but if we do we will never get outside our own minds. We'll always be wrapped up in our conceptualization of romantic love. Disappointment is a loss of innocence, and that loss can actually wake us up, if we are willing to stick with the situation. There is a choicelessness that grows when you can appreciate the other person for who they are and give up trying to make them fit the image of your fantasy.

When we let go of manipulation, relationships are fundamentally groundless. We have no control over them. In a healthy relationship, you try to support the goodness and dignity in the other person. You don't allow them to cover up the situation again and again; you give up your feeling of betrayal if they do the same with you. You are willing to be a gentle reminder of the way things are, and allow them to be one too. But there are no assurances about your respective roles or the outcome.

Should we cut romantic love out of our lives? Of course not. We are in and of our culture, and we have our neuroses to work with. The intelligent way of working with romantic love is to experience it fully, beginning with romantic passion, and then experience the disappointment and go on from there. We should understand fully what we are doing, being aware of our tendencies toward delusion when we are "in love."

There is tremendous energy in passion. Romantic love is the beginning of understanding the nature of relationship. With it we develop the courage to jump in, and once we are in the ocean, we learn to swim. Without romantic love, we might never have jumped in.

1. For a discussion of this concept, see Chogyam Trungpa, *Shambhala: The Sacred Path of the Warrior* (Boston: Shambhala Publications, 1984).

2. See Denis de Rougemont, *Love in the Western World* (New York: Harcourt, Brace & Co., 1940). Also see C. S. Lewis, *The Allegory of Love: A Study in Medieval Tradition* (Oxford, England: Oxford University Press, 1936).

3. Marge Piercy, "Simple-song," from *Hard Loving* (Middletown, Connecticut: Wesleyan University Press, 1964, 1967, 1968, 1969), p. 35.

Celeste West

My Tantric Flip-Flop

A FUNNY THING HAPPENED to me on the way to facilitate the Engaged Buddhism workshop at the 1988 Celebration of Women and Buddhism Conference. It all began seriously enough. In dutiful preparation, among other things, I read Sandy Boucher's interview with peace activist Joanna Macy in *Turning the Wheel*.[1] Herein, Joanna coins a fine concept called the "tantric flip." This is the judo-like play of moving *through* negative energy rather than resisting it. On the tantric path, one uses "evil" as well as "good" to catalyze the transmutation of dross into gold, of dimness into awareness. A tantric flip rolls *with* the punch so that you flip the problem onto its kazoo and get on with the dance of life.

For example, it is said that a *tantrika* does not see a stand of poison ivy and turn around, nor does she even tiptoe through the ivy to keep on the path. The tantrika plunges directly into the ivy—"So be it!"—even if it takes her *off* the apparent path. Joanna Macy's tantric flip sounded like a marvelous, if madcap, way to say "Yes" to the universe.

I was not prepared, however, to actually be called upon to do a tantric flip in my workshop. So here is the story of what may be called my tantric flip-flop. Being new to tantric ways, perhaps my flip-flop is akin to Naomi Newman's wonderful "Falldowngetup. Falldowngetup. Falldowngetup. This is ALL ONE MOVE!" performance piece given at the Conference.

At first, no one showed up at the Engaged Buddhism workshop.

"Is the engagement off?" I wondered. "What if they gave a war and no one came?" was a happier old thought. But finally five women arrive. I take solace in the earnest political vow: "You work with however many show up." The King Ron and Queen Nancy years had seemingly taken their toll. We smile. At least things will be intimate and relaxed.

Then, like mushrooms sprouting after a rain, the peaceniks begin to pop up. I had forgotten that activists are usually late. When we reach twenty-five women, we meditate together, "May all beings be free from suffering and from the causes of suffering." I begin to feel the wondrous "interbeing" sense of harmony of which Thich Nhat Hanh speaks.

Then—*whammo.*

Who to my wondering eyes should appear but the woman with whom my lover has recently chosen to have an affair. My beautiful interbeing flies like a dove out the window. The high-decibel, vein-popping drama of my mind turns up the jealousy channel. "Why the hell did X come to this workshop, to *my* workshop? There are thirty others she could cruise. Whatever happened to discretion, to old-fashioned, fragrant good manners?"

The dove beats her wings on the window, "X perhaps did not know it is *your* workshop. She's probably been to jail as often as you have, and you know she's a great organizer."

"Well, hell, if it wasn't my workshop, I would just decamp." How I loathe being in the same room with a parvenu. Why don't I just tell Ms. Great Organizer that I am on the high road to a headache and ask her to facilitate? We are all leaders here, after all. My eyes are blood-red, my contacts cracking.

The dove croons through my newly acquired chain-metal helmet, "Whatever happened to sisterhood?"

Me: "This is *sisterhood interruptus.*"

Dove: "Whatever happened to *metta?* Whatever happened to Joanna Macy?"

Me: "Is she in heaven or is she in hell, that damned elusive Pimpernel?"

I, obviously, am losing it. Here I am, a social mutant, sitting with socially responsible, heroic Buddhists who are meeting together to bring peace into the world. They think globally while I think meanly. They are nonviolent, I guzzle blood from the skulls of Kali. They are changing the status quo, I am a cliché of its economics of scarcity.

"SO BE IT," the tantric words ring as the dove flies back in and sits on X's head. I am a jealous fool. Jealousy, the bitterest of emotions because it is allied with the sweetest. SO BE IT. You can flip the tantra, if not the channel. Watch chimera and perfidia. At least we can be grateful X is not kissing the lips of my beloved at the moment arising because X is a prisoner in *my* workshop. Ha! Sit back and enjoy that unreal reality or real unreality. Don't just do something, sit there. Like that damn dove.

I remember my first teacher, Issan, the beautiful Buddhist *bon vivant* of the Hartford Street Zen Center. He always said, *in extremis,* "Just sit." Sit with the separateness, loneliness, and fear. Sit with the despair—and the empowerment. What would Issan do in my chair? He would put his feet on the floor, his tongue in his cheek, and breathe. "The object of Zen is not so much to become a Buddha as to act like one." I remember my gallant grandmother remarking, "Feigning calm produces calm."

Feigning calm, I begin to actually listen to the women, these loving Buddhist agitators, speak about their reasons for being alive, about their fears and hopes, about the children. These women make the world worthy of our suffering. They say that sometimes they too "just sit" with their raggedy feelings. Then the cycle turns and their inner vision manifests in doing social change and direct action.

Some speak of putting their bodies on the line and being jailed for their nonviolent expression of First Amendment rights and adherence to the Buddhist precepts. Women speak of being midwives both of the birthing and of the dying in a society that does not honor passages. One woman makes films that move hundreds while also being a full-time doctor. Another focuses on grass-roots organizing ("the path is under your feet"). Someone else helps give teenagers a forum for their peace concerns. Someone organizes benefits for Tibetan nuns, tortured and denied homeland and religious freedom by the Chinese. We are startled to realize how many of us have been affected by meeting the gentle Peace Pilgrim, an anonymous old woman who crossed and recrossed the country on foot, "being peace." She carried only comb and toothbrush, pencil and paper, and her numinous, living message for peace—a true bodhisattva of our time.

Our stories hearten one another even as we speak of burn-out and despair. Many emphasize that nonviolence begins in the heart, with the people in our path, not over some abstract political issue. We realize how much meditation grounds us for the long struggle. We recognize many small actions can change the world, just as one snowflake can finally add the weight to bring down the rookery of war. One woman remarks that even if we fail, at least she can look at the children, plants, and animals and tell them she tried. "Direct action is never having to say you are sorry."

I hear the dove again—or is it X?—say, "We all share the same heart." Are there no limits to the decency of irony? Perhaps my amuse system is kicking in. . . .

Finally, the workshop with its kaleidoscopic emotions is over. I feel rather buoyant, maybe I'm just drained. There in my path stands X—my living koan. We have never spoken directly to one another. I summon a smile with the last breath in my body and say that we seem to have many things in common—including our taste in women. Is a joke the closest I will ever come to peacemaking? No, I tell her with sincerity that I admire her work. This almost completely defuses the bomb in my heart. The correct reply to all this is probably no reply. X obliges. But the dove on her head winks.

1. See "Despair and Empowerment Work—Connecting with the Great Net of Being," in Sandy Boucher, *Turning the Wheel: American Women Creating the New Buddhism* (New York: Beacon Press, 1993; revised edition), p. 274.

Barbara Gates

Watering the Garden with My Eyes Closed

A SHATTER OF GLASS from the house next door explodes into a cross-fire of shouts: "Bitch!" "Whore!" "Dealer!" I slam shut the window to prevent my six-year-old Caitlin from leaning out. My dog Cleo, barking shrilly, paws at the pane. Caitlin tugs at my shirt and pleads to have a look.

The jumble of shouts in the street is now unintelligible. But through the window I see the three women, as I have on so many other evenings. Against a backdrop of bougainvillea, by the late summer garden of penstemon and gaura, I watch them—three generations—in battle outside my window.

Up on the front porch, littered with splintered glass, Grandmama Darlene shields the broken window. Hastening down the steps, Donna, the twenty-year-old granddaughter screams toward the street, "Get out! I don't need no whore mama the likes of you!" Invariably the protagonist in these fights, Donna's mother Dee hollers up from the street, "Can't I break in my own bedroom window?" Unsteady on her feet—drunk again, and stumbling on her bad leg—she weaves backward toward the corner. She calls up at Grandmama Darlene, "You take in that drug-dealing daughter of mine, but you lock me out to sleep in the street!"

A version of this essay appeared in *Inquiring Mind,* Vol. 12, No. 1, Fall 1995. Reprinted by permission of *Inquiring Mind.*

Caitlin, Cleo, and I vie for space at the window. "What's going on?" Caitlin persists. I cradle her chin in my palm, tuck a strand of hair behind her ear, and with a sweep of my arm, shoo her upstairs to her dad.

My nose is pressed against the damp glass, opaque with dog breath and paw marks. Could someone get hurt? I worry. Should I call the cops? Should I try to intervene? Stepping out on my front porch, I scan the block for help, but the neighboring Victorians are dark, the gardens empty.

Donna suddenly leaps toward Dee. Just then I hear the sirens and two squad cars pull up. As the officer handcuffs Dee and escorts her to the car, she calls out, "They throw me out on the street. Everybody hears it." She points up at me on the landing. "She hears it. Ask her!"

Choked by a conflux of feelings—fear, fascination, anger—I am unable to speak. As I watch Dee pull her bad leg into the squad car, I notice that the hood is up on her jacket. The beat-up jacket seems strangely familiar to me. Just noticing it, with the fake fur lining peeking out around the hood, I feel an ache of tears. Why is this?

I turn away. I double-lock my door.

Both as a mother and as my own caretaker in healing from breast cancer, I am trying to cultivate a peaceful life. I am upset with these women for their ongoing fights, for the people they could draw to the block who might threaten the safety of my family. But I am also upset with myself for my failure to respond. I retreat into my home as my sanctuary, deny that this violence ever erupted. Over the years I have tended to deny much of the violence in the world, finding myself reluctant to drive on the freeway, to watch the victims of riots or kidnappings on TV, to read the newspaper reports of atrocities in Bosnia or the Middle East.

Last spring, when I emerged from a meditation retreat to news of the Oklahoma City bombing, I felt impelled to give attention to some of the violence that I have spent so many years denying. I took on a new practice: each morning I would read the newspaper with a particular eye for the articles that I might in the past have glossed over.

Then I would write my responses in my journal. The fight on the street I just described found its way into my journal. Sometimes when I began to write, I would be overcome with resistance. Once I even got back in bed and crawled under my quilt, barely able to fight off sleep, even though it was midday. Yet I persevered. Although I wasn't clear on why, I felt that this process would be crucial to my healing.

As I have continued this practice, I have begun to see how futile it is for me to wall up against the violence in the world. I notice that the violence that I shun outside is inside of me. I am surprised to witness this after twenty years of meditation practice and a lifelong commitment to nonviolent causes, beginning with Ban the Bomb marches as a kid.

Even on the meditation cushion, where so often I have sat with grief and longing, I have not been aware of anger. And then I have been shocked by my sometimes vitriolic outbursts at family—my mother, my sister, my brother, my husband Patrick, my Caitlin.

I have so longed to offer Caitlin a peaceful, loving childhood, an oasis from the crossfire of life's dangers and an antidote to my own childhood of slammed doors, fights at the dinner table, yelling, tears, and apologies. Yet even though my family conflicts are fewer and less cataclysmic than the ones of my growing up, the pattern spirals down through the generations.

How different, I ask myself, are my family battles—passing from grandmother to mother, mother to child—from the family battles next door? I don't hurl bottles at windows and fight on the street, but inwardly, I have been ferocious. I attack, defend my turf, shield my broken-open heart.

And I ask myself why some of my explosions with my family have erupted following meditation and yoga practice. The incident that troubles me in particular occurred a year ago on a meditation retreat at Lama Foundation in New Mexico.

◇

While Patrick settles Caitlin to bed in the tent, I begin to sit with the other yogis in the hall. I close my eyes, and sweep my attention again and again, cleansing out the hours of airport diners, changing planes, family spats, and fears about the cancer recently cut from my breast. I rest in the peace I have forged—free of intruding thoughts and feelings.

At the close of the sitting, as I follow the desert path back to the tent, I am absorbed in the deliciousness of the silence. I picture Caitlin, already asleep, Patrick stretched out, waiting for me. Instead, I find them both wide awake in a frenzy of getting comfortable—tossing around sleeping bags, clothes, and stuffed animals. This chaos shatters my hard-won tranquility.

In harsh staccato, I zip up the tent, try to push Caitlin into her bag.

"I can't sleep!" Caitlin yells. "Whisper!" I hiss.

One after the other, Caitlin shouts out her grievances into the silent camp. "I'm hungry!" "My leg hurts!" "I'm afraid of the dark!"

I can feel my body vibrating with tension. "No you're not!" I insist. "No you're not!" I grab her, my muscles tense, my breathing short and fast. I feel I have to control her. I am shouting now too, my nails biting into her wrists.

Shocked by my own fierce grip and acid tone, I begin to cry. As we both weep, we cuddle up together with Patrick, and eventually we are all able to sleep.

◇

As I think back on this incident, I begin to see how, fueled by my drive to heal and my hunger for quiet, I had allowed vipassana practice to slip into a concentrated effort to "win" peace for myself. Here I had been practicing for so many years intending to cultivate mindfulness. But in an unconscious effort to control my experience, instead of training my awareness, I had recently begun training my concentration. And how intensely I had wanted to hold on to the fragile tranquility I'd "gained." How upset I was when Caitlin disrupted it, forcing me to deal with the reality that I could not, in fact, control experience.

In denying Caitlin's feelings, perhaps I was protecting myself from my own. I couldn't bear to hear her shout out the pain I was feeling myself ("I'm hungry!" "I'm hurting!" "I'm afraid of the dark!").

On that Lama retreat, a year ago, I never did fully shift my attention to a more allowing awareness. But very recently, after a similar outburst at Patrick, I did something I have never done before. On a weekend at Green Gulch Farm Zen Center, I found myself meditating on my own violence.

I took off for the weekend still carrying in my mind the echoes of my recent explosion. Soon after I had settled on my cushion for an early morning sit with the Zen students, I began to experience an intense nausea. All the upset from my outburst of anger was stirring in my chest. I swept my attention like surging salt waves in an effort to cleanse out what I felt inside. But my practice in concentration was to no avail. I found it almost impossible to sit through the first period of zazen, to endure the disgust and agitation.

It wasn't until the second sitting that I recognized my intention. Without realizing it, I had been trying to eradicate my feelings. Could I simply witness this—meet it with curiosity? Cautiously, I began to bathe my chest with interest, with kindness. I allowed myself to experience the sensations inside like the swarming of a myriad of tiny flies. Beneath that, the inner flesh felt like dead meat. As I continued to attend, I noticed that my interiors felt cut up as if I had raked them with my own fury. I didn't enjoy this. But I was greatly relieved to stop fighting my feelings.

As my chest softened, memories flooded my consciousness. Among them came the image of Dee's jacket, the one with the hood that had made me cry when Dee and her family were battling on the street. I remembered an incident from three years earlier through which I saw how I was linked to Dee in the dynamics of violence in my neighborhood.

◇

In the midsummer heat of my yard, I am watering my vegetable garden. I love to spray a fantastic whoosh that cascades over the lettuces and squash, back toward the Blue Lake beans, and fans out against the fence between my yard and Grandmama Darlene's.

In the evening, the doorbell rings. Through the fever of Cleo's barks, I open the front door. Dee stands there. "Keep that dog down! That dog don't like Black folks. . . ."

Before I can reply, she tells me, "Your goddamn water done ruined my clothes."

"But I didn't know ... I'm sorry ... where were your clothes?"

"Where you think they were? You know my mother kicked me out! I stack my clothes the other side of the fence." Then bitterly, "Where else I keep them? You see me come here every day to change my clothes!" She sniffs, her lower lip quivers. Then she swings away and clumps down the stairs.

Several months later, the torpor of Indian summer settles over me and the garden. The air is fetid with factory fumes, exhaust, the stink of rotten landfill. Seeking relief, I water. As the exuberant fountain cleanses the air, awakens the wilted lettuce and burnt zucchini leaves, I am renewed.

Two nights later a pounding at the door interrupts dinner.

It's Dee. She braces herself against the evening wind, hugging something in her arms. "You done gone and ruined my whole wardrobe!" I force myself to look more closely as she whips the soaked, muddy clothes from her bundle: a sweater with rhinestone buttons, a pair of jeans, and the hooded jacket with fake fur lining. "You owes me! Didn't I tell you where I keeps my clothes?"

"I'm sorry," I splutter. "Of course I'll pay for the ... I...."

I think of nothing to say. I had allowed myself to forget. I had been absorbed in the world on my side of the fence, exclusively.

◇

How often have I fenced off my own sanctuary in order to win peace? I close my door to the violence on the street in order to keep peace in my home. I cut out the cancerous growth, radiate the precancerous cells, eject sickness from my healthy body. I water my garden to nourish my plants and my own peace of mind, closing off my awareness of the life on the other side of the fence. How often do we all do this, driven by the illusion that if we shut out or eliminate "the other" we will find happiness and equanimity? Grandmama Darlene and Donna lock out the alcoholic Dee to win peace for themselves. And in a family conflict of terrifying scale, Bosnian Serbs "cleanse" their country by exterminating Bosnian Muslims.

As I follow my line of thought, I see also that when I close my eyes and close myself away (on retreat, in solitude), I often shut my heart to the world. Even in the techniques of meditation, too often

I use concentration like a laser, annihilating thoughts and feelings. No wonder my practice often fails to carry into my life.

Three years after I watered Dee's clothes, I am still grappling with what happened. One day I went to the park with my journal and in my scribbling I tried to imagine what it was like for Dee to arrive home on that late summer night to find her clothes in a muddy heap. This was still home for Dee—I had to remind myself—even if the door was locked to her and her clothes were hidden away by the fence. Just as my home is for me, Dee's home—this space between her mother's house and the fence—was her sanctuary. Standing on the street outside her house, Dee would still have been able to feel the inside of the rooms and remember what it must have been like to lie her tired body down on the couch. After a cold walk, perhaps across town, I imagined that Dee would indeed savor the thought of her zip-up jacket, the one with the fur hood, so snug for a chill late summer night.

As I thought about Dee, I saw how, like me, she would need warmth and protection, and that like me she would long for peace. Years back, before she was locked out, I used to see her through the curtains sitting cozy at her kitchen table and gazing out the window dreaming her own dreams.

Beneath the cravings for excitement and pleasure, beneath the impulse to strike out, I believe that *everyone* yearns for peace. As I have reflected more deeply on Dee, I sense this must be true. Grandmama Darlene, Dee and Donna, my mother, myself and Caitlin, the Muslims, the Croatians, the Bosnian Serbs—everyone. And as I recognize this yearning for peace, at the same time I see how easy it is to slip into the fundamental illusion that peace can be won by the violence of shutting anything out.

I am coming to see that when we posit "this" versus "that," the possibility of peace is lost, at least for that moment. True peace has to do with inclusion—with sitting in the midst of everything with our eyes open. I can't find peace in meditation until I open to all that is crying to be heard. And I can't have a peaceful garden unless I water with my eyes open.

I am not suggesting that I never lock my door, that I take down my fence, that I quit going on retreats or that I stop closing my eyes when I meditate. Boundaries have their place. But I want to remember that the walls between me and you—the ones that allow me to pretend that my actions don't affect you—are my own creation.

At my house all of the watering hoses, the showers and sinks and the washing machine, are connected to the same water source. Since the time that I ruined Dee's clothes, I have taken particular care not to splash water over the fence. But because all of the hoses are interconnected, I must muster a tremendous effort to be vigilant. I need to continue to adjust and readjust *all* of the faucets. If I turn off a hose in the front of the house or the washing machine goes into the spin cycle, the water will suddenly surge out of the hose by the vegetable garden. Once again, a great wave of water will spill into the yard next door, potentially destroying someone else's things.

We all draw peace from the same pool. I may go on retreat or close myself in my office. But it doesn't affect me alone. I also run the risk of shutting myself off from Caitlin or Patrick when they need me to hear their cries and tend to their hurts.

So I will teach myself to water my garden with my eyes open. Perhaps I will begin to see through the fences, to recognize the shattered windows and muddied jackets and the sadness of my neighbor as my own.

Maylie Scott

A Short History
of Buddhists at The Tracks

Guided Meditation for The Tracks

Blackbirds squealing on the chain-link fence.
Let us appreciate the ground
that supports us, the breath
that sustains us, the wind
on our faces, the sun
on our backs.

Let us know how this place extends.
How the quick missile sprays dirt,
and flesh. The soft and hard places
where the bullets lodge. The profits,
the jobs provided, the services lost,
the taxes we pay, the governments
we bring down and those we bring to power.

We are here because we know
the facts of inter-being
do not leave us alone.

They have brought us to this ground
where blood has been spilt,
that allows us to sit, that holds
our confusion, our collusion
and failure of intention.
This place where weapons trucks
and trains carry death each day.
Where nothing is disowned;
where, in this moment, we are whole.

IN AUGUST 1987, Brian Willson said of the Concord Naval Weapons Station, "Every train that goes through means people are going to die in El Salvador and Nicaragua. Their lives are not worth less— our lives are not worth more." The CNWS is the main shipping station on the West Coast for nuclear and conventional weapons. Most of the weapons going to Asia and Latin America leave through its port. Trucks and trains loaded with bombs, missiles, and ammunition cross Port Chicago Highway going from base to port many times a week. It has been estimated that 7.5 million people may have lost their lives to CNWS munitions. The CNWS, thirty miles east of San Francisco, is within the radius of the 3 million people in the Bay Area, and yet very few are aware of its existence and its deadly commerce.

On September 1, 1978, Brian and two other men, well schooled in nonviolence, decided to sit on the tracks and block a weapons train. The Base was notified of their intention. Sailors blocked traffic on Port Chicago Highway so the train could cross. The train, which was supposed to travel at five miles an hour when crossing an intersection, speeded up to fifteen. One man jumped off the tracks. Another jumped onto the cow-catcher in front. As he sat in half-lotus, Brian Willson was hit and dragged beneath the train. He sustained a serious head injury. His legs were severed from his body. Miraculously, he lived.

I was introduced to The Tracks in December 1987 by my good friend Anna Graves. In September, two days after Brian's maiming, she had organized a demonstration of 15,000 people who came to protest and witness. Some people stayed and in the next weeks the group, calling itself "Nuremberg Action," began an encampment which was to last until the Gulf War in 1991.

It was a clear winter morning a week before Christmas. A dozen or so protesters were gathered ready to block if a train should come. Port Chicago Highway is a flat two-lane road running north to south. The Naval Weapons Station is set back into the bare, brown hills to the east. A big sign that read "Merry Christmas" with a picture of Santa Claus stretched above its entrance. A chain-link fence blocked the Port to the west. It was a pretty ordinary place, a place you would drive by without any cause to notice. And it was also a place where one man's blood had just been spilled; a place where, for nearly half a century, weapons that caused untold millions of deaths and maimings around the world had been originating.

Thirty or so protesters stood and sat about on sleeping bags and boxes. There was a table with leaflets and posters attached, and a large blue Nuremberg Action banner. An outline of Brian's body was painted in red over the sunk-in track where he was hit. As I walked up and down for the first time, I wondered. How is it that such a place can look so ordinary? How is it that I could have driven past without even noticing? How is it that I can drive home and resume my habits and this unremarkable place by the side of the road will slip out of my consciousness?

A vow is not a private matter, not a matter of will. It is a blessing that opens the way. As I walked up and down, cars driving past, people chatting, blackbirds squealing on the chain-link fence, my feet learned something from the ground and this teaching passed up through my body. The Site was a place of "practice." Just being here was enough. Just to be here was, in some profound and restful way, to be at home. Just the commitment to return would take care of what I needed to do.

I came again on Christmas morning. Brian Willson came too, walking with crutches, making his first reappearance on artificial legs. A crowd of supporters watched him dance a few steps on the spot where the train had struck him. Then we stood in a large circle and prayed and spoke our hearts and were grateful for Brian's life.

Ten to twenty people were living at the Site, some sleeping in a variety of vehicles parked nearby, others sleeping in a row by the side of the road. More people came and went by day. There were endless hours of discussions about tactics, process, and purpose. Every weapons train was blocked and protesters rotated in and out of jail. A log was kept of all weapons shipments, trucks and trains, and the destructive power of their contents. An ongoing dialogue was initiated with the Navy Base personnel, the County Sheriffs, and with the small local community across the highway.

The encampment became a landmark for peace action groups from the Bay Area, from the rest of the country, and, especially during the summer months, from all over the world. Occasionally alcoholics and homeless people showed up and were variously assimilated. The tasks of defining NA's purpose, establishing clear leadership, and reconciling its remarkable diversity defied resolution. Gradually some natural leaders emerged. The basic form of decision-making was a circle of people holding hands. Every morning there was a check-in circle to discuss the issues of the day. In crisis situations— if we were threatened with confiscation, if the port-a-potty had been turned over by vandals and needed a cleanup, if there were serious disagreements, if someone had been hit or threatened by an object thrown from a car driving by—a circle would form to determine what to do.

Hugging was another important form. We hugged as we greeted, we hugged as we departed. Sharing the uncertain and spartan conditions of life drew us together in a powerful way. Due to strong off-site support there was always food. In rainy weather we bailed the Site, which was slightly below road level.

We could not say what we were, but we were clear as to what we were *not*. The Site was the ground on which we said "No" to the violence of our consuming-producing society, "No" to our "institutionalized ignorance," "No" to the violence of weapons.

I began to lead what at first felt like a double life, driving out from my home in Berkeley, spending a day and a night at the Site, sometimes in jail, and driving back home again. After a while it began to seem natural; it was just what I did. In January 1988, I was ordained a priest at the Berkeley Zen Center. My head was shaved and I took the precepts again, as well as the vow to "leave home." I spent many hours in walking meditation up and down the highway in front of the Base, carrying one of the many white crosses we made, each bearing the name of a weapon's victim from Central America, Palestine, and, toward the end, Iraq. I spent more hours sitting on yellow plastic chairs in the Martinez County Jail holding unit, trying to count my breaths and to contain my impatience while the TV blared soap operas. I met many people, heard many stories, encountered unshakable intention and inexhaustible spirit. I learned more about living the Middle Way—how to persist in the midst of trouble with the purpose of an open heart.

Gradually, even in the inherent confusion and chronic frustration, the Site developed a stabilizing effect. Its ritual nature—people acting together from a common intention—became forceful. The core ritual was the blocking of death trains. We didn't know their schedules, but we became sensitive to small, impending signs: the gathering of official cars, a distant train whistle, and finally the formation of twenty or so sailors, helmeted and carrying truncheons, jogging toward us. On our side there was the scurry to gather up Site belongings so they would not be confiscated, the giving and taking of phone numbers of those planning to be arrested, the circle of people gathering on The Tracks around the red outline of Brian's body, singing, chanting, praying. The traffic would be stopped and then there was the bullhorn warning: "One minute to leave before you will be arrested. . . ." The choice.

Brian Willson had brought a lawsuit against the CNWS (he eventually won) and the Navy was very careful about its procedures. The people risking arrest had time to pray and gather their thoughts as they sat. Those who supported stood by the side of the road looking into the faces of the young sailors, men and women, who stood at attention nearby. Other supporters spoke to the passengers in the often long lines of cars waiting to get through. Finally the train made its slow passage like a funeral train come before its time, each car marked with its death potential: "A-1." "B-1." "Inert." "Empty."

Larger than us all was the ritual of the passage of time and season. Sun rising over the east hills where cows still graze. The gathering of blackbirds, the recorded trumpet reveille from the Base, the sleepy-eyed shaking out of sleeping bags, and the circulation of hot coffee. The heat, the ants, the sunburn. The sulfurous wind from the oil refineries and industrial sites that pollute the North Bay. The salty breeze from the mud flats. The rain, followed by the lake of water lapping at the Site table. Winters brought bone-piercing cold countered by blankets, mittens, and wool caps, runny noses, and evening huddles around propane heaters.

After the first year the encampment began to decrease in size. The flow of weapons would not stop. The Navy's plan to build a $10 million bypass did not materialize. Less than ten people continued to live at the Site and not many more came to visit, unless a larger protest was scheduled and publicized. How is intention sustained in the midst of change?

I felt particularly allied with Sidney Vilen and Diane Poole, both residents of The Tracks, both Buddhists. Sidney slept in her car, later her camper. Diane slept on the railroad tracks, or in whatever sleeping vehicle was available. We began to sit zazen together. We made several zafus and stuffed them with cattails that grew in the nearby marsh. In February 1990, we decided to institute "Saturday Night Sittings." Beginning late Saturday afternoon, we meditated until 9:00 PM and began again Sunday mornings from 6:00 to 9:00. We made a prayer flag from a pole found by the road and hung it first with Tibetan flags and then flags of our own making. Gradually an altar of found and donated objects spread at its foot. If it rained we sat in Diane's tent, or later Sidney's camper. Everyone at the Site was invited to our silent suppers of rice and beans and our instant oatmeal breakfasts. Occasionally we were five or six, most often three. Two was fine.

For more than a year, the local Buddhist Peace Fellowship group sponsored a "Morning of Mindfulness" group one Saturday a month. We sat in a circle, rain or shine, as cars passed, drivers honking approval or yelling their often obscene disapproval. We walked with crosses and ended by chanting the *Metta Sutta*.

The sustained vigils ended in February 1991 with the onset of the Gulf War, despite the enormous increase of weapons traffic coming through. Diane had moved on. Sidney was sick. The windows of her camper were broken twice. The fury of people driving by was unnerving: Was it war-frenzy? Some kind of twisted patriotism? Generalized fear? Increasingly violent threats and objects hurled from cars—eggs, steel pellets, rocks—made our continued presence fool-hardy. Greg was shot at and yet he, who had lived at the Site since the beginning of the encampment, hung on. "It gives my life meaning," he said.

For some time I continued to go out occasionally to block trains and trucks with a small group that gathered on Thursdays. I restrung the prayer flags and restored the picture of the Dalai Lama when it was torn off, as it frequently was. (Such a sweet face is hard to resist!) I repainted the red, purple, and golden rocks that supported the flag pole. In August 1992, twenty participants of the Buddhist Peace Fellowship's Meditation in Action Conference drove out. We hung new flags we had made the day before and sat and walked and talked together about our understanding of "engaged" action.

Most lately I have gone out only occasionally. The anniversary of Brian's maiming is always observed. Forty or fifty people come. If he is in the Bay Area, Brian comes too. There is no longer anything to mark the former site of The Tracks, no table, no drawings, no prayer flags. Port Chicago Highway is no longer a through road; it has been closed off just east of the CNWS. Weapons trucks and trains can cross it now with no disturbance, except on Mondays when Abraham, age ninety-three, blocks, and Dorothy, sixty-seven, who is on probation for blocking, supports him.

Beings are numberless. I vow to save them.

Anne Teich

Frontier Buddhism

I AM GRATEFUL for this opportunity to write about my experience as a pioneering student of Buddhism in America, and about the frontiers visited and yet to be visited. I begin with a bow of respect and gratitude and offer salutations to my teacher, Rina Sircar, who I believe to be one of the most accomplished Buddhist women alive today. It is due in large part to her unceasing efforts, begun in 1973, and to the presence and blessings of her teacher, my Preceptor, the Very Venerable Taungpulu Tawya Kaba-Aye Sayadaw, that the Theravada Buddhist tradition ("The Way of the Elders") has come to be established in this country.

Called Visakha[1] by her teacher, this senior female practitioner of the Buddhist Way is, in addition to being a Ten Precept Holder,[2] a professor, a meditation teacher, and a healer. Wherever Rina presents herself—on whoever's heart and head she places her hand, with whatever words of comfort or advice she speaks—crisis moves to resolution: fear, anger, uncertainty, and dis-ease give way to relief, acceptance, and peace of mind. Through the years of watching her work quietly, resolutely, and patiently, Rina has become for me The Remover of Obstacles.

To Meet a Saint

I have developed a Buddhist perspective and lifestyle out of my Western experience. I know that I have adopted this spiritual path rather than coming to it by birthright. Here in America, perhaps more so than anywhere else, it is easy to *try on* others' ideas. This is one of the few advantages of being part of a young, undeveloped, and still restless culture. I, like so many others, have taken full advantage of the possibility to explore and experiment in ways that a more established, traditional culture would not have allowed.

As a child I was fascinated by all religions. The great variety of beliefs, practices, regions, and distinctive architecture of churches, temples, and synagogues awakened in me the mystery of the sacred, and I was always ready to join my friends' religions. This generosity of spirit lasted until age eleven, when a teacher at St. Peter's Lutheran school told the class (with a particularly lethal dogmatism) that only Lutherans would go to heaven when they died. My hand shot up: "What about all the people in China?" Then there were the Catholic school children I rode the bus with; they told me that only *they* were going to heaven.

My anxiety increased as year after year, pastors and Sunday School teachers told us that we had only *this* life to repent, to believe, to be good, to be saved. Try as I might, I could not understand what was required of me. I squeezed my eyes shut trying hard to believe, all the time wondering about the fate of the Chinese and how God could possibly have left them out of his heaven.

I moved to San Francisco a year after graduating from college and began to study Eastern philosophy, psychology, and meditation at the California Institute of Asian Studies; I was introduced to yoga psychology, Tibetan and Zen Buddhism, Sanskrit, hatha yoga, acupuncture, and Ayurvedic medicine, and joined other curiosity seekers who visited any and all gurus who passed through the Bay Area. Eventually, I dropped yoga, discontinued staring at mandalas, and stopped fidgeting through zazen. In 1975, still free-floating and "unenlightened," I began taking classes in Theravada and *satipatthana* meditation with Rina Sircar, who had joined the school in 1973.

The notion of a spiritual life for me had always included a secret wish: to meet a living saint. I could not think of any other way to judge the truth of what the texts talked about unless I experienced such a being with my own eyes and ears. I had no idea who I was looking for, what to expect, or that wishes like these are sometimes actually granted, so I was in no way prepared for who I actually met.

So long as the Sasana Era[3] endures, there will always arise from time to time a few developed beings who are venerated by others. Such a person was my Preceptor, the Very Venerable Taungpulu Kaba-Aye Sayadaw, a Burmese forest monk. In his young days people had remarked, "As the dawn so the day," and at his passing, the late Venerable Kalu Rinpoche commented to Rina: "He now fills the earth and the sky."

Though Taungpulu Sayadaw was considered in the Burmese tradition to be an *arahat*, there was lively discussion immediately after his death that he may have taken the Bodhisattva Vow.[4] This meant, of course, that Sayadaw's life had not been his last, and this assertion stood in contradiction to the arahat ideal of the Theravada tradition, where *nibbana* is achieved at the end of the life and there is no more rebirth. This possibility was based in part by a statement made by the great monk and meditation teacher, the Venerable Mahasi Sayadaw of Rangoon, who, together with Taungpulu Sayadaw, had studied under the guidance of Mingon Sayadaw, who died an arahat. Mahasi Sayadaw said that Mingon Sayadaw requested one of his students to take the Bodhisattva Vow and that Taungpulu Sayadaw had done so. No agreement has been reached among the followers of Taungpulu Sayadaw, but everyone understood his power and believed that he could determine his destiny.

No one who has ever met the Venerable Sayadaw could deny that they were in the presence of an extraordinary being. His body, totally without tension yet completely disciplined, radiated loving-kindness and moment-to-moment mindfulness. These qualities allowed him to look at everything and everyone as if for the first time, every time. Though he was not a tall man, his limbs were quite long, and he looked much taller sitting down. He never had a gray hair, and his teeth were intact when he died at the age of ninety-one. No one doubted that he lived on the pinnacle of spiritual achievement, and that he was looking out at our world from a very different, supramundane inner world.

Taungpulu told us not to live on the *bhavachakka*—the wheel of suffering existence—but rather on the *dhammachakka,* the wheel of truth. It was his way of inviting us to join him. In his presence cares melted, time stopped, and the liquid balm of peace spread throughout the whole body. It was a cooling experience to sit in front of him, and when he smiled, everyone smiled. The sound of his voice, softened by twenty-five years of silence, was heard in the ears but felt just as much in the heart. It is not surprising that he was awarded the title Kaba-Aye ("world peace"), for he was a living example of his own teaching: that world peace starts with inner peace; and inner peace, according to the Sayadaw, comes from the practice of generosity, virtue, and the meditative life.

The Venerable Taungpulu Sayadaw endeared himself to everyone, but especially to women. When he died in 1986, his body lay in state in Rangoon before being brought back to the village of his birth, Tezu. As the procession bearing his body traveled from village to village on its way back to Tezu, everyone lined the streets to bid tearful farewells. But as the monks carried the glass coffin containing his body the last several hundred yards to the funeral pyre, women began crying loudly and uncontrollably, shaking in a frenzy of anguish, their long hair tumbling down. It was the wailing of mothers who have lost their only, most precious son.

Taungpulu Sayadaw recognized, honored, and trusted women's abilities; his relationship to Rina is a great testament to this. He encouraged her to continue her college studies, he advised her to accept the job offer in the United States, he instructed her in Dhamma, gave her permission to lead retreats, counseled her in her healing practice, and told her to keep up her meditation practice. From his point of view, the Theravada bhikkuni order—the order of nuns— had long since passed away, and could not be revived in this Sasana Era, but for him this did not cancel the ability of women to practice intensively or achieve spiritual heights.

For Sayadaw, the fundamental ingredient to spiritual progress is momentum—the ability to keep up the practice without lapse—and this had nothing to do with gender. If you have momentum, you can achieve success using even the simplest practice. Even by taking Refuge in the Buddha, Dhamma, and Sangha and observing the Five Precepts,[5] Sayadaw maintained, a devoted practitioner can attain the first stage of sainthood *(sotapanna)*, and can be reborn in the heavenly realms. Sayadaw used to ask us to observe mindfulness for the duration it takes to snap the fingers ten times *(thakana)*. A life, he said, even with only a small amount of mindfulness practice was infinitely superior to living 100 years without any mindfulness.

The critique of the arahat ideal and the one-lifetime goal of reaching final liberation from the wheel of existence, which began shortly after Buddha's death, foretold the era of the Great Vehicle—the path of Mahayana Buddhism. Within two centuries of the Buddha's passing, the arahat ideal was described as a "selfish" way to seek enlightenment because it meant focusing only on yourself, and forgetting the suffering conditions of those around you. In this view, enlightenment (nibbana) is seen as an escape, a compassionless route away from the suffering world to get to some eternally peaceful Nowhere. The arahat—slayer of the enemies of greed, hatred, and delusion—became a primitive prototype, a narrow understanding of how to go about seeking enlightenment.

It did not take many years for ardent American students of Theravada Buddhism to find out that attaining enlightenment "in this very life" is quite a difficult task—selfish or not—and that sitting on cushions is an essential but not sufficient part of the psychological process of liberation. This was not a new discovery. Taungpulu Sayadaw always encouraged people to try to reach the initial stage of sainthood—that of streamwinner (sotapanna), not arahatship, which is the fourth and final stage.[6] He said that going from the stage of infinite rebirths to that of having only seven lives remaining (sotapanna) is comparable to a person carrying a heavy load who suddenly becomes the size of a fly. As the stages of sainthood progress, a fly stays the same size, but its wings and legs become paralyzed.

The rise of merit-making activities and the popularity of the bodhisattva ideal in Buddhist cultures attest to the unsuitability of monastic practice for the vast majority of people. Perhaps only a few persons in an entire generation of practitioners reaches the stage of arahat.

The Great Wisdom Being, the bodhisattva, exemplifies a multilayered spiritual ideal. In all three vehicles of Buddhism, the bodhisattva works toward the goal of enlightenment. There are two understandings of the bodhisattva ideal. In the Mahayana tradition, these beings vow to remain outside the Transcendental Gate (of nibbana) until all other beings have been liberated, thus guaranteeing help to suffering populations for a very long time. In the Theravada tradition, the bodhisattva works specifically to perfect ten spiritual ideals called *paramis* so that he or she can become a Buddha whose last rebirth will be in a future era.

The bodhisattva career is a progressive, lofty one and provides for the emancipation of innumerable beings. The arahat path, in contrast, is fueled by the urgency to eradicate suffering *now* and applies laser-like effort to the moment. Bodhisattvas abound, the arahat is rare; their separate tasks are taken up according to temperament and life-task, and both are necessary to complete the harmonious manifestation of each Buddha Era.

By meeting Taungpulu Sayadaw, I felt I was meeting an example of the Living Word of the early Buddhist doctrine. I realized that the state of enlightenment can be a *full* rather than an empty one. The mind of a developed being is filled with the Seven Factors of Enlightenment[8] and the Four Illimitables.[9] These sublime mental states are called "illimitable" because they are boundless and the individual who radiates these divine qualities transforms his or her environment and all who enter it as naturally as sun rays soak into the earth and warm it. In the three-dimensional presence of spiritual perfection, discursive thinking and critical debate become less important. The sight, smell, and sound of this perfection remain forever in the memory as confirmation that our minds have power of infinite range.

Setting Up

With the arrival of Theravada Buddhism in America, the three great vehicles—Hinayana, Mahayana, and Vajrayana—now reside alongside one another. Buddhism as a religion and an ethical system thrives in temples and meditation centers throughout the country. In the academic world, Buddhist classes are a mainstay in Eastern religion and philosophy curricula; scholars inform their research of classical texts with fresh insights, and journals and periodicals discuss a wide range of Buddhist topics.

Buddhist principles are a tangible force in social movements such as ecology, feminism, hospice work, and political action; Buddhism has influenced Western science and the healing arts. It has moved beyond being the ethnic religion brought by immigrants or a fad of the 60s Beat Generation. Buddhism in America is a firmly entrenched counterculture which will continue to blossom in as yet unforeseen, positive ways.

Buddhism in the West is completing its foundation stage, in large part due to thousands of American students who have devoted years of study and practice in the most dedicated way—by immersing themselves in the culture of their chosen tradition. I am one such student, and along with many others, began a pursuit of enlightenment by "setting up" in a very grand way.

We purchased houses and properties, built meditation halls, pagodas, *stupas* (monuments), and retreat centers. We listened to the teachings and augmented our study with long meditation sessions and ordinations. We studied languages and traveled abroad to the homelands of our teachers. We learned to chant, attend long ceremonies, teach, publish, welcome strangers, and fundraise. We put on ethnic religious dress, and learned to cook and eat Asian food.

It would seem we accomplished a great deal in a short time. We thought we were learning Buddhism and moving ever closer toward enlightenment, but in our enthusiasm as a founding generation of Buddhist practitioners, we were also creating the institution of American Buddhism. I consider this work not just a cultural accomplishment but a meritorious deed, complete with the opportunity to practice detachment from the results of one's actions.

Theravada teachings and practices have been brought to the West by several movements. The great Thai forest monk, Venerable Achan Cha, trained his American-born student Venerable Achan Sumedho in Thailand, but established from the beginning a separate community for Western students. He knew that Asian monastic Buddhism would have to adapt to the West in ways which only Westerners could determine.

The Venerable Taungpulu Sayadaw, on the contrary, kept everyone together. He always encouraged men and women to wear the robe, even for one day. In addition to offering great benefits to the practitioner, the Venerable Sayadaw wanted a sangha of Americans to grow and carry on the Sasana in the West. Quite a few individuals experienced monastic life, but there was never any organized attempt to train Westerners to teach other Westerners, and a cohesive group of Western monks and nuns did not develop. Over the course of time at the California monastery, the Asian and American cultures stratified. Religious festivals were attended almost exclusively by Asians, while meditation retreats were attended only by the Americans.

Taungpulu Kaba-Aye Monastery in Boulder Creek, California— established in 1981— is one of the earliest attempts to provide a permanent monastic setting for Westerners in the United States. Through the years, Asian and American students, both male and female, have become monks and nuns, but only a few have been able to remain in the robes for long. It has been a brave first attempt. No serious student of monastic Buddhism ever desired to spend the start-up years in the United States.

The Insight Meditation Society of Barre, Massachusetts, Spirit Rock Mediation Center in Woodacre, California, and the Friends of the Western Buddhist Order have brought the teachings of Theravada to Westerners without the complication of cultural trappings. Lay teachers conduct retreats, give meditation instruction, and teach classes. Their organizations share teaching events with monks and nuns who visit from time to time.

The evolution of these forms continues to be a spectacle of ethnographic interest as a whole generation of Buddhist practitioners adds a unique chapter to Western religious history. In the most privileged and difficult of times they struggle to plant and cultivate a precious spiritual tradition. Conflicts, which arise as a part of the life of every movement and organization, secular or religious, inevitably attend such fledgling efforts. As everyone knows by now, Frontier Buddhism has not been without a few "Donner Parties."

Falling Down

I had been working in the same dedicated way as had other Dhamma brothers and sisters throughout the country. Under the leadership of Taungpulu Sayadaw and Rina, our project focused on founding a forest monastery in the Theravada tradition. I believed that as the monastery moved into the future, it would undergo a gradual evolution best suited for its survival. Normal ups and downs accompanied our organization's growth through its first eleven years. We were supported by a culturally diverse population, we had resident monks, large numbers of visitors at the regularly held festivals, students who came frequently for individual retreats or temporary ordinations, and a donor base which helped support ongoing projects.

With the exception of a few Burmese and Chinese members, the board of directors were American. There were five resident monks who came from Burma and two Americans. In the eleventh year, without the Americans' knowledge, members of the ethnic Burmese community began a group of their own, established, they claimed, in order to help look after the monks' needs. At the largest festival of the year—the July celebration marking the beginning of the annual Rains Retreat—several members of this group set up a table and began collecting donations. The board's treasurer did not object to this, since she fully expected that the group would hand over the donations at the end of the day. When they refused to give her the $2,000 they had collected, everyone understood that this group had its own agenda.

Confusion and disbelief at this turn of events led to anger and confrontation between the incredulous board members and the resident monks, who had assembled in the shrine room to discuss the matter. One by one, the most senior monks left the room until only three younger monks remained; it was obvious who was behind the bid for power. When questioned later, the abbot said that he had not objected to the formation of the Burmese organization, but he told them not to collect money. This new revelation—that the younger monks and their new supporters ignored the wishes of the abbot—was a new source of distress.

The abbot, who had his own monastery in Burma, had accepted the assignment of heading this monastery from Taungpulu Sayadaw. He had done so out of respect for his teacher. Unfortunately, his temperament was not ideally suited to the unforeseen demands of this position. While everyone appreciated his great spiritual strengths—equanimity, loving-kindness, and patience—the fact that he was not able to exert authority became something of an "Achilles' heel" for us.

The months immediately following the attempted coup were full of tension and incidents. The board was accused of not knowing how to take care of the monks, and worse, of not reporting the finances in a timely or accurate manner. Rina's picture disappeared from the entry hall, and she received threatening phone calls. She was referred to as the "General Ne Win"[9] of the monastery, and eventually she stopped visiting altogether.

A Burmese visitor who had come to the monastery to ordain temporarily, already distraught with personal problems, further deteriorated in the chaotic environment. Egged on by his Burmese acquaintances, he became even more undone, taking a swing at one of the board members with a broom, getting into a screaming match with another, taking photographs of everyone, and producing a tape recorder in the midst of conversations. To everyone's relief, he disappeared after several weeks.

The phrase that came to mind during those months was: "Hard to make, easy to break." Donations plummeted; festivals lost attendance. Throughout the entire crisis, Rina remained unshakable in her determination not to "hand over a ready-made monastery" to this or any other group who wanted to wrest control of the leadership, even though several of her own board members encouraged her to do so. She would always refer to Taungpulu Sayadaw's founding vision of having a forest monastery for Western students:

> The monks from Burma will be staying here only a short while. Most of the Burmese monks don't want to stay in America, and will eventually go back to their native country. Therefore, in the long run, the Americans who become monks will carry on the Sasana. They are the only ones who can really establish the Sasana in this country. People from outside, from far away, cannot really do much.[10]

The board members responded quite conservatively: they chose not to enter a lawsuit in order to retrieve the money, opting instead for a series of discussions with the group and generally waiting it out. Eventually, after a year, the money was returned, and the Burmese group moved to its own location in a Bay Area suburb where it maintains a house for one or two monks.

The troubles that beset the monastery did not develop suddenly, nor for readily apparent reasons. In this case, the Burmese and Sino-Burmese supporters had immigrated to the United States because they were displaced by a military government. Like Rina and her family, they were forced to leave their homes, settle in a foreign country, and become part of a cultural and religious minority. Burma is neither overpopulated nor under-resourced, but under Ne Win's regime it became so badly managed that thousands fled as the political and economic climate destroyed the quality of their lives, and in some instances, even threatened their lives. I have witnessed on more than one occasion people who, after being separated for many years, meet one another again while visiting the monastery. These people, having lost their property, their fortunes, their livelihood, their status in the community—in short, their entire way of life— rely heavily on the monastery as one of the few remaining links to their homeland. It takes great resourcefulness to start over, and there are many success stories. There are others, however, who cannot accept their disrupted life and live with great anger, sadness, loss, and alienation.

All the Burmese individuals who formed this group were initially devoted to the monastery; some had even been board members. They saw Anglo-Americans playing at roles they were born into, and not always doing a good job. These neophytes made decisions, handled the finances, planned the projects, supervised the festivals. Certainly, this must have appeared to them completely upside-down. To the more conservative individuals of their community, the *real* Theravada tradition was slowly being lost at the hands of inexperienced, disrespectful young Americans, and they felt something must be done to save the purity of the tradition.

I had certainly experienced all this to be true, but had never registered the violation as something that needed to be remedied. After all, this is *America,* where nothing remains pure for long; we are, as a people, in fast motion with regard to cultural and spiritual identity. I had been watching for years as Westerners acted both appropriately and inappropriately in their efforts to absorb an understanding of Buddhism; it was all part of the melting pot in which borrowed traditions undergo the alchemy of generations.

Another contributing condition was that monasteries in Asia are always—as prescribed in their monastic rule—the province of the monks, and it is their prerogative to run things accordingly. Our "petri dish" monastery, dominated by a secular board of directors, having a woman co-founder, and in which monks were "tenants," was, I am sure, more than they could endure.

No amount of sociological analysis, however, tempered my own reaction to the incident. Bewilderment gave way to a red-hot anger which, like a river of slow-moving lava, engulfed my white Anglo-Saxon Protestant sensibilities in a sludge of righteous rage. I ruefully pondered the dissolution of my good intentions and my labors of the last eleven years before my very eyes.

Duped, I thought, *taken in. I did not sign up for this!* I fumed. Hadn't I avoided organized religions because of the authoritarianism, the hypocritical behavior of the ministers and congregation, the materialism which in the name of religion fattened the church coffers and compromised everything truly spiritual? And here I was, *secretary* of just such an organization.

The worst blow during this time was the realization that some of the monks were behind this sordid affair. Thus did I encounter "The Patriarchy." You may ask how I could have for so many years been oblivious to a state which for the rest of the female population (including, and perhaps especially, the female Buddhist population) was so glaringly obvious. In fact, women had been talking and writing about it for years. My naiveté lasted as long as it did because Taungpulu Sayadaw was the first monk I had ever met, and I projected his sublime qualities onto every other monk. Since patriarchal forms arise only in the absence of spacious, sympathetic, balanced, or enlightened states of mind, and since Sayadaw lived always in such positive states, I was completely unprepared for encounters with selfish, politically minded Sangha members who justified their every action by pointing to their robes.

After months of smug indignation and wounded pride—a sure sign that my spiritual aspirations had not advanced far toward enlightenment—something inside me said *Adios, frontier.* Go back to the teachings: the rising and falling of the breath, the rising and falling of thoughts and feelings, the rising and falling of experiences, of decades, or eras, of worlds. The Middle Way became my own beating heart thumping out a rhythm: elation-disappointment, effort-defeat, happiness-anger, doubt-faith, aspiration-discouragement. "Let's just see what happens," it beats on, "all this is just wet clay."

At times I visualized Taungpulu Sayadaw giving one of his favorite teachings: "There is no practice that excels patience ... like the fire that will burn everything, from the finest sandalwood to the most repugnant dead bodies without protest, without saying anything, practice patience."

I longed to "roam alone like the rhinoceros,"[11] to be free from the dense web of social life. I knew that institutions are society's vessels for preserving and transmitting knowledge of great value, and that institutions which run poorly for whatever reason become the antithesis of the very knowledge they are entrusted to protect. Even periods of peace and calm—when everyone seems to be practicing—can be the gestating periods for future calamity. But somehow I also knew that spiritual life and work—with or in community—is the collective, objective expression of the interconnectedness of life. The best of times and worst of times will always be associated with community endeavors; it is always a "mixed bag."

If I dwell on the mistakes, the failings, the misguided intentions, and willfulness of individuals, I can always be in the safe harbor of the one who has been wronged. This is a comfortable, ego-bolstering position. I will have my own and everyone's sympathy. I will not have to inspect myself, I will not have to examine what role I played in the failure, and, best of all, I will not have to change. I have long since abandoned my overconfidence about the way things will be or should be in the future.[12] However, I still cherish the role that a monastery plays—encouraging practice, learning, and healing.

The capacity for Americans to fulfill the role of monastery stewards remains to be seen. Those who live by ascetic practices or have undertaken monastic practice for any length of time understand well the hardship, hunger, and loneliness, the untamed mind with no avenues of distraction, the dependence on others, and the physical privation that monastic life entails. Whether or not you are practicing detachment or denial is also difficult to discern. But the benefits and positive achievements of such a life—simplicity, having few wishes, lightness of mind, wakefulness, quietude, and insight—keep the monastic Sangha alive as a viable path for spiritual progress.

If monks and nuns practice earnestly and show gratitude to their benefactors, a strong spiritual symbiosis develops between lay and monastic Sangha members. It is a delicate balance, difficult to strike, hard to maintain, and right now there is not a large monastic community in America. With few exceptions, monks and nuns operate as ministers serving a congregation, rather than living communally.

Taking Root

Gotama Buddha appeared in India during a time of philosophical ferment and rigid social stratification. His all-embracing compassion countered the injustices which were the warp and woof of the social fabric: the caste system and the belief in karma as "fate."

His discriminating wisdom punctured the belief that rites and rituals and paying the priests would bring salvation. But it was his teaching of *anatta* (non-self) and nibbana that overturned Krishna's claim to Arjuna, "Never was there a time when I did not exist, nor thou, nor these rulers of men; nor will there ever be a time hereafter when we shall all cease to be,"[13] and marked the Buddha's teaching as a wheel-turning moment in the evolution of human consciousness, setting it apart, forever, from all other spiritual paths.

As Buddhism moves into the Christian West, it will not be embraced for its philosophical expressions of anatta and nibbana, for there is no greater love than the love of self, and we are still struggling to understand "no-self." The *Abhidhamma,* the Theravada psycho-ethical system of psychology, unequaled in its precision, offers still under-explored transformative potential for Western practitioners. Within Buddhist psychology lie the doctrines of karma, rebirth, and dependent origination. In this respect, the *Abhidhamma* is not strictly religious but a highly analytical, integrated system which demonstrates that the mind is very vast and a vehicle of infinite potential. The teachings of the *Abhidhamma* offer a panoramic view of human consciousness, from depraved to sublime states. This system is at once philosophical, psychological, ethical, and spiritual, and there is no analogous paradigm in the West.

The *Abhidhamma-pitaka,* literally "the basket of Higher Teachings," is the third part of the Pali Buddhist Canon. It consists largely of abstract formulations, questions and answers on certain topics, and long lists of categories and combinations of categories. The *Sutta-pitaka,* the basket of the Buddha's discourses, reveal his teachings in a simple, conversational way. Nevertheless, as present feminist scholarship reveals, these conversations reflect the gender limitations of what Rita Gross calls "androcentric recordkeeping."[14] The *Abhidhamma,* however, treats everyone, regardless of gender, as a collection of psychic factors and elements.

The Buddha of the early literature proclaimed his mission tersely: "I teach suffering and its end." The Buddha taught the importance of cultivating a discriminating mind. If cultivated properly through the practice of mindfulness and clear comprehension, it is our most powerful guardian: it prevents suffering states from arising and relieves suffering states that have already arisen. This quality of discrimination is understood through the study and practice found in Buddhist psychology.

The Buddha's position on suffering is one which has over the years received its fair share of misinterpretation. The most common one—all of life is suffering—occurs when people try to summarize the First Noble Truth:

> What, O monks, is the Noble Truth about suffering? Birth is suffering, sickness is suffering, old age is suffering, death is suffering. Grief, lamentation, mental unhappiness are suffering. Not getting what you want is suffering. In brief, the five groups of clinging are suffering.[15]

The Buddha did not say that happiness is suffering, or that success, friendship, and joy are suffering. Only very specific states are suffering, and these states are experienced universally by all creatures. Even a fully enlightened being will experience physical suffering, but not mental suffering. It can be argued that because the Buddha taught the way to end the cycle of birth-rebirth that he rejected the physical world. Yet he achieved his enlightenment on the earth, in a body. After achieving nibbana, he lived at least forty more years as an example of noble living to those all around him. His *parinibbana* expressed one of the Great Mysteries which captivates the human heart: the extinguished flame which goes to rest and cannot be defined.

There is no Pali word for "spirituality," but the Western term "embodied spirituality," I believe, describes for our times the positive, life-affirming notions found in the Buddha's teachings. Buddhist women will play a major role in shaping a new paradigm. Materialism in its most lethal form—no respect for the life-force—is now upon us, and women, with their capacity to incubate and bear new life, are endowed by Mother Nature with all the tender and terrible qualities necessary to protect life.

Noble Living, from the Buddhist point of view, is an ethic-based psychology; it is the cornerstone of Buddhist practice and will evolve despite substantial disappointments that have plagued the early Buddhist movement in this country—notably, the behavior of teachers who have misappropriated philosophical teachings (such as emptiness and nonduality), or used their institutional authority abusively in their relationships with students.

"Nirvana and samsara are the same [therefore, whatever I do doesn't really matter]" and "The teacher is the embodiment of Truth [therefore, whatever he or she says or does is above reproach]" are two examples of how teachings can be exploited for ego-centered purposes. Using a position of authority to take advantage of someone is one of the oldest, saddest, and most universal of exploitative behaviors. Fortunately for the future of Buddhism in America, the fundamental importance of ethical behavior is being more and more understood, appreciated, and required.

The psychology of early Buddhism claims that we can acquire a special kind of knowledge called *insight,* which is a discriminating kind of seeing. We acquire this knowledge through direct experience; it has a truth and power not necessarily obtainable through the discursive states of mind we use when we read or study. In the *Kalama Sutta,* the Buddha advises us not to believe a doctrine just because it comes from tradition, scripture, or even a trusted teacher. He gives the criteria for judgment: actions fueled by desire and greed, dislike and hatred, illusion and ignorance—do such actions lead to happiness or unhappiness? More important, the Buddha concludes that good judgment lies within our own experience. Personal experience is highly valued by the Buddha as a means of attaining psychological insight:

> By living together with a person one can find whether a person is consistent in his actions and if so whether he is a virtuous person;

in the same manner a person's integrity can be tested by having dealings with him; and a person's fortitude can be tested in a crisis situation and his wisdom in conversation. The way a person acts in a particular situation or a series of similar situations over a certain length of time gives us an indication of the character of a person. It is also said of the Buddha that his preaching and actions are consistent *(yathavadi tathakari)*.[16]

There are other appeals to innate, common-sense knowledge. Do we have to cut off our limb in order to know that a person with a severed limb suffers?

The ability to discern what leads to harm and what leads to happiness atrophies when mental culture *(bhavana)* is neglected. Our culture advances a techno-glut atmosphere which mesmerizes the senses, keeps our focus outward, and forces us to think and move faster and faster, so that we spend our days reacting rather than interacting. In such an environment, it becomes more and more difficult to cultivate a strong inner life.

It is my hope that all the Buddhist havens already established will continue to offer their sacred spaces as zones in which the qualities of peace, simplicity, humility, stillness, and clarity can be nurtured. Places for solitary and group meditation provide an antidote to the speed of modern life, and offer a highly therapeutic environment, a quiet place where people can rediscover and rejuvenate the mind and body. The insight-knowledge gained in the quietness of meditation is a source of great healing—which is a primary purpose of Buddhist practice.

These last few decades of Buddhism in America have provided us with unequaled adventures, both pleasant and unpleasant. We still look forward and backward at the same time: we no longer resemble the parent generation of teachers who brought the word from native lands, but we are nevertheless Buddhists. Buddhist schools no longer face the physical challenge of building a vessel, but they face unanswered questions: How will Buddhism inform the Western perspective of ego and soul? Will the languages of the sacred texts live on? What will be the role of the monastic sangha? Can Buddhism help decrease violence in this country? Can a Bodhi tree grow here?

As with all other spiritual movements, the institution of Buddhism and the practice of Buddhism will remain in some ways separate. Practice starts in the silent witnessing of the mind and ends in silent witnessing; institutions start with talking, and never stop talking. It is an easily proven fact of history that good people—even saints—arise despite and sometimes at the very center of the worst-run "spiritual" institutions.

The contribution of Buddhism to the next generation is not grace but graciousness, an ethic that is not choked by dogmatism, but informed by psychological insight, a mode of action whose power is not destructive but rebalancing, and a wisdom that does not exclude but *creates* spaciousness. As Buddhist women in America, our efforts will not only be on behalf of ourselves, our families, and communities, but on behalf of Mother Earth in crisis. As she witnessed for the Buddha, we must now witness for her: In the midst of talking, observe the silence. In the midst of action, observe the stillness. In the midst of meditation, observe.

1. Visakha was the main benefactress of the Buddha and his disciples. She provided for them whenever she saw a need.

2. The Ten Precepts, or *Dasa Sila*, are to abstain from killing, stealing, incelibacy, untruthfulness, intoxicants, eating food past noon, singing, dancing, and entertainments, wearing make-up, ornaments, and unguents, sleeping on a high and lofty bed, and handling gold and silver. Rina also observes the ascetic practice of eating one meal, at one sitting, in one vessel.

3. The period of time—thousands of years—that the Buddha's teachings exist.

4. The practitioner undertakes the path of practice leading to Buddhahood in a future era. This includes the perfection of ten spiritual qualities *(paramis)*: generosity, morality, renunciation, energy, patience, truthfulness, resoluteness, loving-kindness, equanimity, and wisdom. After this is accomplished, the being takes rebirth in a heavenly plane until informed by other heavenly beings that the time is ripe for rebirth on earth as a Buddha.

5. The Five Precepts, *Panca Sila*, are to abstain from killing, stealing, sexual misconduct, false speech, and intoxicants.

6. Ledi Sayadaw of Burma (1846–1923), wrote that "Freeing or deliverance from the plane of misery is the First Nibbana," in *Manual of Insight* (Kandy, Sri Lanka: Buddhist Publication Society, 1961), p. 46. "This," the editor notes, "refers to the first of the four stages of emancipation, Stream-

entry, where rebirth in the lower worlds is excluded. Since, already at this stage, the final attainment of Nibbana, at the latest after seven existences, is assured, the author calls it, in anticipation, the First Nibbana."

7. In Pali, *bhojjanga:* investigation of the Dhamma, effort, mindfulness, concentration, one-pointedness, joy, equanimity.

8. In Pali, *brahma-vihara:* boundless compassion, sympathetic joy, loving-kindness, and equanimity.

9. The military leader who seized power and nationalized Burma in 1961.

10. Quoted in an interview with Taungpulu Sayadaw in the newsletter of the Taungpulu Kaba-Aye Monastery, *Forest Light News,* January-February 1984.

11. The full quote is: "Cold and heat, hunger and thirst, storms, sun, insects, serpents, too—Overcoming all of these, roam alone, like the rhinoceros." Narada Thera and Bhikku Kassapa, *The Mirror of the Dhamma* (Kandy, Sri Lanka: Buddhist Publication Society, 1970), p. 22.

12. As of June 1996, the monastery thrives under the direction of a newly arrived, energetic, and no-nonsense head monk.

13. Rita M. Gross, *Buddhism After Patriarchy: A Feminist History, Analysis, and Reconstruction of Buddhism* (Albany, New York: State University of New York Press, 1992), p. 20.

14. Eliot Deutsch, translator, *The Bhagavad Gita* (New York: Holt, Rinehart and Winston, 1968), p. 38.

15. Rune E. A. Johannson, *Pali Buddhist Texts Explained to the Beginner* (Stockholm, Sweden: Scandinavian Institute of Asian Studies Monograph Series, 1973), p. 23.

16. Padma Di Silva, *An Introduction to Buddhist Psychology* (New York: Barnes & Noble Books, 1979), p. 15.

Sandy Boucher

Not to Injure Life:
A Visit with Ruth Denison

I HAVE COME TO UNDERSTAND, in the last fifteen years, that my spiritual practice with Ruth Denison in the Mojave Desert is sustained by two major elements: first, my relationship with this quite innovative and unpredictable teacher, and secondly, by my experience of the unique environment of the desert with its fragile flora, its startling extremes of weather, its animals and snakes and birds, on Copper Mountain Mesa where Ruth's Dhamma Dena center is located.

I have meditated and studied Buddhism in many other settings, even as far away as Sri Lanka, but I always return to the desert and to Dhamma Dena. I come home to the little cluster of low buildings off a sandy dirt road; I come home to the concrete-block zendo, to check in with myself.

In 1984 I thought I would write a book about Ruth Denison's work and life. What developed out of that impulse was the idea for *Turning the Wheel*,[1] and I left the material I had written on Ruth to investigate the overall phenomenon of North American women's participation in Buddhism for that book. But recently, having come upon the ten-year-old manuscript about Ruth, I saw how it expresses her environmentalism, her conserving of resources, her connection with all living beings and her care for them; and I discovered in it her explanation of how she came to teach some all-women courses (she was one of the first teachers to do so) and her complete acceptance and welcoming of lesbian women.

Ruth's being and her behavior at Dhamma Dena have taught me that whatever our spiritual attainment, we are one with the conditioned world, and how we greet and care for and respond to that ordinary world provides the crucial ground for the honing of our practice.

◇

Already the sun rides high, assaulting my eyes as I look out on the miles of low chaparral, the chalky round sage bushes, the tall creosote bushes scattered among the sage, their skinny stems gray with black circles like the joints of a puppet's arms, their yellow flowers bobbing in the steady wind. Far out, the low brown-blue shapes of mountain ranges rise, wrapped in haze: presences always there at the horizon like friends who attend and watch over you but never come close.

A rich deep sound fills the sky, pushing at its boundaries, awakening a throbbing in my body. I am lifted up into this guttural song, and then it fades and is gone. It comes at intervals during the day, a motif to remind us where we are. This particular stretch of dry earth extending out before me is near neighbor to the Marine Corps Base at Twenty-nine Palms, not far from the Flight Test Center at Edwards Air Force Base; to the north are the U.S. Naval Weapons Center, the Irwin Military Reservation, and the Randsburg Wash Test Range, from which come echoing booms.

Two hours' drive to the west is Los Angeles and the shimmering Pacific, and an hour up the coast, Santa Barbara and Lompoc, where at Vandenberg Air Force Base they shot off the MX missiles to arc out over the ocean and drop on the Marshall Islands. Here in the high desert on Copper Mountain Mesa, just north of Joshua Tree National Monument, suffering and impermanence are close companions. A shirt left outside for two weeks is eaten by the sun, its cotton hanging in shreds; an unwanted dog thrown out of a passing car wanders in confusion and hunger until it steps into the cruel jaws of a trap set for small animals; plants shrivel, skin puckers, eyes are stunned by the flashbulb-intensity of the sun.

I am picking up my notebook and readying myself to leave my private place behind the shed when a long-skirted figure appears from around the woodpile. She is short and square-shouldered, her hair covered by a white scarf tucked up behind, her long-sleeved white blouse and tan skirt fluttering against her body in the wind. On her face is an expression of satisfaction as she looks down at the desert tortoise clasped in her outstretched hands. Behind her waddles an ancient dachshund whose deep throaty cough accompanies his steps as he hurries to catch up.

The sound of the passing jet gradually grows transparent and fades into silence as they approach.

"Ah, this is where you are hiding!" For a moment she stops and stands looking at me, as if she cannot decide whether to talk to me or go on about her business. The tortoise swims energetically, its head thrust out of the shell.

Ruth grins down at it.

"Look at her! I found her caught in the junk pile, yah, in the wire under there. She couldn't move. I come out here sometimes just to check on her."

She approaches me, walking in a wide-legged sturdy gait with a slight limp, holding out the tortoise for me to see.

It is about the size of a small round casserole dish, its greyish shell like joined domed plates of armor, each section outlined in darker gray. Its head wags from side to side, and as Ruth sets it gently on the earth, its legs scrabble for traction, lifting its weight on its horny toenails.

"She is hungry." Ruth says, folding her hands before her. "I am going to take her to the house and give her some salad."

The dog comes up to peer at the turtle with its bluish old eyes, and I smile, remembering Ruth's remark yesterday about the tufts of black hair above its eyes. "Special eyebrows," she had said, smoothing the strands of coarse hair, "I call them the Suzuki eyebrows. Have you ever seen a picture of that great Zen scholar D. T. Suzuki? He had eyebrows that *stuck* into the universe." She paused, tilting her head as she surveyed her handiwork. "Yah, they formed an umbrella over his eyes."

Now the dog, whose name is Uliloo, seeks out the shade under the overhang of a makeshift wooden platform someone has built to support a mattress. His shaggy brown muzzle peeks out, alternately pointing to the tortoise and Ruth.

"Want to sit down?" I ask, moving over to accommodate her.

"No, darling, I have many things to do. I must get back up to the house and then we have a sitting at nine, *hmmm?*"

But instead of hurrying off, she stoops, her skirt spreading on the dry yellow dirt, to stroke Uliloo's head. "He's really a sweetheart, you know. He's not supposed to eat now because he goes to the vet. He's looking at me. You see how dependent animals are? He cannot speak. The desire is in front of him: to eat. And he just can look at me, he can't be angry, he can't take anything for himself. You see, the dependency is enormous, we are not aware of it. But this feeling only comes when you really begin to see the suffering in the world."

Uliloo flops on his side, panting so heavily that he begins to choke again.

Ruth perches on the edge of the platform and, shaking her head, looks with great solicitude at the dog. She is a sixty-year-old woman with a strong-boned, lined face. Her bangs, visible beneath the edges of the scarf, are the dull blond of antique gold touched with red. During the first year I knew Ruth Denison I never saw her without one of those little scarves tucked up in back, and eventually I began to wonder if she were bald. But actually she has long golden hair twisted and tucked up under the scarf. "Not a gray hair in it," she told me. "In my family we do not get gray." Once on a visit to the Woman's Sangha in Berkeley she wore a dress of some deep color and let her hair down over her shoulders. The effect was startling, as if I were seeing her naked, as vulnerable as a young girl.

Now her eyes squint against the sun, the dark eyebrows above the deep sockets wrinkled, her bright blue gaze shadowed. Her skin is very pale, with deep furrows from her nostrils past the corners of her thin-lipped mouth down to her jaw. A fold of loose skin extends from her chin to the base of her throat. Her jaw is a proud hull, her face a ship cutting through turbulent waters.

She has lost all incentive to get back to the house now, I see, for she is looking at the objects in a pile near us, no doubt devising a use for each. To our right stands a freezer, maybe eight feet long, gleaming white in the sun. Next to it rears a stand-up refrigerator which faces the wall of the shed, its motor and cooling elements like intestines obscenely exposed. Behind us is a junkyard of old wood, shiny household appliances, coiled wire, doors of various shapes, casement windows, pieces of metal, all neatly stacked or propped or stood in rows and piles. The detritus of the desert, gathered from abandoned houses or bought for almost nothing from some settler who decided to give up his place and go back to Los Angeles or San Bernardino where the sun is not so blistering or the wind so vicious. "Gifts from the universe," Ruth calls these objects.

I'm feeling grumpy and tired, having struggled through the early morning meditation session, and afterwards castigated myself that I am not really a very religious or spiritual person. She, on the other hand, was always drawn to religious practice, always devout. She was even attracted to her husband Henry because he was so "spiritual" (he had been a Vedanta monk). Adjusting my now-stiffening buttocks on my makeshift seat of piled boards, I look over at Ruth, who has picked up a piece of rusted metal and sits examining it with the shrewd eye of one who knows how to recycle everything. Suddenly I wonder how it happened that she conceived the idea of offering all-women retreats besides her regular mixed courses. Certainly she is a feminist, but those of us over the years who have tried to subsume Ruth under our particular political categories have found that she never comfortably fit there or answered our needs in quite the ways we required. She is known as a loner, a renegade.

At my question she looks up to fix me with intent eyes. She has placed the piece of metal on the ground now and smoothes her skirt over her knees.

"Through a student of mine," she answers. "Her name was Carol Newhouse, and she belonged to the founders of Womanshare, a farm up in Oregon. She came to me and invited me to a little farm, she said, where only women live. Seven. Whether I would do that. My classes were big. I had ninety students at times. So she was rather very modest and expected nothing, huh? And shy asking me, but would I come? And I said yes. Also I knew there were only seven on a little farm, but you see because I said yes was not because they were just women or feminists, but it struck me seven people in a community, in a farm, and want the teachings ... huh? That was very touching to me."

I sit forward, elbows on my knees, interested. "So you went up there?"

"I think I was three or four times there, then, and I got very friendly with them and had good relatedness to it. I called those my black-market courses, you know, because I would just sneak away to do them. It's near Grant's Pass and then about two hours to drive. I lived in a little chicken coop where I could hardly stand up. They had nicely cleaned it up and made a bed for me. There was no electric light, and I had to go into the forest for the outhouse. Our outhouses here are *salons,* compared to that: it was just a board where you sat in open space all around you. A beautiful forest, and they lived really narrowed down, and oh, many people, there were more than seven because they had invited others from the surroundings, and they came. There's a picture of this in the album in the dining room. Didn't you see me sitting on the ground? We had no space where to eat, and it was warm. With what was around there, some boards and round old spools from telephone wire, I created somehow a table on the ground, and we sat around and did blessing and we held our bowl, and it was very ... yah ... ceremonial, despite the hard primitive condition there."

Ruth fiddles with the eyeglasses that hang on a chain around her neck, a mannerism which sometimes annoys me. Today I simply watch her strong blunt hands lifting and toying with the earpieces.

"They liked it and I liked it. I liked the spirit, and then I felt they were moving toward wanting to create better conditions and living also as a model somehow. What I got there was that they were in a minority and they were somehow not approved of by neighbors, and then I found out they were lesbian. I must tell you, I had heard of homosexuality but I had never really gotten acquainted with this field and acting among women. But it didn't cost me any special thing. It was just ... they were beautiful people and however this intimacy is arranged, that's a personal thing, let them do it the way they like."

"But how did the all-women's retreats get started *here* at Dhamma Dena?" I ask.

"By then I knew some women already, you see," she says. "The groups got larger in Oregon. There were seventeen women there at one time, and it was very crowded, and I think I just said now I am not coming anymore, you come here. I don't really know how that happened, whether they asked me or I asked them."

"Is it different teaching all women?"

"Yah, a little. One speaks so much of woman-energy. I think to be among women it is just natural that one feels more comfortable perhaps. There is some flowingness among women, some energy where it's always uniting. Well, you know, it's really very primitive instincts in us; this is our group, you see, we belong to it, we are one and the same."

The two black dogs arrive panting around the corner of the shed. Both are nearly grown puppies, one with a shepherd's high pointed ears, the other with round fluffy ears and brown markings on muzzle and feet. One jumps the other and they proceed to wrestle, bumping up against the freezer, feinting, baring their teeth and growling, now and then biting each other, rolling over on the crumbly earth. Uliloo simply goes on sleeping, but the turtle contracts head and legs to become as innocuous as a rock.

Ruth pays attention to the dogs for a time, smiling faintly at their antics, and then as she moves her body, turning more toward me, I know she has returned to our conversation again.

"It wasn't a big deal being women alone. You see, I am actually raised with women. I grew up in East Prussia, where you live in a small village where you go out to Sunday School and everybody knows you are there. It was a beautiful little church. We were friends with the minister. His wife was a very active and artistic woman, she had her woman's group, you know. *Frauenverein,* we called it, and my momma was part of it. We children—me and my brother and sister—they would train us for some theater and dress us. And then, I also belonged, when I was a young woman, to the *Glauben Schonheit* association. Only women, you know. We did all kinds of beautiful things together—hiking, swimming, building rafts, dancing on floating rafts with lovely wreaths in the hair, and jumping naked into the water and swimming out. So you see it wasn't so unusual to be with women, only that we weren't lesbians. What I felt when I became acquainted with the lesbians here in the women's retreats at Dhamma Dena was that there was a little too much emphasis on the sexual orientation. It was very much stressed then. And I think that has subsided. You see there is something added now to their life, we have added the Dhamma."

The dogs lie panting, across from each other, their eyes alert, their bodies ready to spring up again. Ruth squints out at the mountains, her face thoughtful.

"Certainly I am a woman who is not totally dependent on the man. Before I married I was a very independent woman too, I was a schoolteacher and a principal, so when I married then I ... without any kind of ill feelings or so, just took that wifely role for a while because I didn't need to work. But as you can see, I didn't stay in that role, so there is some blood in me. But I must say, I have one thing which is remarkable, which is, I have no revenge or this need to pay back something that is done wrong to me or to my group. I could really be nasty to men, you know, I was raped and violently handled by men through the war situation, by Russians and also Western men, but mainly by Russians. So I could be having a real turn-off to men, but I don't see it that way. In many ways I have brought good karma forces with me, with natural balance, with a sense of justice coming from a deeper soul or ground, and a great compassionate feeling. I have a love for life, *hmmm?* which brings with it sensitivity and care, *real* care. So when you have that certain sense you cannot really charge back, no matter how wrong it was done to you. Because when you charge back, you see that you injure life. And the principle then is not injuring life."

We sit in silence, and I hear a faint rustling to my left. I turn to see a strip of paper, a length from an adding machine roll, caught in piled boards, tugging at its mooring. Farther away, another long ribbon of paper wraps about the base of a creosote bush that bobs in the wind, its flowers sedately dancing. To my right the metal siding of the shed squeaks, worrying at itself.

Then suddenly Ruth's voice comes. "Oh, but do you have a watch, darling? It must be late ... the sun so hot now!"

"It's five to nine."

She stands up quickly. "Then I must go, and get this turtle to her breakfast. You are going to the sitting, no?"

She stoops to prod Uliloo, who snorts and stretches his stumpy legs.

"Yes, I'm going into Dukkha House first to leave my notebook."

"See you in the zendo," she says, as she strides briskly away, the tortoise held out before her, Uliloo struggling up on his legs to follow. Now in this headlong flight, body tilted slightly forward, the skirt billowing about her legs, the little cap gleaming in the sun, Ruth looks like one of the factory women in a Kathe Kollwitz lithograph, someone sturdy and strong-armed and reliable, whose life is labor.

1. *Turning the Wheel: American Women Creating the New Buddhism* (New York: Harper & Row, 1988. Revised edition: New York: Beacon Press, 1993).

Shosan Victoria Austin

Suzuki Sensei's Zen Spirit

I FIRST MET SUZUKI SENSEI IN 1976. At the time, I was a very young practitioner. Although I had often noticed a petite, quick woman who looked like she might have been in her fifties or early sixties, we had never exchanged personal words. She would greet the birds and flowers and pick up stray coffee cups. Or sometimes I might hear the very distinctive sound of her slippers on the floor—*pssh, pssh, pssh.*

I heard from other students that the mysterious woman was the widow of Suzuki Roshi, who had died in 1971. In many ways an ordinary Zen priest, Suzuki Roshi was unusual in his desire to teach Zen in America. After many years of wanting to come, he had been appointed abbot of Sokoji, San Francisco's Soto Zen temple, in 1959. In the morning he sat zazen and welcomed anyone who wanted to join him. Many "hippie-*san*" came, and because of their beginner's mind and intense desire to learn, Suzuki Roshi decided to stay and teach them. In the late 60s, after having practiced for some time with the Japanese congregation at Sokoji, the zazen students decided to buy their own building at 300 Page Street so they could establish a more intense residential practice.

Of Mrs. Suzuki I knew very little. She and Suzuki Roshi had noticed one another at Rinso-in, Suzuki Roshi's temple in Japan, where she was kindergarten principal. Seeing each other in action, they had been struck by each other's wonderful qualities, so they'd married. Though she hadn't shared his desire to come to America, she'd been willing to join him if his term at Sokoji were extended to teach Americans. Much of her family and also his had stayed in Japan. After Suzuki Roshi died, Mrs. Suzuki thought she should go back to Japan, but everybody at Zen Center had been so sad about her leaving, she'd decided to stay.

The year I met Suzuki Sensei, I was sewing and stuffing zafus (round meditation cushions) at Alaya Stitchery, Zen Center's cushion and meditation clothing business. My fellow students and I had just begun to make *hipparis* (wrap-around work jackets) and were wondering how they were traditionally made in Japan. One day I was asking a sewing question of another student. Suzuki Sensei came in, small in stature but big in presence. Though she was quiet, her presence filled the room. She said, "I teach a sewing class. Would you like to come?" So I did. The class met in the Buddha Hall at Zen Center. We spread out mats and sewing boards, and would hand-stitch *juban* (wrap-around undershirts), hipparis, and half-kimonos to wear to tea ceremony. Suzuki Sensei instructed and corrected us bit by bit.

The very first day, when I picked up the piece of fabric and stuck the needle in it, she said, "Everything Americans do is backwards!" I had lifted the cloth exactly upside down and backward from the Japanese point of view. We continued in that vein for quite some time. When I cut the fabric, something would be wrong. When I went to thread a needle, something would be wrong. The way I made a knot in the thread was "wrong." Also, I was a lefty, but the Japanese way is to sew with the right hand.

There's a special stitch for the yoke, another for the collar, and a third for the end of the row. All were hard to learn. Because I was so confused, Sensei would let me sew no more than two or three inches, then look and correct my stitches. Sometimes all that was necessary was a look. I would notice her expression and ask, "Should I take this out?"

As a Zen priest, I keep very few things. But aside from a few pieces I gave to other students, I still have everything I sewed in that class. Each time I look at all the different stitches I remember the teaching, as well as the hands that helped me sew. Suzuki Sensei's hands are small and very well kept. When she picks something up, even if it's as seemingly insignificant as a pin, her hands and the object seem to know each other. The way a pin or a piece of fabric is held becomes a teaching in such hands.

By 1980 Suzuki Sensei had to end sewing class because her eyes were getting so tired and her vision so blurry that she could no longer see the fine stitches. One day just after class, in which we had been sitting about three hours in *seiza,* on our knees, I was staggering upstairs, pulling myself up by the banister. Behind me I heard Suzuki Sensei's slippers on the stairs—*pssh, pssh, pssh.* Then she said something. Because I was in pain, I was unable to hear her right away. It was taking all my concentration just to drag myself upstairs. Then I realized she was saying, "Why don't you study tea?" I had never thought about *chanoyu* (tea ceremony) and didn't really know what it was. I hesitated. Then she prodded: "You don't like green tea?" I said, "Okay, I'll study tea."

The next day I asked Suzuki Sensei how to prepare. "Please buy some *tabi* (starched white socks with a notch between the big and second toes), take a bath, and wear juban and half-kimono." And I did. When the appointed time came, I put it all on and stood outside her door. I felt large and awkward, and my feet felt like they would trip in the unfamiliar tabi. After almost ten minutes of hesitation I rang the bell. She said, *"Hai!* (Yes!) Come in!" I opened the door.

My first impression was of immaculate spring light and a sweet smell. Water was bubbling in a large iron pot, and steam mingled with fragrant incense. Under a scroll was a polished piece of wood on which a single flower in a vase stood. The floor was four-and-one-half tatami mats (each mat is about three by six feet), so clean that they seemed to glow. Next to the door was a set of plain wood shelves with mysterious bowls, ladles, and bamboo utensils whose colors seemed unusually vivid for such subdued, natural shades. All these impressions registered in my stomach in an instant. Before I had a chance to think, Suzuki Sensei said, "Please wash your hands with soap and dry them on the towel next to the sink." Then she taught me how to say "good morning" and ask for her teaching in Japanese: *"Ohayo gozaimasu, Sensei. Onegai itashimasu."* She brought out a thermos, a bowl, and a tray, and taught me how to receive a tea cake and how to eat and drink. She assigned me a partner, another student who looked as awkward as I felt. We practiced saying the unfamiliar words.

Over the next few sessions I realized that teaching tea wasn't easy for her. Just as in sewing class, here too our instincts were all backwards from her teaching. Despite my intention to change my habit, day after day I would impolitely reach for tea objects with my left hand. From seiza, Suzuki Sensei would tap my hands with a ladle handle or a fan. "Vicki-san! Every time the same mistake! Why do you want to study tea?" Another time as I was scooping some powdered tea into the tea bowl, I accidentally dropped a small amount onto the tatami mat. She silently brought a damp cloth, then wiped up the mess, while I sat there feeling like an idiot. I had ruined the whole occasion. I didn't know what to say. She said, "Please apologize," and I did. Once someone dropped the tea bowl and it broke. Half-laughing, Suzuki Sensei said, "In Japan you would have to commit suicide if you did something like this." Many years later, she fleetingly considered teaching us *kaiseki,* the formal meal service that precedes the tea ceremony. "No," she decided. "I don't want to go crazy, and I don't want you to go crazy."

Prodding ladles, persistent left-handedness, my awkwardness and the knee pain from sitting so long—sometimes I would get so frustrated and impatient, and in my discouragement I would think, "This is too hard, too foreign. It's obvious I'll never get it. I should just quit right now." Again and again I watched Suzuki Sensei pick up the bowl, the fan, and the ladle in the proper way, with presence and dignity. As I practiced her corrections and imitated her example, eventually I realized that the difficulty had become a challenge and the foreignness, a broader perspective. But my mental and physical attitudes took a long time to change. Only now am I beginning to see the kind of patience that allowed her to sit next to me and correct me all those times.

A few years later my knees got bad enough that I had to stop studying tea for awhile. I practiced yoga and by 1991 I had healed enough to begin again. About that time, Suzuki Sensei turned seventy-seven and decided to retire. Even though I could no longer study formally with her, she still continued to train me informally, as she

trained everyone she encountered through her example and kindness. All in all, Mitsu Suzuki Sensei stayed and taught us for thirty-
two years. I studied with her for eighteen years.

In 1980, speaking of the principles of tea, Suzuki Sensei said:

> The most important principle of tea ceremony is tranquility, quiet-
> ness, nonattachment to the world, and it can be summarized as no
> false thoughts.
>
> In establishing a company, the host and guest work together
> to build up the occasion of a single meeting, a particular occasion
> that will never occur again in one's whole life.
>
> The master said, "Make tea so that it tastes good. Place the
> charcoal so that the water boils, and arrange the flowers to suit the
> flowers. Keep cool in summer and warm in winter. There is no other
> secret than this."
>
> The way of tea is the way of knowing contentment.

What do these principles look like in action? In fact, they don't
look different from ordinary life—it's more that they bring out the
meaning and depth of ordinary life. Even when she and I used the
same type of tea, hers would taste particularly good. Sometimes she
would invite me to her kitchen for tea—not formal tea, but the kind
you make at home for yourself. Suzuki Sensei didn't keep a particularly special kind of tea for everyday use. As the master said, she
simply made ordinary green tea so that it tasted its best. We'd sit at
her kitchen table. She would warm the pot with a little bit of boiling water. Then she'd warm the cup. When the pot was happy and
the cup was happy, she would pour the water out. She'd let the boiling water cool just a little bit so the tea leaves would be happy, too.
Then she would pour a little, slowly enough so that the leaves wouldn't
jump around. She'd let it sit a few minutes, then pour the happy tea
into the warm cup and hand it to me. It tasted so good! We would
be chatting, but as she prepared the tea she was silent, just making
the tea. She was teaching Zen spirit. Even the plain boiled water she
served after tea carried the subtle flavor of the teaching.

One morning in the summer of 1993, when we both knew that
soon it would be time for her to leave for Japan, I knocked at her
kitchen door. She invited me for breakfast and said, "Please sit." She
took out ingredients both Japanese and American: miso, tofu, green

onions, Tassajara potato bread, and English strawberry jam. Handing me a knife, she said, "Suzuki Roshi always used to cut the grapefruit. Could you please cut the grapefruit?" While I detached each section of the inner rind, trying for a perfect triangle to let her know I cared, she pulled down a jar of cabbage pickles she had made herself, low salt because of her tendency to high blood pressure. A canister of tea, a thermos, dishes, silverware, and condiments went on the table, each carefully in its place. While the bread was toasting, I watched her make the miso soup. From a few vegetable pieces she made stock, and then slightly poached the tofu, stirred a small amount of hot stock in the miso, and let the green onions cook just enough to become bright. Then she turned off the heat and stirred in the miso mixture. Breakfast was interesting and flavorful, but the soup was the best I had ever tasted. I asked her, "Suzuki Sensei, when I watch you make miso soup, it seems so simple, but mine never tastes this good. Could you tell me your secret?" She responded, "Your miso soup of course does not taste the same as my miso soup. It is simple, but simple is not easy."

I saw how she carried simplicity, stability, and grace into her daily life. Monday and Tuesday were for washing and ironing, doctors' appointments, and so on. She would wash her laundry in the tub with bluing, hang it up outside on the roof, and starch and iron everything immaculately. Wednesday was for sewing and mending, and her tea class. Thursday without fail she cleaned the whole house. Friday she went shopping and put out fresh flowers, and Saturday and Sunday she had events with tea companions and friends. She would ask us to drive her here and there, and often hand someone a small treat as a gesture of appreciation. If she received a gift, she kept it on the altar for a day before opening it.

In the mornings, in her room, she regularly made a little offering to Suzuki Roshi. She set out a small portion of her breakfast, lit a stick of incense, and softly rang the bell three times. Then she ate her own breakfast. Later she might go around the building and appreciate people and things, or to the courtyard to visit the baby birds while her long hair dried in the sun. Every day she freshened the flowers in the *kaisando*, the founder's hall, and she exercised: 2,000 marching paces in the hallway or up on the roof; chi kung;

self-massage. She watched Japanese TV programs. Speaking English was hard for her. Somehow she managed with a simple gesture—setting out a single flower, or saying hello to a bird—to make every act a meeting between host and guest, a unique occasion in life.

Zen lore has a story about this spirit:

> Attention! Ummon introduced the subject by saying, "I do not ask you about fifteen days ago. But what about fifteen days hence? Come, say a word about this!" He himself replied (on behalf of everyone), "Every day is a good day."[1]

That is what Suzuki Sensei showed us with her schedule here. She made every day a good day. And when she greeted a person or a bird, that act of attention and care transformed the day for us all. With her attention to tea, sewing, and each second of life, she brought to life Suzuki Roshi's teaching: "Each day is its own past and future and has its own absolute value."

In a 1970 lecture on "Every Day is a Good Day,"[2] Suzuki Roshi compared change to "flowing water . . . which reveals its true nature in its eternal travel," and pointed out that "this kind of travel might make one feel lonely or helpless." I think of the twenty-three years of the sound of Sensei's slippers in the hall after Suzuki Roshi's death, of the absolutely present quality of her hands on a tea bowl, of the sense in the tea room that there was only one being present, which each of us could find only by deeply entering his or her own experience. In discussing this lonely travel through life, Suzuki Roshi talks about *wabi* and *sabi,* Japanese cultural terms of primary importance that literally mean "lonesome" or "monotonous." He says:

> In the strict sense, wabi and sabi mean reality which does not belong to any category of subjectivity or objectivity, simple or fancy. However, it is this reality which makes subjective and objective observation possible, and not only possible but perfect, and which makes everything simple or fancy able to come home to our heart. In the realm of wabi or sabi, even in one drop of dew you will see the whole universe.

When Suzuki Sensei saw large, clumsy American students like me enter the tea room, she wasn't repulsed or disturbed. She didn't reject or grab onto us. Instead, she simply showed us the next step of the tea ceremony. She taught our feet to touch the floor when they walk and our hands to feel the warmth of the bowl changing as we hold it in our hands. She lived Suzuki Roshi's words:

> In the world of wabi and sabi, there is no attempt, no attainment, no anger, joy, sorrow, or any waves of mind of this kind whatsoever. Each existence in this world is the world of subjective self-training and objective pure and direct understanding....
>
> The savor of fruits comes home to our heart, and confirmation of reality takes place. We observe falling flowers at their best. By repeating this kind of direct experience, one may have calm and deep understanding of life, and deliverance from it, like a traveling monk who has full appreciation of everything, and is nonetheless completely detached from it.

And this was her practice and its fruit: her hands on a tea bowl, the appreciation of a moment as it happens and before it's already gone, and the ability to let go.

Recently Suzuki Sensei returned to visit us for two weeks. One night we were at a party where delicious hot tea was served. She said something in Japanese to one of her friends and nodded at me. She was pointing out that my hands were holding the bowl quite naturally, the way she had taught.

1. *The Blue Cliff Records (The Hekigan Roku)*, translated by R. D. M. Shaw, D.D. (London: Michael Joseph Ltd., 1961), p. 42.
2. From an unpublished lecture by Shunryu Suzuki © San Francisco Zen Center.

Nina Egert

Coming Home

AMA YESHE, my Tibetan landlady, pounds on my door, just as I have completed my morning practices. "Mommy, Mommy," she insists—meaning that my folks have finally succeeded in making it through the Indian telephone system. I run up to my landlady's apartment and pick up the phone.

"Darling, I certainly hope you're planning on coming home soon," my mother pleads.

"Just as soon as my research is finished," I reply.

"I really want you to be home by May third. Our synagogue choir is performing a new jazz version of the Friday night Sabbath service," Dad booms from the bedroom phone.

"That's her birthday, you know," Mom reminds him.

"I'll do my best," I answer.

◇

Still blurry with jet lag, I pull my best dress, unworn in many months, out of my suitcase. I fix my hair and put on light make-up, as if all of this had been the uninterrupted routine in my life.

Mom and I drive the half-mile down the hill to synagogue, where my dad meets us at the door and shows us to the seats he has saved for us. A vocal ensemble of sixteen adults is seated on the altar platform, next to a set of trap drums, two saxophones, an acoustic bass, and a set of keyboards. On the other side, at the pulpit, stands the female cantor that I have been hearing about for the last several years. (My parents, having finally made the jarring adjustment to the gender of the person in charge of the musical portions of their worship services, have praised at length her musicality, vitality, and active presence within the community.) She stands before the members of the congregation and warns that tonight's service is going to be quite different than what they are used to hearing. The children's choir joins them on stage, then the whole ensemble breaks out singing the praises of God in a lively, newly-composed, upbeat tune replete with saxophone solo.

This is my first time back in the prayer hall of my childhood in perhaps twenty-five years. As the music proceeds, a wave of memories flood over me—sleepless hours lying in bed pondering the meaning of life, arduous conversations in my Sunday School classroom questioning the existence of "God," giggling teenage girls chatting about cute boys and sneaking glances at risqué novels tucked into prayer books as a way to counter boredom with the uninspired and repetitive recitation of prayers and dull sermons. (My dad's comment about why he liked the former rabbi who had provided me with my early spiritual training was that he had the good sense never to talk about religion, only politics, during his lectures.)

The service continues. This week's Bat Mitzvah girl ascends to the pulpit, tall and lithe and full of poise. She is the daughter of Russian Jewish immigrants who have joined the temple in the intervening years since I last attended. Gracefully and flawlessly, she holds up a large silver cup containing wine, and recites the proper blessing. Words that I had not recalled in decades rise from my bone marrow to my lips.

The Bat Mitzvah girl sports a gold six-pointed star suspended from a chain around her neck. It's been many months now since I have thought of that symbol as a Star of David. To me, just returning from months of training in ritual performance at a Himalayan Buddhist monastery, this star symbolizes the *chos 'byung*, the "arising of Dharma," the insignia of the dakini, or female principle.

The irony of the situation hits in full.

In my late teens I had walked away from this environment in search of "deeper" spiritual meaning. After detours through existential depression and hippiedom, I located some small relief from my angst in the words of Shakyamuni Buddha and the meditational practices of some the most powerful lamas of Tibet. Their words and meditations soothed my soul and intellect. Yet for many years, still reeling, I suppose, from the alienation from religious rituals I developed in my childhood, I continued to be perplexed by the Himalayan propensity for ceremonial pomp and circumstance. Having developed over time some experientially based faith in the profundity of my teachers' words, I figured there had to be something to all this ritual stuff or the lamas wouldn't be pushing it so hard.

Assuming I was not alone in my quandary over the relationship of ritual to meditation—that other American converts to Buddhism might be in a similar boat—I decided to explore the topic as the focus of my doctoral dissertation in anthropology at the University of California, Berkeley. In the end my studies took me to the Himalayan foothills, where I spent the better part of a year and a half training to prepare and lead the regularly performed rituals of one lineal tradition so that I might discuss the perceived meanings of ritual performance as it is practiced in its indigenous cultural context.

Assigned to study under the community's ritual master, I at first had no idea how my gender would affect my work in the field. Himalayan Dharma in this country has essentially developed according to our value system of gender equity. Of course, one could argue over fine points of residual patriarchy, but essentially American women are taught the same practices and participate in the same activities as their male counterparts. Knowing Himalayan attitudes toward women to be somewhat less than egalitarian, I anticipated running aground of resistance to my work. Surprisingly, perhaps because the head lama of my religious training center *(gompa)* had given his blessing to my project, I found the residents of the gompa greatly cooperative and generous in their sharing of information.

Only rarely did gender figure into the mix. For example, I was permitted to learn certain types of chanting on the promise that I would not perform it publicly, as my voice was too *chung chung,* meaning "high pitched," for the proper production of lower vocal resonances. This was a physiological fact that could not be denied. (This is not to say that my gender did not figure into other areas of social interaction during my fieldwork stay, but that subject remains to be discussed elsewhere.)

Rather than hostility, I met with significant support for my efforts, both from the monk/ritual specialists with whom I trained as well as the laywomen I met. From an indigenous perspective, it was not at all inappropriate for a woman to be learning to lead ritual performance. While the actors and musicians I observed in rituals attended by mixed company were all male, there was significant precedence for women to lead rituals when groups of nuns were gathered for group practice. (Especially popular with both robed and lay female practitioners were various traditions of the *gCod* ritual, which focuses on a female deity.)

Other lay women, who were too involved in childrearing and housewifely duties and/or some kind of outside employment to participate in much formal practice, were especially appreciative of the fact that someone had come from so far away to study performative and textual material of which they had little knowledge or understanding, despite having grown up in the culture. Consistently, local residents spoke of how few of them possessed any understanding of the philosophical basis behind whatever religious activities they performed. Few had taken or were able to take the time to learn the classical Tibetan in which religious texts are written; in any case, being able to read these texts did not necessarily imply that one had the ability to comprehend their content. Yet these individuals faithfully performed their daily offering rituals, came to visit the gompa on important holidays, and commissioned rituals to be performed by small groups of monks on special occasions, truly believing that these would effect a kind of magic on their lives—that they would experience comfort, wealth, and good health in the present, while establishing "meritorious" conditions so that these would continue in the future. But for layperson and cleric alike, the fact that I would take on the study of any part of these activities was, in their eyes, unquestionably meritorious and valorous.

◇

Only a discreet few lamas and nuns have gone on to access the meanings of the texts behind the ritual activities—texts containing a mixture of visualizations, confessions, supplications, and offerings which hark back to more formal teachings linked to the most profound levels of meditational experience. Some of the more scholarly types tend to pooh-pooh actual ritual performance; as I did before my arrival in the village, they regard performance as extraneous to the activities that bring one closer to the liberation of the mind.

I, on the other hand, have grown to appreciate the communal bonding that occurs when a group of individuals come together to perform a ceremony. Whether or not one chooses to accept the possibility of super-normal results from performing ceremonies, there is an undeniable magic that arises as the result of a kind of transformative blending of adrenaline-charged energies. This is similar to the level of bonding I have experienced time and time again when giving some sort of dramatic or musical performance on stage at home. By the end of a day of chanting, praying, and evoking remorse for your less skillful actions, you become too exhausted to maintain the outer levels of your ego boundaries. You become a drop in the ocean of good feeling among those with whom you have shared the performative experience.

But the bonding comes out of more than just a sense of shared experience. We, the *tshogs pas,* have enacted words, gestures, and music descended from a line of great masters—and in performing the ritual, we, too, have entered that lineage. We are part of a large family, bound by common practices and goals. With each ritual performance, we become just a bit more comfortable within ourselves, as if we have once more settled in to a deep and soft old armchair. One lama in our lineage describes this as "relaxing like a child coming into its mother's lap."

◇

This week the sermon is not presented by the rabbi. Rather, the cantor gets up and introduces a young man with wavy long hair who I do not recognize. It turns out he is a well-known local jazz pianist who went to Sunday school at my parent's synagogue. He stands behind the pulpit and rambles casually and personally—as jazz musicians are wont to do. Finally, he calls up the band and improvises on a familiar Hebrew song. It's a hit with the congregation, even though he goes overtime.

Here, too, the music evokes a sense of lineage, a sense of belonging. Everyone knows the tune, even if it is embellished with extended chords and looped runs. The sax takes off on an extemporaneous solo with gutsy timbres that have never resonated through this prayer hall before. This is a sound that for me also speaks of bonding, but with jeans-clad musicians in smoky night clubs, the spiritual meeting of the minds of those who follow the Muse.

I am of many minds. The feisty feminist in me brims with pride that the synagogue has arrived at something close to gender parity with the hiring a female cantor. As a musical composer, I am intrigued by a new and experimental musical setting for the same old service. As a social scientist I note with pleasure how amazing it is that the daughter of former victims of the Soviet regime may ascend to the pulpit with the careless ease of one born possessed of the entitlement of religious choice.

Like this child, I have exercised my splendid American inheritance of entitlement. I have traveled a half a world away to learn the inner workings of my chosen spiritual path. Perhaps someday, like the cantor, I, too, will lead my sangha through a religious service. I may even someday find it appropriate to develop musical settings that resonate in the hearts of Buddhist practitioners raised on Beethoven, Madonna, and Miles Davis. But for now, I just ease into the groove and sink back into the soft velvet of the synagogue pew.

Thubten Chodron

You're Becoming a What?
Living as a Western Buddhist Nun

A WOMEN WITH a shaved head and maroon robes is not a common sight in the West—although sometimes a stranger will compliment me on my hairdo and outfit. Since people often ask me why I became a Buddhist nun and what my experience is, I would like to share this with you.

I grew up near Los Angeles, doing everything most middle-class American children did. My teenage years coincided with the Vietnam War and the protests against racial and sexual discrimination widespread at that time. These events had a profound effect on an inquisitive and thoughtful child, and I wondered: Why do people fight wars in order to live in peace? Why are people prejudiced against those who are different? Why do people who love each other later get divorced? Why is there suffering? What is the meaning of life? How can I help others? There had to be more to life than having fun, making money, raising a family, growing old, and dying.

Wanting to learn, I turned to my parents, teachers, and religious teachers for guidance. But their answers did not satisfy me. I could not understand why a compassionate God would punish people, and why, if he were omnipotent, he did not stop suffering. While the instruction to "love thy neighbor as thyself" made sense, no one could explain how to do this, and I did not see much tolerance or love in society. I could not put my questions aside, for I believed that investigation and understanding, not blind faith, led to wisdom. For lack of a sensible and comprehensive philosophy to guide my life, I abandoned religion.

In 1975, while doing graduate work in education and teaching elementary school, I went to a meditation course taught by two Tibetan Buddhist monks. I was surprised when the teachings by Ven. Lama Yeshe and Ven. Zopa Rinpoche proposed answers to the questions that had been with me since childhood. Rebirth and karma explained how we got here. Attachment, anger, and ignorance as the source of our problems explained why people are dissatisfied and quarrel with each other. The importance of a pure motivation showed that there is an alternative to hypocrisy. The possibility to abandon faults completely and develop good qualities limitlessly gave purpose to life and showed how each of us can become wise, compassionate, and skillful.

The more I investigated what the Buddha said, the more I found that it corresponded to my life experience. When I practiced the techniques for dealing with disturbing attitudes such as anger and attachment, my life and relationships became more harmonious. The Buddha encouraged us to ask questions and to accept things only when we understood them. He also emphasized changing our attitudes and our heart, not simply adopting an external religious appearance. I began to examine my life from the perspective of the Dharma. The teachings resonated within me as I thought about human potential, the value of life, and the fact that at death our possessions, loved ones, and body—everything we hold dear—could not come with us. I knew that the Dharma was extremely important and did not want to miss the opportunity to learn it, so I left my job and went to Nepal to study with Lama Yeshe and Zopa Rinpoche.

Once there, I participated in the community life of work, teachings, and meditation at their center. The Dharma continued to affect me deeply. I saw that attachment, anger, ignorance, and self-centeredness dominated almost all my actions. Due to the karmic imprints collected on my mindstream through my unrestrained thoughts and actions, a good rebirth would be unlikely. And how could I help others when my own thoughts and behavior were polluted?

I wanted to change; the question was how? Although many people can live a lay life and practice the Dharma, that would be difficult for me. My disturbing attitudes were too strong and my lack of self-discipline too great. I needed to make some clear, firm ethical decisions, and I needed a disciplined lifestyle that would support, not distract me from, spiritual practice. Monastic life and the ethical discipline its precepts provide was a viable option to fulfill those needs.

My family did not understand why I wanted to take ordination. They are not spiritually inclined and knew little about Buddhism. How could their daughter leave a promising career, friends, family, and financial security to become a nun? I listened and considered their objections. But when I reflected upon them in light of the Dharma, my decision to become a nun only became stronger. It was clear to me that lasting happiness did not come from possessions, reputation, loved ones, or physical beauty. If my mind remained attached to external things and relationships, how could I develop my potential and help others? It saddened me that my family did not understand, but I believed that in the long run I would be able to benefit others more through holding monastic precepts. Ordination did not mean rejecting my family. Rather, I wanted to enlarge my family and develop impartial love and compassion for all beings. With the passage of time, my parents have come to accept my being a Buddhist nun. I did not try to convince them, but simply tried to live the Buddha's teachings as best as I could. Through that, they saw that I was happy and that what I did benefits others.

Taking Ordination

In 1977, with much gratitude and respect for the Triple Gem and my spiritual teachers, I took ordination from Kyabje Ling Rinpoche, the senior tutor of His Holiness the Dalai Lama. People ask if I have ever regretted this. Not at all. I earnestly pray to the Triple Gem to keep my ordination purely and be able to be ordained in future lives as well. Having precepts is liberating, not restricting; they help free me from acting in ways that, deep in my heart, I do not want to. As a monastic, I endeavor to live simply—without many possessions, entangled emotional relationships, or preoccupation with looks, and so I have more time for the inner exploration Dharma practice requires and for service-oriented activities. If I had a career, husband, children, and an extensive social life, it would be difficult for me to travel to teach or to receive teachings as much as I now do. The precepts also clarify relationships. For example, my relationships with men are much more straightforward and honest now. Wearing robes and shaving my head, I am not concerned with my looks. If people like me, it will be because of inner beauty, not external appearance. The benefits of simplicity are evident in my life while I live according to the precepts.

Monastic ordination centers around four root precepts: to avoid killing, stealing, sexual relations, and lying about spiritual attainment. Other precepts deal with other aspects of life: our relationships with other monastics and laypeople, what and when we eat and drink, our clothes and possessions. Some precepts are designed to protect us from distractions that destroy mindful awareness. My personal experience has been that much internal growth has come from trying to live according to the precepts. They have made me much more aware of my actions and their effects on those around me. Keeping the precepts requires mindfulness and continual application of the antidotes to disturbing attitudes. It necessitates the transformation of old, unproductive emotional, verbal, and physical habits. Precepts force me to stop living "on automatic" and encourage me to use my time wisely and make my life meaningful. My intention as a monastic is to purify my mind and develop my good qualities in order to make a positive contribution to the welfare of all living beings. There is much joy in ordained life, and it comes from looking honestly at my own condition as well as at my potential.

Ordained life is not clear sailing, however. Disturbing attitudes follow us wherever we go. They do not disappear simply because someone takes precepts, shaves their head, and wears robes. Monastic life is a commitment to work with our garbage as well as our beauty. It puts us right in front of the contradictory parts of ourselves. For example, in one part of ourselves we feel there is a deep meaning to life and we have a sincere wish to actualize our human potential. The other part of us seeks amusement, financial security, reputation, and pleasure. We want to have one foot in nirvana (liberation), the other in samsara (the cycle of constantly recurring problems). We want to change and go deeper in our spiritual practice, but we do not want to give up the things we are attached to. To remain a monastic, I have to deal with these various sides of myself and to continuously clarify my priorities. I commit to going deeper and peeling away the many layers of hypocrisy, clinging, and fear inside me. I am challenged to live my faith and aspiration. And I have found that with effort, there is progress and happiness.

While Catholic nuns enter a particular order—one dedicated to teaching, contemplation, or service, for example—Buddhist nuns have no prescribed living situation or work. As long as we keep our precepts, we can live in a variety of ways. During the nineteen years I have been ordained, I have lived alone and in community; I have studied, taught, worked, done intensive and silent retreat; I have lived in the city and the countryside, in Asia and in the West.

Buddhist teachers often talk about the importance of lineage. There is a certain energy or inspiration that is passed down from spiritual mentor to aspirant. Although previously I was not one to believe in this, it has become evident through my experience in the years since my ordination. When my energy wanes, I remember the lineage of strong, resourceful monastics who have practiced and actualized the Buddha's teachings for 2,500 years. When I took ordination, I entered into their lineage, and the example of their lives renews my inspiration. No longer afloat in the sea of spiritual ambiguity or discouragement, I feel rooted in a practice that works and in a goal that is attainable—even though one has to give up all grasping to attain it!

Being a Western Nun in the Tibetan Tradition

As one of the first generation of Western nuns in the Tibetan Buddhist tradition, I face certain challenges. For example, because our Tibetan teachers are refugees, they cannot financially care for their Western ordained disciples. Their primary concern is to rebuild their monasteries in exile and to take care of the Tibetan refugee community. Therefore, Western monastics have no ready-made monasteries or support system. We must provide for ourselves financially, although it is extremely difficult to maintain our precepts if we have to put on civilian clothes and work in the city. If we stay in India to study and practice, there are the challenges of illness, visa problems, and political unrest. If we live in the West, people often look at us askance. Sometimes I have heard a child say, "Look, that lady has no hair!" or a sympathetic stranger approaches me and says, "Don't worry, you look lovely now. And when the chemotherapy is over, your hair will grow back." In our materialistic society, people often ask, "What do you monastics produce? How does sitting in meditation contribute to society?" The challenges of being a Buddhist nun in the West are many and varied, and they have given me a chance to deepen my practice.

A great part of Buddhist practice is concerned with overcoming grasping at an identity, both an innate feeling of "self" and one that is artificially created by the labels and categories that pertain to us this lifetime. I am a Western nun in the Tibetan Buddhist tradition, a phrase that contains many categories. On a deeper level, however, there is nothing to grasp in being Western, a nun, a Buddhist, or from the Tibetan tradition. The essence of monastic life is to let go of clinging to such labels and identities. Yet on the conventional level, all of these categories and the experiences I have had due to them have conditioned me.

As a Westerner I have been conditioned to believe in democracy and equality. Yet I have chosen to become a monastic, and thus some people associate me with an institution that they see as hierarchical, and thus negative. There are two challenges here: one is how I relate to the hierarchy, the other is how I am affected by Westerners who see me as part of a hierarchical institution.

In many ways the hierarchy of the monastic institution has benefited me. Being a high achiever, I have tended to be proud, to add my opinion to every discussion, to want to control or fix situations that I do not like or approve of. The Dharma has made me look at this tendency and reflect before acting and speaking. For example, during bhikshuni ordination in Taiwan, I participated in a thirty-two day training program in which I was one of two foreigners out of 500 ordainees. Each day we spent about fifteen minutes filing from the main hall into the teaching hall. I could see a quicker, more efficient method of moving many people from place to place, and my impulse was to correct the waste of time and energy. Yet I was clearly in the role of a learner, and the teachers were following a system that worked for them. Even if I could have made my suggestion known in Chinese, no one would have been particularly interested in it. I had no alternative but to be quiet, to do it their way, and to be happy doing so. In terms of practice, this was a wonderful experience, one which I now treasure for the humility, openmindedness, and acceptance it taught me.

Westerners sometimes create their own hierarchy in Buddhism, using ethnicity and culture as the discriminating factors. Some Westerners feel that if they adopt Asian cultural forms they are practicing the Dharma. They assume that Asians—being foreign and "exotic"—are holy, while Westerner practitioners, who grew up watching Mickey Mouse, are ordinary. In fact, spiritual qualities depend upon an individual's practice. Fascination with the foreign or exotic obscures us from understanding the path. Spiritual practice is about transforming ourselves into kind and wise people, not idolizing a teacher or adopting another culture. On the other hand, a reverse hierarchy—in which Westerners think that Asians do not understand Western ways—must be avoided. The real spiritual path does not depend on culture; it cannot be seen with the eyes, for it lies in the heart.

As a Westerner, I have a unique relationship with the Tibetan Buddhist religious institution. On one hand, I am a part of it since I practice in this tradition and have high regard for its spiritual masters and the teachings they preserve, and I have taken ordination in its monastic institution. On the other hand, I am not part of the Tibetan Buddhist institution because I am a Westerner. My knowledge of Tibetan language is limited, my values at times differ from the Tibetans, my upbringing was different. Early in my practice, when I lived primarily in the Tibetan community, I felt handicapped because I did not fit into the religious institution. However, over the years the distinction between spiritual practice and religious institutions has become clearer to me. My commitment is to the spiritual path, not to an institution. Of course it would be a wonderful support to my practice to be part of a religious institution that functioned with integrity, but that is not my present circumstance. I am not a full member of any Tibetan religious institution, and Western ones have either not yet been established or are still young.

Making the distinction between spiritual path and religious institution has allowed me to see the importance of constantly checking my own motivation and loyalty. It is essential to discriminate Dharma practice from worldly practice. It is all too easy to transplant attachment for material possessions, reputation, and praise into a Dharma situation. We become attached to our expensive and beautiful Buddha images; we seek reputation as a great practitioner or as the close disciple of one; we long for the praise and approval of our spiritual teachers and communities. We think that because we are surrounded by spiritual objects and people we must also be spiritual. But we must return to the reality that practice occurs in our hearts and minds. When we die only our karma, our mental habits and qualities, come with us.

Being a woman in the monastic institution has also been challenging. My family believed in the equality of men and women and expected me to have a successful career. However, the Tibetans' attitude toward nuns is different. Because the initial years of my ordination were spent in the Tibetan community, I tried to conform to their expectations for nuns. During large religious gatherings I sat in the back of the assembly; I spoke softly in public and did not voice my views or knowledge very much; I became a follower and did not initiate activities unless directed to. After a few years, it became obvious that this model of behavior did not fit me. My background and upbringing had trained me to take a more active role. Not only did I have a university education and a career, but I had been taught to be vocal, to participate, and to take the initiative. The Tibetan nuns have many good qualities, but I had to acknowledge that my way of thinking and behaving, although greatly modified by living in Asia, was basically Western. Subsequently I adopted what seemed to me to be the best from each culture: the straightforward communication and initiative valued in the West and the humility and gentleness valued in the East.

I also had to come to terms with gender discrimination in the Tibetan religious institution. At first, the monks' advantages in the Tibetan community made me angry—they received better education, more financial support, and greater respect than the nuns. Although among Western monastics this is not the case, when I lived in the

Tibetan community, this inequality irritated me. One day during a ceremony, some monks stood up to make the personal offering to His Holiness the Dalai Lama and then distributed the offerings to the greater assembly. I became angry that the monks had this honor while the nuns had to sit quietly and meditate. A thought shot through my mind: if the nuns were to make the offering to His Holiness while the monks meditated, I would have become angry because the women worked while the men meditated! Suddenly, my anger evaporated.

Having my abilities as a woman challenged by whatever real or perceived prejudice I have encountered in the Asian monastic system and Asian society in general (not to mention in the West) has been good for my practice. I have had to look deeply within myself, learn to evaluate myself realistically, let go of attachment to others' opinions and approval, and establish a valid basis for self-confidence. While I still encounter prejudice against women in the East and the West and try to do whatever is practical and possible to alleviate it, Dharma practice has lessened my anger until it is largely absent.

Being a Buddhist Monastic in the West

Being a monastic in the West has its unique points. Some Westerners, especially those who grew up in Protestant countries or who are disillusioned with the Catholic Church, do not like monasticism. They view it as hierarchical, sexist, and repressive. Some people think monastics are lazy and only consume society's resources instead of helping to produce them. Others think that because someone chooses to be celibate he or she is escaping from the emotional challenges of intimate relationships and is sexually repressed. Curiously, while women's issues are at the forefront of discussion in Western Buddhism, once a woman becomes a monastic, she is seen as "conservative and traditional," qualities often disdained by Westerners who practice Buddhism. At times this has been difficult for me. Having spent many years living as a foreigner in Asia, I looked forward to being at home in Western Dharma circles. Instead, I have sometimes been marginalized by being considered part of the "sexist and hierarchical" monastic institution.

Again, this has been an excellent opportunity for practice. I have had to reexamine my reasons for being a monastic. The reasons remain valid and the monastic lifestyle definitely benefits me. It has become clear that my discomfort is due to attachment to others' acceptance, and part of my practice is to subdue such attachment.

Nevertheless, I believe it is important to present a variety of lifestyle options for Western Buddhists. While some think that the monastic model is stressed too much in Asia, we must be careful not to swing to the other extreme and present only the lay model in the West. Because people have different dispositions and tendencies, all lifestyles must be accepted in the panorama of practitioners. We need to avoid making one better and another worse, and recognize that each of us must find the practice situation that is best for us. I especially appreciate the perspective of a non-monastic Western Dharma teacher who said, "At one time or another, most of us have thought of becoming monastics—of creating a lifestyle where we have less commitments to work and family and more time to spend on practice. For whatever reason we decided not to take that route now, but I treasure that part of myself that is attracted to that lifestyle and am glad that other people live that."

Other Western practitioners share some of the challenges I face. One is establishing a safe environment to talk openly about difficulties in the practice. Asian practitioners, raised in a Buddhist culture, lack many of the doubts Westerners have. Also, Westerners relate to their emotions differently, and our culture emphasizes growth as an individual in a way that Asian cultures do not. This can be both an advantage and a disadvantage in spiritual practice. Being aware of our emotions enables us know our mental processes. Yet we are often aware of our emotions in an unproductive way that increases our self-centeredness and becomes a hindrance on the path. There is the danger that we may become preoccupied with our emotions and forget to apply the practices the Buddha taught to transform them.

Similarly, the Western emphasis on individuality can be both an asset and a hindrance to practice. On one hand, we want to grow as a person and tap our potential to become a Buddha. We are willing to commit ourselves to a spiritual path that is not widely known or appreciated in our society. On the other hand, our individuality can make it difficult for us to form spiritual communities in which we must adapt to the needs of others. We easily fall into comparing ourselves to or competing with other practitioners. We tend to think about what we can get out of spiritual practice or what a spiritual teacher or community can do for us, whereas spiritual practice is more about giving than getting and cherishing others more than ourselves. His Holiness the Dalai Lama talks about two senses of self: one is unhealthy—the sense of a solid, separate self which we grasp and become preoccupied with. The other is necessary—a valid sense of self-confidence based on recognizing our potential to be enlightened. Practice can help us rethink the meaning of being an individual, thus freeing us from an unhealthy sense of self and helping us develop the valid self-confidence that enables us to genuinely care for others.

As Buddhism comes to the West, it is important to preserve the monastic lifestyle as a way of practice that benefits some people directly and the entire society indirectly. For those who find strict ethical discipline and simplicity helpful for practice, monasticism can be wonderful. The presence of individual monastics and monastic communities also affects society, serving as an example of people living their spiritual practice together, working through the ups and downs in their own minds as well as the continuous change that naturally occurs in community. Sometimes just seeing a monastic can make us slow down from our busyness and reflect, "What is important in my life? What is the purpose of spiritual practice?" These questions are important. They point to the essence of being a human being with the potential to become a Buddha.

Michele Benzamin-Masuda

Fertile Ground for a Warrior

I WALK UPON the rich soil of many traditions, cultural and religious. My mother was Japanese and her root religion was Shinto, later to be Catholic. My father was born and raised in America of mixed parentage—Czechoslovakian Catholics on his mother's side, and on his father's side Spanish Sephardic Jews. He is Catholic.

My parents met in Japan during the Korean War, and were married in a Catholic church in Kobe. My mother and father traveled back and forth several times to America and Japan trying to decide where to put down roots for a family. I was born on one trip to America, my sister was born a year later on the trip back to Japan, and there we stayed until I was almost four.

When I was a small child, this crosscultural heritage was my playground and I was happy in it. As I grew older I felt my parents' discomfort as they adjusted to a biracial marriage and their decision to raise us in America. I found myself having to pledge allegiance to only one country, America, and profess only one faith, Catholicism. This created in me confusion, frustration, and, worst of all, a sense of oppression.

I learned early on that I had a natural ability for drawing. Whenever I needed to escape the limitations of the real world, I would retreat to my world of art. It was my haven, a source of joy, my outlet for expression. Within my drawings and paintings were hidden symbols and self-portrayals, a diary of secret journeys within an imagination that was too wild to be expressed verbally at the time.

A field of all possibilities, where I could go beyond race, religion, and economic class to a place much like a borderland. I lived here, in between, not completely American or Japanese. I walked a path in the middle of the two worlds, where I need be loyal to no other authority other than my own heart.

A trip to Japan at twenty-one, my first time back since I was three, stirred up childhood memories and reunited me with a part of myself I had disowned. It was strangely familiar, walking inside those enormous hollow bodies of bronze Buddhas in Kamakura, Nara, and Kyoto. I was amazed to see my mother resurrected there in her homeland, after suffering the many hardships of adjusting to life in America. I watched her reconnect to her heritage and root religion, and regain personal sovereignty. Despite language barriers, I too reclaimed bonds to my Japanese family that would later change my entire view of life and spirituality.

I came back to America and continued seeking ways of enriching my experience in Japan. I began training in the martial arts, starting with karatedo, and soon after that I took up vipassana meditation. My father had studied martial arts and meditation while in Japan, and had taught me some basic self-defense when I was a girl. When my mother was a young girl, during the war, it was part of physical education training in school to learn how to use a short staff and some fighting techniques. It was in my blood, so I felt right at home in the martial arts.

I was fond of my first teacher in karate, but became dissatisfied with the classes' constant emphasis on sparring for competition. I enjoyed the lessons I learned from sparring, but cared not a whole lot for being a champion in any tournament. Sparring taught me that more than physical strength, technique, or even speed, it is the state of your mind before and during the fight that determines the outcome.

Two and a half years into my karate training, I moved out of the area and had to find another teacher. I visited a school that offered training in several kinds of martial arts, and felt moved to take up aikido. I needed something to soften the hard edge of fighting in me. Aikido filled that need.

Shortly before my transition into aikido, I discovered the benefits of meditation. I walked into a Buddhist temple in Los Angeles with a friend who had invited me to attend a yoga class with her. Here I was, once again, standing in front of an enormous Buddha statue, more colorful that the ones I had seen in Japan. Then a bald man in ocher robes approached us and said, "Come in, you are early, we start in half an hour." We both felt this was probably the wrong place for a stretch class, but the man was interesting and we were adventurous. So began my vipassana practice.

Inside the enormous body of the Buddha, inside the Dharma, I found there was room for everything. I was now embarking on the well-trodden path of integrating the martial arts and mediation, as well as beginning to put together the puzzle-pieces of my life. I could recognize my relatives from Japan and America, my relation to Pearl Harbor and Hiroshima, Jesus and Mary, Shakyamuni and Tara, angels and bodhisattvas. In the body of the Dharma, all the opposites of my life merged. I signed a peace treaty with all the warring factions inside myself, and became aware of the path set before me.

I am a warrior. The word "war," from the Old English and Old French *werra*, means "bring into confusion." In times of great anguish and confusion—times like ours—warriors are born, arise, and called forth into action to help restore peace and bring about understanding and clarity.

It is easy to fall asleep in the middle-class comfort and convenience of late twentieth-century America. Whatever our economic background, we are living in an era in which leading a simple and content life is neither valued nor supported. In order to be happy, we constantly try to upgrade our lifestyles. We buy consumer conveniences that are supposed to save us time, yet we find ourselves so busy trying to keep up with our possessions that we have lost contact with one another, and lost touch with what we are doing to the planet. Our communication falters and our patience with one another wears thin in a world of fast food, mini-malls on every block, "instant cash" to immediately gratify every whim, and "virtual reality." These things are seen as progress, designed so that we cannot see the long-term effects of living this way.

When we create a closed system where only human values and desires are honored, we sever our relationship to this planet. We see the planet and every other life form as either a commodity or a resource to use as we see fit. It is a point of religious argument that humans are at the top of a spiritual hierarchy that renders the earth as our domain. Even the point of view that we are caretakers, in a role of stewardship to the planet, breeds arrogance. We are a part of the planet, in symbiotic relationship with and interconnected to *all* life—human, animal, vegetable, and mineral.

In Revelations, it says: "Know ye the grasses and trees.... Then know ye the worms and the moths, and the different sorts of ants.... Know ye also the four-footed animals small and great, the serpents, the fish which range in the water, the birds that are borne along on wings and move through the air.... Know ye the marks that constitute species are theirs, and their species are manifold." This is a good place to start.

There is a similar message in Buddhism, in the practice of looking deeply into the nature of things so that "ye shall know thyself." Buddhist scriptures talk much about awakened mind, "enlightenment." Here I find the danger of interpreting this to mean mind separate from body, setting up an epic battle between the "defiled" body and the "supreme" mind. When we view our bodies just as a vehicle for enlightenment, not intrinsic to the very *experience* of enlightenment, we turn them into a spiritual commodity. We may use spiritual practice to disengage and retreat from the world, if we see the world, like our bodies, only as a field of endless suffering (samsara). There is the danger of splitting mind from body, nirvana from samsara, a danger of repeating the battle of duality from other "civilized" cultures and religions: the Greeks' psyche and soma, Christianity's Spirit and the flesh, the Victorian division between reason and emotion. As Sam Keen writes, "If we were fully integrated persons we might refer to ourselves as being bodyminds, rather than as having bodies." We would then engage in life fully and compassionately, understanding that samsara and nirvana coexist, as in the Gospel of John: "And the Word became flesh and dwelt among us, full of grace and truth." In the words of Lama Anagarika Govinda: "To the enlightened man ... whose consciousness embraces the universe, to him the universe becomes his 'Body.'"

If we continue to exist in a way that disconnects us from our bodies and the planet, we will soon die as a species. We have already created a legacy of suffering that will last a long time after our extinction. Is this the function of a spiritual life? Perhaps we feel helpless or overwhelmed, and would rather leave it up to someone else stronger or more capable to change our situation, or, as some would have it, to "just leave it in God's hands."

The most common and convenient denial for Buddhists is not to be attached to anything, even to this life, this planet. Yet we *are* attached, interconnected, and inseparable. We are in a constant flow of interconnection: this very body, this life, this world, is the body of the Buddha, the Dharma, and the Sangha. We create more suffering, more karma, by continuing to separate ourselves and act as if our actions don't count. Thich Nhat Hanh has said, "Someday there will be an instrument that can measure the effect of a leaf falling to earth on a distant star." I see mindfulness as that instrument. With our mindfulness we can see that our intentions and smallest actions have an effect on the world.

I see the interrelationship of our complacency, denial, and fear, hidden sometimes behind the mask of "spiritual detachment," with the destruction of life on earth. It recalls to me the image of a frog immersed in a kettle of lukewarm water on a stove, the flame low, simmering, slowly being cooked. The frog does not realize its imminent demise, and so has no reason to jump out of the kettle. Are we dead already? Dead Buddhists? Or is it time to wake up and smell the toxins, act before it is too late? The action can be as simple as a shift in the way we view our part in this world, not as spectators but as active participants in the world as it is, in its present state.

In each warrior is the seed of compassion. The seed lays dormant in the fertile ground of the heart waiting to be broken open by the fires of delusion, greed, and enmity. The warrior learns by taking action from this place of compassion, and his or her actions are tempered by the wisdom of knowing the task ahead is not futile, but endless. As a warrior, you cannot become attached to outcome, cannot allow yourself to be ambushed by the failure of your hopes and become ineffective. We must remember that to act is a choice. During a heated discussion on the fate of the planet, poet Nanao Sakaki said, "You know, we don't have to survive."

The path of the Buddha Dharma has brought the sword of compassion and wisdom into my martial arts training. With these tools a warrior can develop tireless energy and a clear focus in action. She or he has the inner strength to be steady and still at times, sustaining an immovable gaze, and the freedom and abandon to jump in and take risks when necessary. To know intimately the beauty of failure. To let go of attachment to outcome only after having given everything you have to give. The warrior realizes the only true enemy is complacency and self-righteousness.

Without compassion and wisdom the warrior loses sight; energy and zeal turn into a destructive, out-of-control force. With misguided passions, she or he can be bought and soldiered into acts of self-righteous "benevolence," lashing out irresponsibility without understanding the full consequences of their actions. When there is an enemy to fight against, we are for the moment safe from having to look into our own deep wounds. But we do not heal, and the problem remains.

I have been teaching meditation and contemplation on compassion along with the nonviolence principles of aikido for some time now, and countless times I am asked if I would kill someone in order to protect myself or a loved one. I've answered, "I would kill. I'd kill their action, not the person." Yet now, as I write this, another thought enters my mind: Yes, I could indeed kill the person. I feel this is important for me to acknowledge. I am reminded of a story a friend told me. He was participating in a peace rally, and someone angrily threw a question to him: "What would you do if you met the person who killed your loved ones? Don't tell me you wouldn't be angry and want to take their life!" He replied, "Yes, but then I would count on you, brother, to restrain me." We are not alone in our struggle; it is necessary to know to ask for help.

As I walk the path of the warrior, I find love and tolerance to be my great teachers. I call myself a "warrior" because I am a woman who is discovering her strengths, who has taken up a path traditionally walked by men. In doing so, I am uncovering a long lineage of female warriors, and bringing these archetypes of strength back for myself and other women. I feel strongly that women need to acknowledge their personal power.

Everyone has a legacy of stories and rituals deriving from their culture, background, and lineage. These myths give us security and identity, but they can also create intolerance, selective blindness, and rigidity. As women we need to uncover our own myths, handed down through history and by our families. If we understand how our actions have been controlled by these myths, and ask the question "For whom does it serve," and the reply is not "women"—ourselves—then it is time to reevaluate and rewrite them.

I feel my role as a woman in Buddhism is to pay homage to, honor, and love deeply my own mother, grandmother, and the ancestral mothers and sisters within the Buddhist tradition. If we as women can do this, we can begin to reclaim and bring back to life the rich heritage of women's participation in Buddhism, often obscured in history, and blaze new trails for ourselves as well as the mothers and daughters of the future.

This earth is fertile ground for a woman warrior to walk upon.

Ji Ko Linda Ruth Cutts

The Dark Clue

I AM SO GRATEFUL for this practice, grateful to have been exposed to the teachings of the Buddha and the practice of sitting still—sitting upright in the middle of life. Many times, however, I know that this simple practice can become difficult to understand. "What am I doing here?" "What does this have to do with anything?" We may feel bewildered, confused, as if we have lost our way in a maze. The word *maze* refers to an intricate network of pathways in which it is easy to get lost. The older meaning of the word maze, and also of *amaze,* is to bewilder, to stupefy, to daze. In our life and in our Buddhist practice, we sometimes feel exactly as if we are lost in a maze in the dark.

Autumn is the time of year in this hemisphere when things turn toward the dark. The nights get longer and all the plant and animal life begins to go underground—hibernation—wintering. The plants' main activity is underneath the ground, in the roots. The root systems are growing and strengthening, but not much is going on above ground. So, even though things may look lifeless, vital work continues in the dark. It is important to know the difference between deadness and dormancy.

We too are drawn toward the dark. We begin to want to pull closer in, closer to the fire. In the practice of the tea ceremony at this

This essay is adapted from Dharma talks given by Ji Ko Linda Ruth Cutts at Green Gulch Farm, Marin County, California, in fall and winter 1995.

time of year, we change the way the hearth is arranged in the tea room. Instead of the open, above-ground brazier used for spring and summer, a sunken hearth or firepit is made for fall and winter gatherings. The guests come closer and draw around the fire for warmth. Everything is moving in close—turning toward the dark.

This is traditionally a good time for a more intensive period of meditation, study, and quiet. We are pulled toward this. In the dark of the year we feel some strong calling toward turning in, slowing down, tending parts of ourselves—the roots—that are hidden below the surface and with which we are not so familiar. This is natural. We see this reflected in the natural world around us, yet our society does not always honor this calling.

When we enter into this kind of activity, we do not necessarily know what is going to happen to us. There is no guaranteed outcome. This is like going into a maze or labyrinth.

The labyrinth is a very old multivalent symbol, found in almost all traditions throughout the ancient world. It resonates powerfully with the spiritual path, especially with the particularity of the spiritual path of women. The oldest meaning of the labyrinth is associated with nourishing cosmic waters and the uterus, the original mysterious source of birth and death. In excavated sites in Old Europe that date from thousands of years ago, many examples have been found of the maze-like spiral, meander, or labyrinthine design on vases, tablets, discs, altars, plaques, masks, and especially figures of the Great Goddess. One striking instance of this is the large number of sculptures found at a shrine in the former Yugoslavia, dating from 6000–5800 B.C.E. Many of these red sandstone sculptures with fish-like faces were placed at vulva/uterus-shaped altars, and were engraved with labyrinthine designs.

In present-day South India, at the fall equinox when the days are becoming shorter, Hindu women draw labyrinths on the thresholds of their doorways. This seems to indicate the labyrinth, spiral, or meander as a symbol used at this time of year to honor turning toward the dark and facing the unknown.

In the underground level of Chartres Cathedral, an old labyrinth dating from the year 1220 was discovered, inlaid into the stone floor. Part of Christian religious practice in the Middle Ages was the ritual of contemplatively walking the labyrinth as a pilgrimage. This practice has been taken up by members of San Francisco's Grace Cathedral, where indoor and outdoor replicas of the Labyrinth of Chartres are available for retreats focusing on spiritual renewal through walking meditation.[1]

The Palace of Knossos on the Mediterranean island of Crete was itself called the Labyrinth. The ancient civilization of Crete begins around 6000 B.C.E., and for over 4,000 years a culture characterized by its peaceful devotion to the Great Goddess, great artistic achievement, and its women-centered society developed there. The Great Goddess was worshipped as the source and giver of all—birth and death. The palace was the abode of the "Mistress of the Labyrinth," or High Priestess, or Queen, and it was the site of religious rituals including the famous bull-jumping ceremonies performed by both women and men.[2] The word *labyrinth* is akin to the Greek *labrus*, which means "double ax." The sacred symbol of the double ax is found throughout the Palace of Knossos.

The palace building itself was created in an organic series of hundreds of well-lighted and well-ventilated corridors and rooms, decorated with wall paintings executed with great attention to detail. The palace had no walls of fortification. Entrances were unobtrusive and led in a meandering way to the Central Court. The maze-like construction of the Palace of Knossos, its motif of the double *labrus* or ax—the labyrinth—became synonymous with Crete for the ancient Greeks.[3]

The Greek myth of Theseus and the Minotaur takes place in King Minos' Labyrinth, below the Palace of Knossos. This relatively recent tale (considering the antiquity of Crete) dates from after the Greeks conquered the island in 1450 B.C.E. and subsequently overturned the goddess traditions which were replaced with the Greeks' patriarchal system of dominant male gods. This famous myth does not reflect the extraordinary history of the preeminence of women in Cretan culture and religion, but I bring it forth intentionally, nevertheless, because the labyrinth image it describes is so useful.

Theseus was a hero from Athens who volunteered to come to Crete to slay the Minotaur, a half-bull, half-lion monster that was kept in the Labyrinth and fed seven maidens and seven youths every year as tribute to King Minos. Theseus was seen by Ariadne, half-sister to the Minotaur, who fell in love with him and vowed to save his life. She went to the designer of the Labyrinth, Daedelus, and asked him how someone could find their way out of the maze. Daedelus told her the only way to get out of the Labyrinth was to have a *clew* (clue). He gave her a clew: a ball of thread (the Greek word for thread is *klua*), and told her it must be fastened to the doorway and unraveled while walking into the maze, and then you would be able to find the way back out.

Ariadne took the clew to Theseus and he followed her instructions. He fastened the clew to the doorway and went into the Labyrinth not knowing when or where he might find the Minotaur. After wandering for a long time in the maze, he finally came upon the creature and killed him. With the help of his clew he was able to find his way back, and he led the other young people in the Labyrinth to safety as well.[4]

Down underneath in the dark can be a very complicated place. When you are meandering around the maze, without a clew, you can get into a lot of trouble and despair and not know what to do. But if you have your clew in hand, even though the way is complicated and you do not know what to do, you can continue ahead.

A woman was talking to me recently about her sense of being in a new situation, a new life of relationships and practice, and that she couldn't go back to her old way of life. The old way didn't make sense anymore and this person no longer wanted to live like that; yet in a new situation, she found that she was afraid and filled with anxiety. She didn't really know how to act ... she didn't have a clue. This person had dropped a lot of her old, familiar habits of body, speech, and mind, and yet she was afraid of the unknown, afraid that if she kept going in the new way she would find out something about herself that she wasn't really sure she wanted to know. She was afraid that she would meet some part of herself that was sure to be really terrible. This to me was an almost perfect description of what it's like to be in the maze, in the labyrinth—not being able to go back out, not necessarily wanting to go forward, not knowing what's around the next bend, not knowing when you are suddenly going to meet your Minotaur. The inner work we can do in the labyrinth is essential, and it is hard work, like labor.

The labyrinth as uterus and place of the double ax points to the ancient teaching and functions of the Great Goddess. This teaching has been powerful for me in valuing and validating the feminine, honoring Buddhist practice in this female body, and consequently in more thoroughly studying the self. Tara Buddha, the compassionate female Buddha especially revered in Tibetan Buddhism, vowed to always be reborn in a female body. She chose this form to teach, benefit, and awaken all beings. I find great strength and healing, both psychologically and spiritually, in relating to mythic and symbolic female beings and consequently connecting with the wisdom and compassion of the foremothers of many spiritual traditions.

The Great Goddess' functions are life-giving, death-giving, and regeneration. This corresponds to the moon's cycle of waxing, waning, and renewal, as well as the round of the seasons, the cycle of sprouting, growing, fullness, dying, and rising again. The double-edged ax, ancient symbol of feminine power, cuts both ways: it is both giver and taker of life. Resonant with this symbol is the figure of Manjushri, the Bodhisattva of Wisdom, whose image is traditionally placed in the Zen meditation hall. Manjushri carries a double-edged sword to cut through delusion. This is the wisdom that takes the old life and gives the new; the new life that rises up is free. This is the full circle of our inner and outer life—birth, death, and regeneration. The double ax, graphically represented by two triangles placed point to point, also resembles a butterfly, and the butterfly has long been a symbol of transience, emergent life, and liberation.

We usually think of butterflies as having the spirit of a Walt Disney movie, fluttering about to the tune of "zip-a-dee-do-da." But recently I was in a very intense discussion with a gardener friend of mine who was experiencing a strange sense of fear and discomfort about the butterflies she was studying. She couldn't figure out what was going on and why she was having this peculiar and strong reaction to butterflies. After doing some research, I found that butterflies are strongly associated with impermanence, the evanescence of life, and the inconceivable transformation of death and life. In many cultures the butterfly is an object of fear.

The etymology of the word preserves this ancient meaning: the Greek, Germanic, and Slavic words, *mora, mara,* and *morava,* respectively, mean both "nightmare" and "butterfly." The Breton and Irish word *maro* means "death" (as Goddess), and the Lithuanian word *moré* means Goddess of Death. The German *Mahr* and French *cauchemar,* "nightmare," are further derivatives. The blending of death, fear, and the butterfly are clearly evident in these languages. No wonder my friend was having this reaction: she had tapped into the ancient meaning and manifestation of the Goddess of Death. Butterflies are beautiful but they do not live very long. Brightly colored and attractive, they are poisonous to birds. Some butterflies travel for thousands of miles on nectar alone. They are mysterious and terrifyingly beautiful creatures.

The butterfly symbol holds not only the death function of the Goddess, but also the function of regeneration. This emblem of the Goddess has been found in Neolithic agrarian settlements on figures and pottery. In the important excavations of the town site of Catal Huyuk, in present-day Turkey, archeologists found frescoes dating from the seventh century B.C.E. which depict butterflies. Although the symbol of the butterfly was fused with that of the double ax in Crete, it originated long before the development of metallurgy and the invention of the ax as a tool or weapon. The butterfly and its association with new life are very clear in many Cretan artifacts. A beautiful example of this is a decorated sarcophagus, or box-like tomb, from about 1200 B.C.E., which is covered with row upon row of butterflies rising up out of sacred horns with patterns of flower buds and shells.[5]

The butterfly, a being that embodies the world of transformation and regeneration, is also reflected psychologically in the individual entity of the soul or psyche; the word *psyche* itself means "butterfly." How marvelously rich and deep this symbolism is! In her book *Woman Changing Woman,* Jungian analyst Virginia Beane Rutter describes a three-part pattern that is always present in women's initiation ceremonies: the first is containment, then metamorphosis, and finally emergence.[6] This pattern could also describe the life cycle of the butterfly, the gestation and birth of a baby, and indeed, the initiation of the psyche (butterfly), or soul. I see these three parts repeated in the path of the Buddhist practitioner, with the intention and vow to practice with "imperturbable way-seeking mind."

The initiation of the psyche is necessary. We all long to go deep within, to realize what we need to realize in this world, so that we may live gently, in peace, and find our way together in harmony. This is, for each person, an initiation—entering the labyrinth, facing what we must face. But we need a clue. We need some thread that will help us. This clue is not permanent, but conditioned and very particular to you. When you are through with it then you give it to someone else. It is not something you need to hold on to forever and ever.

The first part of the process, containment, can happen in many ways. When you enter an intensive practice period, a sesshin or retreat, you voluntarily place yourself in a contained situation with temporal boundaries of the daily schedule, physical boundaries regarding place, maintaining silence, etc. Choices and decisions are reduced; food and drink are simple; distractions are few. It is very important and necessary to have this time of containment in which you feel supported to do the hard work you need to do. Entering the labyrinth *is* hard work: you never know what is just around the corner—you don't know what is going to confront you.

The butterfly's life cycle also includes a period of containment in a firm case called a chrysalis or cocoon which is spun by the caterpillar itself and serves as a kind of womb for its transformation. We use the word "cocooning" nowadays to mean getting some good food and a good video and sitting cozily on the couch at home. Some may feel that going into a retreat or an intense period of practice is a form of cocooning or escapism, just vegging-out—sitting around like a couch potato, or a zafu potato. But such periods of containment are actually more like being a *real* potato. In the spring we plant hundreds of potatoes at Green Gulch Farm. First you put the seed potatoes in the earth and cover them up, and then you step on them. We walk the rows of potatoes and press them down firmly into the soft earth. It is vital and alive down under in the earth, in the dark. This is true vegging-out! A period of containment is closer to the real life of the potato and the vegetable. And the real life of cocooning is not to escape, but to give yourself the time to do the growing and transforming you need to do.

Our word *larva,* another name for the caterpillar, comes from Greek and means "disembodied spirit or mass." Inside the cocoon you have a not yet quite formed, not yet connected-up being. This may be an accurate description of someone who needs to spin a cocoon, needs to create for herself a firm chrysalis of practice. *Chrysalis* comes from the Greek word that means gold—*khrusos*. This container is pure gold, a golden time to do the work you must do without distraction. Just turning inward and doing this vital work—by yourself, with everyone else—is transformative. Straw into gold—inside and out.[7]

There are many experiences we may have that create containment. I have recently spent a lot of time in the hospital visiting my parents, who have been ill. It reminded me very much of a sesshin or retreat. I know many people have done day-to-day caregiving for someone who is ill. You go to the hospital every day, the same room at a certain time, and come in, take your seat, and settle in. Then all day you just attend to the details of bodily functions, checking them: amount, color, quality, time. Details. Being present for someone without averting, without asking anything. Both the cared-for and the caregiver are contained and transformed.

However, this is not easy work to do; many caretakers may not know how to take care of themselves during these times. Paying close attention to the details of your own day and your own body is an important clue. We need clues to help us find our way here, also. It is difficult to go back to the hospital every day; it is not particularly fun. It is necessary to make an effort not to turn away from someone you love while they go through their transformations and rapid changes right before your eyes. That is our vow.

The second part of the process is metamorphosis. Inside the chrysalis a lot is going on, but when you look at it from the outside it just seems to be hanging there quietly, doing nothing. We sometimes say that zazen is "sitting quietly doing nothing," like a potato under the ground. Yet the potato is multiplying, growing. The larva is transforming. The butterfly that emerges is a totally new creature. It can fly.

People change. Conditions change. People do drop away old ways of acting, habitual ways of thinking, routinized postures and attitudes of body, speech, and mind. This is metamorphosis—very fresh and surprising and scary. There's the dying of the old form of life and a new form of life wants to come forth, wants to break out and emerge. It is an emergency.

The third part of the process is this emergence. In the coming-forth out of containment and metamorphosis into the world something has changed, and we may not even be able to say what it is. When Shakyamuni Buddha emerged from his containment, metamorphosis, and realization under the Bodhi tree, he was asked to teach and turn the Wheel of the Dharma for the sake of the world, and he could not refuse.

When you emerge you can carry on your work for the benefit of the world and respond to the requests of your life. This work can be almost anything. The sutras name many vocations that people can do that are of great help to sentient beings, including nursing, teaching, economics, architecture, and the arts. This is what I call the fourth part of the process of initiation, "returning to the marketplace with gift-bestowing hands"—and wings.[8]

The butterfly also responds to the requests of her brief life. As she goes about her daily activities, flower to flower, she pollinates, bringing her gifts with no thought of giver or receiver. This is the perfection of giving. The whole world wants us to pollinate, too—to help pass on the teachings and bestow the gifts of our kind speech and actions with no thought of gaining something for ourselves. It's up to us.

But in order to reemerge from the labyrinth, from the chrysalis, we need clues. What are the clues we have? For some, hearing something that another person says can be a clue that they carry for many years. I remember vividly a phrase from one of the first Dharma talks I ever heard: "If you take pencils from work you will not be able to sit zazen." I was astounded to realize that every aspect of my life mattered and could be filled with awareness. Unforgettable. Maybe there is something that someone once said to you that made a difference and that will be helpful for a long time, until it is time to give it to someone else.

In zazen, cross-legged sitting meditation, we form our bodies into a maze-like shape and there we are: a labyrinth. There are clues for this sitting practice that have been given to us by compassionate teachers for over two millennia. "Be sure your ears are in line with your shoulders"—that is a clue. "Sit still." "Your eyes should always remain open." "Sit upright in correct bodily posture." "Eat and drink moderately." "Neither lean to the left or the right, nor forward or backward." These clues are very simple, but it is not necessarily easy to hold the thread.

A clue from the eleventh-century Zen Master Yuan-wu is: "The essential point to learn in Zen is to make the roots deep and the stem firm. Twenty-four hours a day, be aware of where you are and what you do." Zazen posture, upright sitting, is the full expression of keeping your roots deep and your stem firm—the rooted feeling of your body and firm, flexible mind. A friend of mine told me that due to various excesses of her behavior, she once found herself with a stranger in an unfamiliar apartment, and she did not know how she had gotten there. How disturbing and frightening this was for her. She realized with searing clarity the consequences of her actions. This may sound like an extreme example, but when we live without awareness, we live dangerously. "Twenty-four hours a day, be aware of where you are and what you do."

To be aware of where you are and what you do, you have to admit what it is you are feeling, what is going on for you, what you are up to. Most often, this will mean admitting the pain you are feeling. The word *admit* means acknowledgment or confession. To confess or to admit that you have done something is to acknowledge thoroughly. *Confess* comes from the root "to speak"; to speak with intensity is to confess. When you admit, when you acknowledge where you are and what you are doing, at that same moment you allow yourself in to the fullness of your life. This is another meaning of admit—to let in; to enter; admittance.

Admit thus has a dual, turning meaning: to admit where you are is to be where you are fully. Whether you like what you are doing or not is not so important. What is important is to admit what you are doing or thinking or feeling. And then immediately, you are fully there. If you don't admit, if you don't acknowledge, you cannot actually enter your life—you don't have the admission ticket. It takes heart and courage to make your roots deep and your stem firm, and study who you really are.

In the Buddhist tradition, there is a ceremony for admittance and confession. In this ceremony, after confession, one traditionally takes refuge in the Triple Treasure: the Buddha, Dharma, and Sangha. That is the next step. *Refuge* means "to fly back." In Japanese, the phrase for "I take refuge in the Buddha" is *Namu Kie Butsu*. The word *kie* is in two parts: *ki* means to unreservedly throw yourself into, and *e* means to rely on. So to take refuge is to unreservedly throw yourself into and rely on—just this—not holding back anything. This is taking refuge in the Buddha, Dharma, and Sangha. First you fully admit and confess where you are, who you are, and this creates a firm basis for unreservedly throwing yourself into your life. This is fully meeting your life and meeting the Triple Treasure in your life.

There is a Japanese Zen teacher who lived to be ninety-six. When asked what his secret was for living such a long life, he said he always ate three meals a day. He commented that this may sound very simple, but to actually do it is not so easy. Imagine living a life that has the calmness and order and space in which we would be able to have three meals a day. This person was fortunate to have access to three meals a day, while millions of people do not. But to have access to three meals and to actually have your three meals a day—what would this mean? Think of your life and the changes you would have to make in order to have three meals a day—no more, no less. If you pick one part of your life and do just that thoroughly and carefully—eat three meals, sit zazen at a certain time, take refuge, follow the precepts—then everything begins to orient around this activity or vow, and your life will greatly change. This is a clue.

When someone finally emerges from the labyrinth-uterus, they speak with an authentic voice, just like a newborn baby. When you hear this full expression from someone else, you feel that you can be yourself, too. I too can admit who I am, and speak from there. The *Metta Sutta* says "This way of living is the best in the world." This doesn't mean any particular lifestyle, but a way of living in which we meet fully all parts of our life—the happy parts, the painful parts, the Minotaur. May we meet fully each thing as the Buddha Dharma, not turning away from what life brings forth. And with this comes a further wish: that all beings may be happy and live in this way, awake, "body exposed to the golden wind" of the teachings of the Buddha.

In closing, I offer this poem by Emily Dickinson, who was contained most of her life and metamorphosed, transformed, and emerged through her poems, her gifts to the world.

My Cocoon tightens — Colors tease —
I'm feeling for the Air.
A dim capacity for Wings
Demeans the dress I wear —

A power of Butterfly must be —
The Aptitude to fly
Meadows of Majesty implies
And easy Sweeps of Sky —

So I must baffle at the Hint
And cipher at the Sign
And make much blunder if at last
I take the clew divine —

1. See Lauren Artress, *Walking a Sacred Path: Rediscovering the Labyrinth as a Spiritual Tool* (New York: Riverhead Books, 1996).

2. The bull was the principal sacred animal for the Great Goddess. The head and horns of bull have a stunning resemblance to the uterus and Fallopian tubes of a woman. The horns are also closely associated with the "horns" of the crescent moon, and therefore are part of the cluster of symbols that celebrate the cyclical nature of life. See Marija Gimbutas, *The Language of the Goddess* (San Francisco: Harper and Row, 1989), Chapter 24, "Bull, Bee, and Butterfly."

3. For more discussion of the remarkable Cretan civilization, see Riane Eisler, *The Chalice and the Blade: Our History, Our Future* (San Francisco: Harper and Row, 1987), pp. 29–41.

4. Daedelus, as we know from the myth, was punished for helping Ariadne; he and his son Icarus were put in the Labyrinth. Of course, he couldn't get out without a clew, so he made wings for them both to fly to safety. Icarus flew too close to the sun and plunged to his death.

5. See Gimbutas, *The Language of the Goddess*, Chapter 24.

6. See Virginia Beane Rutter, *Woman Changing Woman: Feminine Psychology Reconceived Through Myth and Experience* (San Francisco: Harper Collins, 1993).

7. In ancient Goddess cultures, the chrysalis and caterpillar are also familiar motifs that symbolize the process of becoming. A gold chrysalis bead with clear markings indicating the eyes, wing casings, and abdomen, as well as gold pendants shaped like chrysalises were found in a chamber tomb at Mycenae (c. 1500 B.C.E.). Caterpillars are found on pottery, vase painting, and funerary urns dating as early as 4500 B.C.E. Many examples show the caterpillar in a procession with other animals (similar to a zodiac), reflecting and celebrating the cyclical nature of life. See Marija Gimbutas, *The Gods and Goddesses of Old Europe: Myths and Cult Images* (Berkeley and Los Angeles: University of California Press, 1982), p. 186.

8. The phrase "returning to the marketplace with gift-bestowing hands" refers to the tenth of the Ten Ox-Herding Pictures, a pictorial representation of the structure of the religious quest, where one finally returns full circle, back to everyday life, with no trace of attainment. It is recited in the San Francisco Zen Center's ceremony upon formally taking leave of the monastery or temple.

Susan Moon

Wholeheartedness

COMMITMENT IS NOT a particularly Buddhist concept, but it is certainly a concept which bears on Buddhist practice. When I hear the word *commitment* I think first of the context of intimate relationships, marriage being the most obvious example. But of course we can speak also of commitment to work, or to a spiritual practice, among other things. We're familiar with Freud's definition of mental health as the ability to love and to work, and I would add to that a third sphere of human endeavor, and that would be the ability to have some kind of life of the spirit. In all three of these areas, I believe that the concept of commitment has relevance.

What do we actually *mean* by commitment? I like the word "wholeheartedness," which is perhaps a more Buddhist way to think about the same thing. The word "commitment" implies engagement with an activity over a long period of time. Wholeheartedness implies a depth of engagement at a given moment in time. Maybe we could say that commitment is a horizontal kind of engagement, and wholeheartedness is a vertical kind of engagement.

Am l committed to Buddhist practice? I started sitting at the Berkeley Zen Center twenty years ago. I have often been uncertain, wondered whether it was right for me, been beset by doubts. Somewhat

---

A version of this essay appeared under the title "Thinking About Commitment" in *Inquiring Mind,* Fall 1989. Reprinted by permission of the author.

unaccountably, after eight years of practice, I felt ready to have what we call lay ordination—that is, to take refuge in the Buddha, Dharma, and Sangha, take the Ten Precepts, the Four Vows, and receive a Buddhist name. It was a subtle and unconscious transition for me, like finding oneself hungry and sitting down to a bowl of cold cereal. No big deal. No big decision. It didn't mean that I would do anything any differently from before. I was not becoming a priest. I would look just the same. But it was a way for me to make a statement to myself and to my community that I am committed. It was a way to let go of doubt, to make some room for wholeheartedness and faith. I felt different afterwards. I now say, to myself and to anybody who asks me, that I'm a Buddhist. Looking back, I have to conclude, as a historian, that, yes, I must be committed to Buddhist practice, just because I *am* still doing it. But can one be retroactively committed? This sounds like an easy way out. Can one even be committed to something without knowing it consciously?

I know from painful experience that in personal relationships you can't make yourself be wholehearted. I've tried: "What a terrific guy! He's single, straight, and considerate—I should fall in love with him." It doesn't work. You can't make yourself feel certain things, no matter how much you want to feel them. But if you can't just decide to be wholehearted, can you just decide to be committed? Perhaps if you make a commitment, the wholeheartedness will come after, in the space you've safeguarded with the commitment, like a plant in a fenced garden. Like an arranged marriage. Or must both commitment and wholeheartedness grow without being pushed, unnoticed, organically, like mushrooms in the dark?

My strongest experience of wholeheartedness and commitment in personal relations is as a parent. My children are grown up now, and the unhesitating commitment their presence has called forth from me, from the very bottom of my heart, has surely been one of the liberating experiences of my life. It's easier for me to be wholehearted when there's no choice, no exit.

As for Buddhist practice, I think you can't just decide to be wholehearted about that, either. But what you can do is put yourself into certain situations which foster wholeheartedness, which force you to burn yourself up, leaving nothing behind.

Beating the drum for service, for example. Sitting zazen, it's so easy for me to lose my concentration, to sleep, to daydream, to plan. But when I'm hitting the *mokugyo,* I can't think about what I'll cook for dinner. I am completely wholehearted, beating the drum and chanting the *Heart Sutra,* and the drum itself seems to be my heart. I am no more beating the drum than I am beating my heart.

I used to do rock climbing, and the wonderful thing about it, too, was the wholeheartedness it required. Definitely no daydreaming as I clung by my fingernails to a pimple of granite in the sky, but rather a quite enthusiastic feeling of commitment to staying alive. The challenge, of course, is to be wholehearted about our humdrum everyday lives lived at sea level. And every moment that my whole heart is beating within me is another opportunity to be wholehearted. Or to recognize that I already *am* wholehearted.

I have studied hand bookbinding, and in bookbinding the word *commit* is used when you are pasting two surfaces together. Let's say you are making the book cover. You have your bookcloth, all measured and cut. You have your cardboard all measured and cut. You brush the paste on the cloth. You brush the paste on the cardboard. Then you pick up the limp cloth and hold it exactly over the cardboard which will become your book cover, and when you're ready, you *commit it*—that is, you lay it down in one smooth unhesitating movement. If you stop in the middle and wonder what you're doing, it will stretch or wrinkle or buckle or warp. So you just jump in and go for it, with your whole heart. The worst that can happen is that you may have to do it over, but if you waver and are tentative, you will *surely* have to do it over.

So the important thing is to be wholehearted at the moment that you are doing something. The idea that you are committing yourself to something that stretches way ahead of you into the future is perhaps not so helpful. Or maybe we focus too much on that aspect of commitment—the part that goes on over time. Two people can commit themselves to each other very sincerely, with the idea that it is for a long time, even forever. Or a person can commit herself wholeheartedly to a new job. And in the moment these commitments are made, they are made wholeheartedly. Then things change, unforeseen circumstances arise, people change, the couple separates, the person leaves the job. Does that mean the commitments were in any way false? What counts is making the commitment *now,* without covering over the wholeheartedness with too many layers of ideas.

Commitment has been an issue for me in terms of my work, as well. I have worked at a number of things in my life, in the fields of publishing, education, and political activism. I have suffered a great deal from my own uncertainty and changing focus. I've always wanted to write; I've always dibbed and dabbed at it, but I never, at the deepest level, committed myself to it, because I was afraid. Nobody was asking me to write, the world wasn't crying out for my material, it wasn't going to save anybody from starvation, I would have to do it all alone, and then persuade people to read it. My self-doubt kept getting worse and worse. And then one day, I couldn't stand it any longer. I just knew I had to commit myself to writing anyway—to put myself on a schedule, to do my work no matter what, to be completely and utterly wholehearted about it. Three hours a day, every day, just do it, like beating the drum. Don't do the other things first, the things that people want from me, the folding of laundry, the shopping, the cooking, the driving, the meetings, the political work. Do them after. But every day, first the writing.

It made me feel like a new person. And the funny thing is, I wasn't doing anything dramatically different from what I was doing before, but my attitude completely changed. I surrendered to wholeheartedness.

The task is to focus on one project at a time, and do that with full attention, until it's completed. Then it's time to do the next thing. One thing has a way of leading to another. If you keep walking along a path, you get somewhere. You can always change your course as you go along, depending on the weather conditions, an unexpected rock slide, a beautiful lake that wasn't on the map. I have made a leap of faith—that if I follow my heart, the other things will fall into place. So faith is connected to commitment and wholeheartedness. Faith tides you over when wholeheartedness flags. The days when I sit at my desk and I can't think of anything to say, or I don't like what I *can* think of, I have faith that it's going to be all right, that I'm doing what I need to be doing.

Buddhist practice has helped me to make this commitment. It has helped me with what looks like self-discipline, but which, oddly, is really the kind of faith I was just talking about—it's what keeps you from getting up and leaving the zendo in the middle of the sesshin even though your knees hurt or you're bored or sleepy or claustrophobic. It's what keeps you from leaving your desk to do the laundry even though you can't think of anything to say. I suppose it's what keeps you from leaving your husband even though you just had a fight about whose turn it is to drive the carpool. And Buddhist practice has helped me to be wholehearted about being me, from one moment to the next.

Anne Waldman

Poetry as Siddhi

I'VE BEEN WRITING since childhood, and since 1970 have been a formal Tibetan Buddhist practitioner. I was originally attracted to the ideas and practices of Buddhism because they seemed co-natural with ideas and practices in art. I enjoyed the poetries of Li Po, the T'ang poet Han Shan, the seventeenth-century haiku master Basho. I was drawn to the steadiness of gaze, tightness of construction, and condensation which is a quality in Sappho's generative fragments, Emily Dickinson's elliptical brevity and compacted verse, and in the work of modern American poets such as William Carlos Williams and Lorine Neidecker. Ezra Pound's versions of Rihaku (Li Po) are achingly beautiful, Jack Kerouac's haiku both contemporary and vivid *(in the medicine cabinet / the winter fly / has died of old age)*. I came early upon Japanese Heian court raconteur diarist Sei Shonagon and was impressed by her raging detail, wit, and insight into human foible and ego, measuring the particulars of the world of relative appearance. I imitated her lists.

The heaven/earth/man principal of Chinese aesthetics is both a poetic and spiritual practice. In fact, the two are inseparable. It is "man's" duty to join heaven and earth. Human beings are the intermediaries between the vast and the particular. The poet's imaginative eye triggers the synapse creating a complete universe, a bubble of perception which brings the vision of an infinite reality, or construct, together with tangible detail. It's up to us (the human realm) to make the connections.

Later, while studying shamanism and ethnopoetics, I was attracted, by contrast, to Arthur Waley's translation of the "Nine Songs" from China, Mira Bai's delirious hymns to Krishna, Native American (particularly Navaho) chant, and the Songs of Milarepa, all primarily longer-limbed ecstatic forms. This tradition—a poetry of ecstasy and a poetry that is itself energetic, activating, and animating—manifests in many cultures and individuals through time.

As I studied Tantric Buddhism I became aware of how the mind relates to various psychological energy principles, both peaceful and wrathful. I also looked into the tradition of the *doha*, a song of realization that acknowledges an encounter with a master teacher, traditionally a guru or lama, and explores a particular wisdom and teaching transmitted through a kind of call-and-response duet format. The doha also describes the trials and hardships of the adept or initiate. This form of poetry exacts strong devotion from the practitioner.

The pivotal word for me, in terms of how I relate my Buddhist practice to a practice of writing, is *energy*. The energy itself manifests in a basic sense as passion, which is one of the ingredients in the doha form. The Tantric understanding of energy is actually related to the experience of duality, contrast, extremes. From the Tantric perspective, it first would appear that you exist as a solid entity, and others outside you are separate and solid as well. In fact you see your own thoughts as solid, as "real." You create elaborate structures out of thin air. But what you come to in practice is to see the deceptive nature of these kinds of projections. Once you start to examine your own mind you see how insubstantial thoughts are, which is not to denigrate them but simply to see them as they are. We are all just conglomerates of psychological tendencies—very tenuous, as a matter of fact. You start to see the emptiness, the emptiness of "ego," in yourself and in others. You start to see through the thickness of those fabrications.

"I write because we're all gonna die," said Jack Kerouac. Many writers have had that *satori*-like insight, a realization or impermanence, of the terrible beauty and fragility of our existence. It propels us to write, possibly in the hope or giving weight and meaning to experience, of acknowledging the moment as it is passing. But at a deeper level, in writing we are performing a necessary ritual, just as in meditation practice we ritualize our breathing. In a sense, the ritual helps us to really understand breath, or in further practices beyond sitting meditation, to understand how energy works. We meet our *yidam,* our basic nature. The act of writing also shows us who we are, what life is, what time is, what sound is. We are writing inside our own death. This is not morbid; on the contrary, it is profoundly inspiring. All meditation, all writing, starts with the contrast.

The deceptive existence of "I" and "others" seems to rub together. What interests me is how and where the rub takes place between my so-called "self," or whatever that consciousness or perception is, and the phenomenal world—and the words and images and arrangements and collidings that occur, that come out of this chaos. There is an unconditioned spark happening, and how we relate to this experience can actually exist inside language itself, in how the sounds collide. All this seems consistent with many Tibetan Buddhist practices, which are themselves explorations and transformations of energy. Energy is just energy. It is non-conditioned except through our neurotic and grasping egos. This pure self-existing energy is also the potential of what in Sanskrit is called *siddhi,* which literally translates as "magic." We might consider poetry a kind of siddhi.

This ability to use the existing energy of the universe may be where poetry touches on the play of duality. How we handle or transcend it, or feel the gap that arises where duality seems to come to a standstill—this interests me as well. That powerful spark, the original spark of insight or realization where the poet or adept or student suddenly "gets it." The poem is the celebration or process of that instant, of the gap that can occur. I am intrigued by the history and lineage of a tradition that supports this kind of active practice, which is based on an older oral tradition of storytelling. It is a communal poetry as well, a public expression of siddhi.

The Mahasiddhas of India actually composed teachings through songs, or dohas. They were composed in the popular style of the period. There is complex esoteric symbolism which relates to particular Vajrayana teachings; there is an outrageousness of imagery. And yet there's an incredible immediacy of expression—spontaneity, rather than originality. The form is more about what is going on in the moment, and the poet might be drawing on what he or she has just understood in terms of the particular teaching and realization. So the poet seeks to communicate an experience of understanding and realization in the most direct and spontaneous way possible, rather than trying to be "original." You might be echoing your teacher, using his or her words or those of the teacher before them, and so on. You might be using remnants of shamanic imagery from the Bonpo tradition, the pre-Buddhist culture of Tibet.

The Kagyu lineage of Tibetan Buddhism begins with Vajradhara, who is not a literal or historical figure but a Sambhogakaya manifestation, or "body of light" manifestation—a figure you might encounter in vision or dream. The two yidams of the lineage are Chakrasamvara and Vajrayogini, and from there the lineage begins with the historical Tilopa who lived in 988. There's a textual canon of Tibetan Buddhist poetry that continues to the present time. The songs of the Sixteenth Gyalwang Karmapa are collected in *The Rain of Wisdom*.[1] This book also includes some dohas by Chogyam Trungpa Rinpoche, the late Tibetan Kagyu lama who was himself particularly interested in the relationship of a meditative poetry to the American tradition.[2]

Trungpa Rinpoche wrote:

The essence of all these songs can be epitomized by the four Dharmas of Gampopa. Gampopa was the student of Milarepa. These four sum up the essence of the songs. These are 1) one's mind becomes dharmic. 2) dharma practice becomes path. 3) in following that path confusion is removed. And 4) having removed confusion, everything dawns as wisdom.

He goes on to say:

The first dharma is the ground where our minds become dharmic, so that we and the dharma are no longer separate entities. We develop true renunciation and have a sense of revulsion towards samsara *(the suffering of cyclic existence)* The second dharma is the path. When our mind goes along with the dharma, the dharma becomes path and any obstacles, whether extreme or ordinary, become a part of our journey. The third dharma is fruition. As the journey is taking place, the process of the journey liberates us from confusion and anxiety. We are delighted by our journey and we feel it is good. The fourth dharma is total vision. When we are able to overcome our confusion and anxiety, even our anxiety is not regarded as anti-dharma or anti-path. And therefore cosmic wakefulness takes place.[3]

The wakeful quality described here is energetic.

As a practitioner I am always curious how others, particularly poets, have come up against the challenges within the Buddhist tradition. If we are supposed to be stilling our minds, why so much verbal display? Are the poems and the poets themselves vehicles for dharmic teaching? Do they necessarily call attention to themselves in that manner? Is all poetry, by definition, sacred?

The wild yogin poet Milarepa is perhaps a good example of a great teacher who taught through his poetry. The Tibetan author of *The Hundred Thousand Songs of Milarepa* lived from 1040 to 1123 C.E. Milarepa's songs are in the form of a dialogue between teacher or guru and student or disciple, a common way of teaching. The teachings, the dohas, are connected to devotion to the guru, so there is a focus on honoring and often invoking the life and teachings of the guru. This is reflected in the following dialogue between Milarepa and a young woman, Paldarbum:

> With great faith, the maiden touched his feet. She invited him in and offered him good hospitality. She requested meditation instruction and offered this supplication.[4]

The text incorporates brief prose parts such as this, which are like directions; it then breaks into song. This format resonates with early folk drama narratives, which are commonly narrative stories of a particular journey. The famous Tibetan story of Nangsa Obum resembles a traditional shaman's journey, such as the classic anonymous Sumerian myth of Inanna. The initiate endures all kinds of hardships—goes to hell and back, in a manner of speaking. She is torn apart, comes back to life, is transformed. In the case of the folk heroine Nangsa Obum, she is married against her will, escapes to practice Dharma, parts from her son (in one of the most moving dialogues between mother and son I've ever encountered), dies, and comes back to tell her story, thus manifesting her faith and devotion in the precious Dharma. Inanna, in another culture, also endures fierce encounters and manifests the complete goddess cycle from prepubescent virgin to mother to old hag. Such narratives are wonderful stories as well as instructive to the persons studying and being initiated into a particular sacred tradition.

When the emotion is intense, the narrative breaks into song, into poetry; the quality of direct transmission, the energy of the exchange, resumes. At one point, Nangsa Obum's mother is advising her to be a housewife. Nangsa replies passionately:

> When the sun stops shining I will stop desiring to practice the
>   Dharma, and stay at home.
> If the sun keeps going,
> I will go also, to the Dharma.
> If the moon stops waxing and waning,
> I will stay at home.
> But if it does continue to wax and wane, I will go to the Dharma.
> If the lotus flower stops blooming in the summer,
> And dying in the winter,
> I will stay at home and not practice the Dharma
> But if it continues I will not stay at home.[5]

In the case of Milarepa and his teaching to the young lady Pal-darbum, whom he has met at a fair, the hearer is meant to experience the same kind of transformation and inspiration as the young woman. She herself becomes a "wonderful yogini, holder of the hearing lineage." He instructs her at one point:

> Look up into the sky,
> And practice meditation free from fringe and center.
>
> Look up at the sun and moon,
> And practice meditation free from bright and dim.
>
> Look over at the mountains,
> And practice meditation free from departing and changing.
>
> Look down at the lake,
> And practice meditation free from waves.
>
> Look here at your mind,
> And practice meditation free from discursive thought.

The lady then, after meditating, offers an examination of her own experience of sun, moon, sky, mountains, lake, and her own mind:

> I am able to meditate on the sky;
> But when clouds arise, how should I meditate?
>
> I am able to meditate on the sun and moon;
> But when heavenly bodies move, how should I meditate?

And so on. Then Milarepa clarifies further.

> If you are able to meditate on the sky
> Clouds are manifestations of the sky.
> Once more resolve this manifestation;
> Once more resolve your mind.
>
> If you are able to meditate on the sun and moon,
> The stars and planets are manifestations of the sun and moon.
> Once more resolve this manifestation;
> Once more resolve your mind.

And finally, in the last part of this section, he says:

> Discursive thoughts are manifestations of your mind.
> Once more examine the root of discursive thought;
> Once more resolve your mind.[6]

The poetry in this tradition, although confirmed in its resolution of purpose and often strong and passionate, is for the most part didactic. It takes one very skillfully and deliberately through the proper Dharmic points and steps. The content—the specifics of the stories in the cases of Milarepa and Nangsa Obum—is often wild and outrageous; the form is more controlled. Again, the aim of a doha is not originality, but being true to one's own realization as part of the specific lineage is. The rub between self and other, the sense of being "put on the spot," is at the heart of this tradition.

It took me a while to appreciate the spirit of the doha form. I was at first more attracted to the simplicity and succinctness of Japanese and Chinese meditative lyrics, and the ecstasy of Sanskrit or Persian poetry has always been more exciting to me personally. Yet I attempted a doha which I composed while participating in a three-month seminary, an intensive Buddhist study and retreat program in 1984. It was a formal request to my Buddhist teacher, relating the history of our relationship. Traditionally, the student requests the teacher to stay around longer in order to teach. The title of this doha refers to the request for higher teaching in which the student takes a particular vow of further commitment. Although it may not display much wisdom, I believe it manifests the qualities of devotion and supplication.

Belated Transmission Request

Do you remember, O Playful One, when you
said to me at Tail-of-the-Tiger in 1970
Stay in New York City & be a warrior!
Why on earth go to Cuba? New York
is a Holy City, take on the poison!
(you were staring at my covered breasts)
You were teaching the spontaneous yogi wisdom
of Milarepa, it was summer, luscious, you
were planting early seeds of Dharma
I sang the Four Dharmas of Gampopa
in a car going north over &
over again with longing
You put this song in my heart

Do you remember, Dear Teacher, Crazy Poet
when as a guest of the Poets' Church
in Manhattan you said I eat I piss
I shit I fuck! Why come to me?
(3 elderly ladies walked out)
My mother was worried you weren't "proper"
How could the daughter of the rational
intelligentsia fall for a showman?
You put the seed of outrageous wisdom in my heart

And when we read poetry together at
St. John The Divine wasn't I nervous
to please you, manifesting power in my words!
Your quirky poetry touched me, awkward & brave
I wanted to be part of your energy
Reluctant, hesitating
I read my poems for you
You put your poems in my heart

I met Geshe Wangyal in 1963 and he said
Your mind can be clear & free
He was like a mirror & whatever I asked
of him was thrown back on me as if
in a spotlight & magnified as if by
a gigantic lens, "Can we change the world?"
"What is L.S.D.?" Naive questions from the heart
I think I knew what he meant when he said
All reality should be regarded as dreams
My boyfriend meditated & stood on his head
We read stilted translations of Gelugpa texts
on cold floors in Philadelphia
I was a teenager
He wouldn't let me wear makeup in the guru's
presence, I couldn't be pious
The little pink suburban house was cluttered
with young monks on Tolstoy foundation grants
& the scent of incense & torma & roasted chicken
permeated the rooms. How could they eat meat?
The shrine was covered with wild & gaudy objects
& pictures. I was attracted to the vividness
Did all the colors & images represent my own mind?

Do you remember, Powerful One, when
you socked me in the chest so hard
I gasped in pain. Did you say Stop
being so New York? Were you referring
to my speed, my clothing, insincerity?
I was filing by to greet you in Boulder
You hit me so quickly I was too shocked
to be scared. My conceptions dropped away
You put the literal ache of Dharma in my breast

During the Naropa Poetry Wars I wanted
your help, your confirmation
I let my confusion & doubt & anger arise
& disappear over & over again
"The truth will be told" you assured me

I defended you unskillfully repeatedly
Everywhere I travelled your name was
on peoples' lips: Canada, Amsterdam, England,
Germany, India, Detroit, Austin, San Francisco
Nothing was ever so provoking as you, Skillful One
You put the thought of Uncompromising Dharma
in their minds

When I served you wine, having looked out
of the suite windows thinking how wise & rich
this landscape is, inside & out, How spacious & sacred
Between when the wine was poured & my presenting
    it to you,
the glass cracked! My heart broke
What an imposter, a weak unworthy vessel I am
I'm a lazy Nyingma, will I never wake up?
You said with a smile It means *drink more*
You are kind & generous, dear Teacher
I was so happy to see you in your
crisp white sheets, so real & Ordinary
You put a sense of humor in my heart

Instead of going to Seminary in 1973
I went to Darjeeling & met Jadtral Sangye Dorje
Why did he seem so familiar to me? His eyes
twinkled in his rugged clown's face,
weathered like a rock by all the elements
Would he make me tend cows for 3 years
in a pasture like the Belgian nun?
He was stern & kind I knew him I hardly knew him
He holds the hat of Sero Khandro
I dreamed of Yeshe Tsogyal
She showed me the world in my cervix
She showed me the word in a black shawl
with diamond flecs that turned into the night sky
She appeared at first like a tortilla lady
Then she had hair like a plant & a rainbow body
My tswai lama is far away

Where are the precious women gurus?
What is my karma towards them and you?

Now after 14 years I wish to receive your transmission
formally. "Further" you said.

It was a relief to write this doha, to clarify aspects of my situation as a student to this particular teacher. I had a fourteen-year history of inspiration alternating with hesitation. Certain lines—"You put the ache of Dharma in my breast"—are acknowledgments of the teacher's profound effect. I felt a reciprocity of energy occurring as I "confessed" to inadequacies and doubts, which in turn seemed to invite the compassion of the teacher. This poem arose spontaneously in a meditative situation. It is autobiographical, personal, and straightforward. There are references to the Lady Tsogyal, Padmasambhava's consort and a great lama herself, and to my own dreams and aspirations. Yet it is also a formal request for further teaching on entering the Vajrayana path. In this doha, I felt I was able to bring the languages of my poetic and Buddhist practices together.

The true "wisdom" or magic of the best poetry seems to go beyond reference points—especially the reference point of "I" and "me." Such a poem breathes on its own, apart from the person writing it, in the sense of Emily Dickinson asking, Do my verses breathe?

The poet James Schuyler wrote in a journal in 1960:

> One is often amazed by the ugliness of things, their great beauty. It is dangerous for art to take a great interest in such appearances since its main interest must be in its own center, which is of course indefinable except by virtue of its existence.
> Words are energy. Physical and psychic heat and force.[7]

His words resonate with the Buddhist axiom: "If you see something beautiful don't cling to it. If you see something ugly don't push it away."

"Appearances" is a key word in Schuyler's passage. The point here is not to get caught in the net of illusion, while delighting in the self-existing energy of the words. In *shamata-vipashyana* practice, which involves the technique of formless meditation in a seated, cross-legged posture (there is a form of walking meditation as well), thoughts naturally arise, but instead of latching onto them and making them solid, the meditator perceives them as fleeting and illusory, and lets them go.

As writers, we might become skilled at catching things as they arise, or pass by, or pass through us. This can be tricky. How do we discriminate? Are we simply mediums? Is anything that "comes up" valid? There are no clear prescriptions. There is love and passion for the words involved which, when the poem (the text) is working, seem to transcend the neurotic self-referential mode, or the cliché mode, or the vague "poetic" mode, filled with abstractions and weak language. Once we start developing our ear, we can hear it.

Reading Wallace Stevens' "Description Without A Place," I am riveted by the word "seems" in its gorgeous play. The notion of appearance has a root in the Sanskrit word samsara. In Buddhism, samsara is the vicious cycle of transmigrating existence, arising out of ignorance and characterized by suffering. Here is part of Stevens' poem:

> *It is possible that to seem — it is to be,*
> *As the sun is something seeming and it is.*
>
> *The sun is an example. What it seems*
> *It is and in such seeming all things are.*
>
> *Thus things are like a seeming of the sun*
> *Or like a seeming of the moon or night*
>
> *Or sleep.*

Buddhists talk about "things as they are," not veiled or colored by our own perceptions. The poem continues:

> *It is a world of words to the end of it,*
> *in which nothing solid is its solid self.*[8]

Here, Stevens seems to be playing in that lively field of form and emptiness, and also delighting in the form, the shape the words take, as wells as the music therein, which weaves its own magic.

In the Tibetan Buddhist Maitri Rooms practice, developed by Trungpa Rinpoche at The Naropa Institute, practitioners assume particular postures in a series of five colored rooms, keyed to the energies and colors of the five Buddha families, which are actually five distinct ways or styles of behavior and perception. Each of the five energies has its neurotic aspects—attached and fixated—as well as its enlightened or sane aspects. For example, the Padma ("lotus") family, is associated with the color red, with sunsets and seduction. In its neurotic aspect, Padma family energy is very grasping and demanding: it wants you for its territory and wants you to buy its "trip." The enlightened aspect of Padma family energy, on the other hand, is what is called "discriminating awareness wisdom"—very sharp and precise.

Vajra family energy is related to intellect and cool precision—a more scientific approach, perhaps. It has been described as having the qualities of icy crystals on a wintry bough. In the blue Vajra room, one assumes a prone position, face down, belly to ground, arms extended, head to one side. As I emerge from the Vajra room, I notice the edges and lines between objects, between emotions, the clear shapes of figures on the horizon, the blocks and edges within speech, the spaces between words on the page—and then the further breakdown of words into phones and phonemes.

In practicing the postures of the Maitri Rooms, one starts to appreciate the world in all its vividness. We seem to pay greater attention to the nuances of phenomena, both material and mental, through the practice of maitri, a word which literally means "loving-kindness." This practice reminds me of William Burroughs' assignment to go out in the street and notice, for example, everything blue. Exercises of the attention. When she was at Radcliffe working with Hugo Munsterberg, one of Freud's protégés, Gertrude Stein came to the conclusion that neurosis was "a disease of the attention." We wish to return to that state which exists, in Robert Duncan's words, "Long before minding everything and finding fulfillment of self in everything." I think the practices of Dharma help.

I view poetry as a kind of *terma,* found treasure. A terma is a precious hidden teaching which can be found or unlocked from rocks, mountains, water, and also from the mind-streams of great masters. Charles Olson wrote, "I hunt among stones." The middle realm between form and emptiness, Sambhogakaya, is the body of light. Keats wrote that he was "straining at particles of light."

The practices and rituals in this particular Buddhist tradition actually show you your mind in all its vividness. The various forms of poetry, including doha, haiku, or ritual chant associated with spiritual practice, can also speak your mind to you. Whether inclined toward Buddhism or not, by practicing basic sitting meditation we can begin to glimpse the nonconditional quality of energy. Thoughts arise—good thoughts, bad thoughts, strong emotions, boredom, fantasies of the next diversion—things so intense they might knock you out of your posture. You see them all simply as thoughts, not so solid after all, and you let them go as you breathe out. This process of watching thoughts arise and letting them go resonates with the practice of poetry. The poet catches the thoughts, refines them in language, and lets them go. Thoughts are not necessarily ideas but that which is noticed. As writers, as poets, we choose to work with them. And from this point of view, all is sacred.

1. *The Rain of Wisdom,* translated by the Nalanda Translation Committee under the direction of Chogyam Trungpa (London and Boulder, Colorado: Shambhala Publications, 1980).

2. Inviting the participation of contemporary American poets, Chogyam Trungpa Rinpoche founded The Naropa Institute in Boulder, Colorado in 1974.

3. *The Rain of Wisdom,* p. iv.

4. *The Rain of Wisdom,* p. 210.

5. Tsultrim Allione, *Women of Wisdom* (London: Routledge & Kegan Paul, 1984), p. 115.

6. *The Rain of Wisdom,* pp. 210–212.

7. James Schuyler, from unpublished notebook.

8. Wallace Stevens, "Description Without A Place," in *The Collected Poems of Wallace Stevens* (New York: Alfred A. Knopf, 1989), p. 339.

Erin Blackwell

The Province of the Saved

The Province of the Saved
Should be the Art — To save —
Through Skill obtained in Themselves —
The Science of the Grave

No Man can understand
But He that hath endured
The Dissolution — in Himself —
That Man — be qualified

To qualify Despair
To Those who failing new —
Mistake Defeat for Death — Each time —
Till acclimated — to —
　　　　—Emily Dickinson, 1862[1]

I NEVER EXPECTED to find myself sitting cross-legged on a black cushion in a bare-beamed hall with a bunch of adepts. I never expected to be invited into the heart of the mystery.

Not just because zazen on a zafu in a zendo is a bizarre Eastern ritual and I'm a child of the West, but because Zen is conceptually perfect and I am really a mess. How could my six-feet-one of flesh and blood, my fickle, fiery Celtic selves ever fold themselves up into a faceless human origami and stay that way for half an hour?

But then, the Dharma has been coming at me from every angle all my life.

◇

My grandmother used to take me to the beach. We lived in Southern California, where she'd moved as a child when things were the way the original inhabitants had left them. Born in Connecticut to an upper-middle-class family of Espicopalians, my grandmother had reinvented herself as a beach rat.

She raised me a beach rat. By the time I knew her, she no longer went for long swims or body-surfed. She took me to China Cove, a small beach on Newport Bay, where the water was warm and the waves gentle. Our view was dominated by a private residence built to resemble a Chinese pagoda. Already the East was there.

Every day, the same ritual. Grachen's aluminum chair, her mat and her umbrella always went on the same spot, well up on the dry sand, against the southern wall. My towel went seaside of her mat. There I was exalted, exultant; there I was safe. We went in the morning and stayed until dinnertime, through sun, clouds, fog, drizzle, and rain. There was no "good day for the beach." The beach was always there, in all its moods and shifts. We were part of that great enterprise.

China Cove is sacred space. An enthusiastic bridge player, my grandmother would not play cards there. Nor would she read. She would write the occasional note to a friend and she would make lists. She knew everyone and greeted them and would gossip some, but she really preferred silence. She really preferred the beach. No one who turned on a radio managed to keep it on. She picked up every piece of paper, plastic, or glass that found its way onto the sand. She was both custodian and queen.

Grachen is the unconditional love of my life, my model for reverence and dignity. The difference in our ages impressed upon me the meaning of space-time. Through her eyes I saw the beach before the advent of jetties, when the natural surf broke for miles and the tidepools crawled with life. If I find her again on my zafu, is it because we sat on a beach together the way you and I sit in a zendo, or because she is my most intractable delusion?

◇

When I left California for New York, I lifted a small paperback from the family library, *The Way of Life* by Lao Tzu. I read the whole thing aloud to myself in the Grand Canyon one sunrise. In Manhattan, I committed the eighty-one fragments to memory and would repeat them to myself when things in the Men's Belts and Accessories Department of Saks Fifth Avenue got weirder than usual. I learned that language "comes out of the womb of matter," that water naturally seeks the common level and so should I, and that no quality can be isolated without calling into being its opposite.

Back in college for a degree, I fell in love with Hegel, the German Romantic philosopher who reconciled the subject/object divide by demonstrating that all knowledge is self-knowledge, and that the actions of consciousness are the same as those of matter.

◇

My next teacher, my next great partner in silence, Nicole, is a junior high school teacher in Brittany, France. Nicole represented everything—lesbian, black leather, desire, physical danger—I had run from. Beautiful and terrifying, she offered me what I had gone to France for: intimate knowledge of the human heart.

She put me on the back of her motorcycle and we rode all over France, Italy, and Spain. Just like Zen, this involved black clothes, sitting, silence, and the contemplation of death. Our first time out, she gleefully explained there's nothing to hang on to—motion is the gyroscope's only stability. Mesmerized by the flying asphalt below, I could only sit there as Nicole passed everything in sight like a video game come to life.

After a while, Death seemed a small thing compared to the discomfort we endured in its pursuit. Since I'm taller than Nicole and the back seat of a motorcycle is typically raised to accommodate "the little woman," my head stuck up and caught the wind factor. Like Grachen, Nicole is no respecter of weather. We rode through pouring rain, strong winds, and freezing cold, averaging 100 mph. Every 150 miles, when the tank ran dry, we'd stop for gas and vending-machine espresso. What joy. Ears ringing, stiff in every joint, feet gone numb, and legs cramping—amazed to be alive—I was forced to recognize the relative triviality of my death wish.

My death-defying mistress taught me that there are always two valid sides to a divorce, and that the world—including my person—runs on contradictions. Guiding me through the uncharted areas of my psyche I'd tried to pretend never existed, she gave a big chunk of me back to myself. Our intense sexual and deep psychic connection proved, to my surprise, that flesh and spirit really are one.

The last trip we took together was a tour of the French Gothic cathedrals, a series of huge, gorgeous, complicated structures dedicated to Notre Dame. I was looking for an alternative to my extreme emotional dependence on Nicole. Notre Dame was my answer. This thirteenth-century French inspiration is goddess, godhead, mother, lover, nurse, companion—the quintessence of beauty, grace, and compassion—a compendium of everything I've ever looked for in a woman and keep forgetting resides in me.

My personal relationship to the Virgin Mary began in Spain, when I was chosen to portray her in my school's Christmas play. At age nine, I had long blonde hair and was taller than most of the nuns. Before and after that experience, unconsciously, I was on the lookout for a manifestation of this Heavenly Mother. When I realized I was a lesbian—long before I knew what that meant—I began praying to the Virgin to somehow rescue me from my inextricably unlovable position.

When I met Nicole, I was terrified. Was she the answer to my prayers? Utterly desirable, she looked like nothing but trouble. She turned out to be a biker with a heart of gold who showered her love on me like grace. By the time I decided to trade her in on some thirteenth-century stone she had opened my heart, been a flesh-and-blood bodhisattva (before I'd ever heard the word), and prepared the way for sublimated worship that doesn't deny pleasure in any of its forms.

Notre Dame didn't replace Nicole; she symbolized her. At Chartres Cathedral, as I stood in the transept in my suit of black leather, I had a moment's regret for having wasted my life. A physical force stopped the thought in transit. This was N. D. fending off negative remarks about her creature, me. At Amiens, I stared and stared at *la Vièrge Dorée* until I recognized myself, until I made the equation *Mary = me*. I was so excited, I went inside and tried to sit through Mass, but the liturgy was dead and dismayingly male. Disappointed, I was not defeated. Just as my years as a French lesbian separatist had shown me there was a good life to be lived parallel to the recognized heterosexist norm, my experience with Notre Dame proved I could participate in a spiritual tradition while dodging the patriarchal spin.

◇

Recently, I found myself back in California, this time in the northern half of the state, in San Francisco, where I became smitten with a German blonde. Britta introduced me to zazen across the Golden Gate Bridge in Marin, amidst the romantic eucalyptuses of Green Gulch. She lent me *Zen Mind, Beginner's Mind.*[2] In it I recognized Hegel and Lao Tzu, but for the first time accompanied by a practical guide to getting the better of my mind. Suzuki Roshi told me how to sit and how not to judge my sitting or anyone else's. I was amazed that such a treasure could still reveal itself to me at the ripe old age of forty-one.

Next Sunday, I bought my own copy. Then Britta broke up with me. It took me a while to appreciate the favor she'd done me by first providing the means for self-discovery and then precipitating the crisis that insured my abject motivation. I started sitting two and three times a day on my futon at home and rereading Suzuki a mindful chapter at a time.

Two weeks later, I attended Buddha's birthday celebration in a state of extreme emotional accessibility. I fantasized I'd been kidnapped by a cult. Alienated from my family, rejected by my lover, a stranger in my own country, I was a quivering child over whom sweet tea was being poured. The metaphors totally worked for me. Ready for Buddha, ready to be Buddha, enchanted to learn we were celebrating my own and everyone else's birthday, I ate several pieces of chocolate cake and bought myself a zafu.

Two weeks after that, I discovered a temple nearer to home. The Zen Center in the city—nestled between the low-income, low-morale housing projects and the freeway—has less atmosphere than Green

Gulch. People there didn't look as pretty or laid-back, and seemed less brilliant and more rigid in their devotions. Just what I wasn't looking for, Beginner's Mind Temple deepened my practice. One of the first things I did was buy ten copies of Suzuki's book, which I gave to people more or less apt to read it.

The library and bookstore needed a volunteer one night a week. In exchange for reshelving books, I would be given dinner and unlimited access to the literature. After my intake interview with librarian Celeste West, the only vestiges of supervision were her weekly notes to me. I lived for them. In spite of the free food, I could barely stand the sepulchral anonymity of the dining room. I took courage from knowing that when I descended the steps to the library I would find a warm and witty note beguiling me to file author and title cards. A subversive spirit, an out and outrageous polyfidelitous dyke, Celeste kept me on the path by demonstrating its all-encompassing width.

My next inroad was a one-day sitting for beginners at Green Gulch. This intensive exercise produced a new kind of high. Our guide was a bright, focused monk named Gaelyn Godwin. Her answers were much more intelligent than our questions, evincing an in-depth grasp I wanted to get closer to. In a rare moment of prescription, she suggested that we not treat the world's religions like aisles in some cosmic supermarket, but commit to a spiritual discipline. As a deprogrammed Catholic and a phallophobic feminist, I'd been wary of getting involved.

My friend Marianne said she'd join me for Gaelyn's weekly evening class on the *Heart Sutra*. Otherwise I would never have committed to driving those miles of winding Marin County road in the dark. I'd been chanting the *Heart Sutra* at home off the xerox I'd saved from Buddha's birthday party. I loved saying the words "No eyes, no ears, no nose," and I was eager to find out what they meant. Although she missed half the classes, Marianne still accompanied me in the form of my disappointment at her absence. She teased me about what she called my spiritual crush on Gaelyn, which irked me. I had to admit, I have a thing for teachers.

One Sunday after the class was over, tea and sublime muffins were being served on the sunny outdoor deck at Green Gulch. I went up to Gaelyn and gave her a handcarved Chinese pedestal I'd found at a garage sale. The old wood had split and the stand was unstable on its three squat feet. "It's fabulous," she said. I told her she was a wonderful teacher and she said, "Erin, you are a wonderful teacher." "Touchée," I said, but I didn't quite get it. Marianne, who'd witnessed everything, later explained that Gaelyn was both acknowledging me and skillfully deflecting my projections of self-love. I still have trouble understanding this lesson, which I guess makes it my favorite.

In the Dharma talk that day, Gaelyn had compared her mother to a sea turtle, the kind who goes to all the trouble of laying an egg and then leaves. Acknowledging that she had been abandoned by her mother, Gaelyn recognized that she had thus also been freed. This message was a big break for mothers around the world, who typically get saddled with their kids' hard karma, and women in general, who are expected to take care of everything in the prescribed "feminine" fashion. When everything is a condition for enlightenment, mothers and/or teachers are wonderful whether or not they give us what we want.

◇

For some reason I signed up for the fall practice period at the Zen Center on Page Street. For an outpatient, I was a regular. There was tea, then dinner, then lecture on Wednesday nights. Dinner and library on Thursdays. Zazen and a student talk every Monday morning. Zazen, service, *soji* (temple cleaning), *oryoki* breakfast, zazen, lecture, and tea on Saturdays. Every month there was a Full Moon Bodhisattva Ceremony and a one-day sitting in preparation for the final seven-day sesshin.

What I hadn't counted on was the cumulative effect of all that time spent not only cross-legged with the Dharma, but in the presence of other people who, unlike me in many ways, share my longing for whatever it is we were there for. My forty-odd years on the planet had convinced me no group of people could be this sweet, this dedicated, this well-organized. After three months of unsentimental togetherness, I gleefully revised my opinion about human beings upward—including myself.

Sesshin was a corker. Like many other first-timers, I was afraid for my knees and my sanity. What would become of me, locked up in a brick building with a bunch of strangers for a week? As a half-measure, I volunteered to work in the kitchen the first four days. That way, I got to trip out on organic produce before settling down to in-depth wall watching.

At tea on the fifth day, after having been served a scrumptious-looking chocolate chip cookie, I had one word in my head: "Mother!" Maybe because hers were the first and finest chocolate chip cookies I ever tasted. Tears spilled out of my eyes. I choked up and couldn't eat my cookie, so I put it in my pocket and ate it later. (It was good.) On the seventh day, when my legs were kindling being licked by small flames, I yelled inside my head, "Take this pain away!"

I was calling my mother.

When I was a child, my mother had taken care of anything that hurt. What she couldn't relieve physically, she would comfort, she would make okay by her presence. It wasn't her fault there was pain, but she took responsibility, body and soul, for my having to feel it. In the context of sesshin, my memory of my own biological and nur-turing mother was my way into the universal sentient experience. The answer to suffering isn't avoidance but compassion. As Ibsen's Peer Gynt put it, "The only way around is through." Every one alone together in that room—engaged in our private communications like travelers in a row of airport phone booths—was suffering and in need of compassion. We were practicing being mothers to ourselves and one another.

I was delighted by my discovery. With tears flowing from the pain in my legs, I broke into a grin. "Tell me more!" I shouted to my self. Suddenly I was rewarded with the jackpot vision of a dragon undu-lating its flashing scales before my eyes—like my favorite part of the Chinese New Year's parade. "A dragon is born!" I'd read that some-where. To me at that moment the dragon symbolized the willing-ness to endure pain for the sake of wisdom.

As one of my final treats of sesshin, I requested *dokusan* (a pri-vate interview) with Blanche Hartman, the seventy-year-old monk who has since become Zen Center's first abbess. Her presence, her status, has had an incalculable effect on me. Seeing a woman in a position of spiritual authority blows my mind. She's like Notre Dame seven centuries on—with a shaved head, wearing Japanese-style robes, and speaking homespun American. Blanche customarily demystifies proceedings without ever diminishing their seriousness.

When I took my cushion across from her, I didn't feel like talking. I just wanted to sit with her. "I'm where I want to be," I said. Some time after I left the room I realized my error. I'd mistaken Blanche for Grachen. I thought we were together again at China Cove.

1. Emily Dickinson (1830–1886) is an example of the bodhisattva as poet. Her great subject is how to negotiate existence during and after intense mental pain. The title of this essay is taken from her poem number 539.

2. Shunryu Suzuki, *Zen Mind, Beginner's Mind* (New York and Tokyo: Weatherhill, 1970).

bell hooks

Contemplation and Transformation

ASKED TO DEFINE MYSELF, I wouldn't start with race; I wouldn't start with blackness; I wouldn't start with gender, with feminism. I would start by stripping down to what fundamentally informs my life, being a seeker on the path. Feminist and antiracist struggles are part of this journey. I stand spiritually, steadfastly, on a path of love—that's the ground of my being.

Love as an active practice—whether Buddhist, Christian, or Islamic mysticism—requires that one embraces being a lover, being in love with the universe. Joanna Macy eloquently speaks of this process in *World as Lover, World as Self.*[1] Thomas Merton also wrote of loving God in these terms. To commit to love is fundamentally to commit to a life beyond dualism. That's why, in a culture of domination, love is so sacred. It erodes dualisms—the binary oppositions of black and white, male and female, right and wrong. Love transforms.

The Buddhist call to move beyond dualisms enchanted and seduced me. While I read about Buddhist thought in my teens, my first direct exposure to Buddhism happened when I was an undergraduate at Stanford University studying and writing poetry. Gary Snyder came to campus and read to us with a passion and calm that was awesome. I already knew he was involved with Zen from his work. He invited me to the Ring of Bone Zendo for a May Day celebration. There were several American Buddhist nuns there who made a profound and lasting impression on me. Since that time I've been engaged in the contemplative traditions of Buddhism in one way or another.

Often black participation in contemplative Buddhist practices goes unnoticed. As a group we are noticeably absent from organized Buddhist events. Many teachers speak of needing to have something in the first place before you can give it up. When interpreted literally to mean the giving up of material privileges, of narcissistic comforts, often individuals from underprivileged backgrounds assume these teachings are not for them. Black folks have come to my home, looked at Buddhist work, and wanted to know, "Give up *what* comforts?" Since much of the literature of Buddhism directed at Westerners presumes a white, materially privileged audience as the listener, it is not surprising that people of color in general and black people in particular may see this body of work as having no meaning for their lives. Only recently have individuals from marginalized groups dared to interrogate the assumption that the contemplative traditions, particularly those from Asia, speak only to privileged and/or white Westerners.

This interrogation is part of an overall rethinking of the meaning of spiritual practice in the West. That critical reflection has been intense within the feminist movement as thinkers have addressed the issue of meaningful spiritual practice within the context of patriarchal culture. Ten years ago if you talked about humility, women would say, I feel I've been humble enough, I don't want to try to erase the ego—I'm trying to get an ego. Now the achievements women have made in all areas of life have brought home the reality that we are as corruptible as anybody else. That shared possibility of corruptibility makes us confront the realm of ego in a new way. We've gone past the period when the rhetoric of victimization within feminist thinking was so complete that the idea that women had agency, which could be asserted in destructive ways, could not be acknowledged. Even so, some people still don't want to acknowledge this.

In a culture of domination, preoccupation with victimhood and identity is inevitable. I once believed that progressive people could analyze the dualities and dissolve them through a process of dialectical critical exchange. Yet globally the resurgence of notions of ethnic purity, white supremacy, have led marginalized groups to cling to dualisms as a means of resistance. In the United States we are witnessing the resurgence of forms of black nationalism that say white people are bad, black people are good, white people are inferior, people with melanin superior. The willingness to surrender to attachment to duality is present in such thinking. It merely inverts the dualistic thinking that supports and maintains domination.

Dualities serve their own interests. In my case, life was easier when I felt that I could trust another black person more than I could trust a white person. To face the reality that this is simply not so is a much harder way to live in the world. What's alarming to me now is to see so many Americans returning to those simplistic choices. People of all persuasions are feeling that if they don't have dualism, they don't have anything to hold on to.

If we are concerned with dissolving these apparent dualities we have to identify anchors to hold on to in the midst of fragmentation, in the midst of a loss of grounding. My anchor is love. It is life-sustaining to understand that things are always more complex than they seem. This is what it means to see clearly. Such understanding is more useful and more difficult than the idea that there is a right and wrong, or a good or bad, and you only have to decide what side you're on. In real love, real union or communion, there are no simple rules.

Love as a foundation also takes us more deeply into practice as action in the world. In the work of Vietnamese Zen master Thich Nhat Hanh we find an integration of contemplation and political activism. Nhat Hanh's Buddhism isn't framed from a location of privilege, but from a location of deep anguish—the anguish of a people being destroyed in a genocidal war. The point of convergence of liberation theology, Islamic mysticism, and engaged Buddhism is the sense of love that leads to greater commitment and involvement with the world, not a turning away from the world. The wisdom I seek is that which enables us to know what is needed at a given moment in time. When do I need to reside in that location of stillness and contemplation, and when do I need to rise and do whatever is needed to be done in terms of physical work, or engagement with others, or confrontation with others?

It is not useful to rank one type of action over the other. Creating such a hierarchy goes back to our relationship with pain. A powerful illusion that is constructed every day in our culture is that all pain is a negation of worthiness, that the real chosen people, the real worthy people, are the people who are most free of pain. We see this denial in a lot of "New Age" thinking, in the rhetoric that connects becoming more wealthy, more happy, and more free from all forms of pain with becoming more spiritual.

To be capable of love one has to be capable of suffering and of acknowledging one's suffering. We all suffer. A culture that worships wealth wishes to deny the fact that when people have material privilege at enormous expense of others, they live in a state of terror as well, with the unease of having to protect their gains, which then necessitates even greater control. That's why we see fascism and a compulsion to control surfacing right now in Europe and the United States. The phrase "New World Order" is significant because it confirms a general sense that life is out of control. Our faith in life is weakened by nihilism. Nihilism is a kind of disease that grips the mind and then grips people in fundamental ways. It can only be subverted by seizing the power that exists in chaos—the power of self-agency, and collective agency too—the idea, as in Nhat Hanh's work, that the self necessarily survives through linkage with collective community.

All this is tied to reshaping Buddhist practice so that one really sees fundamental change. We all have to have a *lived* practice. For example, if we see a female who is powerful yet humble, we can learn about the kind of humility that is empowering, and about a form of surrender that does not diminish one's agency. Our conventional ways of constructing identity must be altered in the very way we structure practice and form community.

A central problem for women is that you can't give up the ego and the self if you haven't established a sense of yourself as subject. Questions of humility and surrender are relevant when we see clearly what we need to give up. I do think that women like myself have to interrogate the processes by which we change, and speak about these processes more. In *Revolution from Within,*[2] Gloria Steinem says that there are many women with skills, resources, careers, and huge salaries who still feel shaky in the deep inner core of their being.

They cannot move forward against patriarchy, for this sense of inner lack binds them to the notion of being a victim. This relates to victimization within any community or group. Many black people who have resources and skills remain convinced inwardly that they lack something. And it is this deep-seated sense of unworthiness that is potentially more life-threatening than structures of domination.

There was a tremendous liberatory moment in my unhappy and painful childhood when I realized *I am more than my pain.* In the great holocaust literature, particularly work written by survivors of the Nazi holocaust, people say, "All around me there was death and evil and slaughter of innocents, but I had to keep some sense of a transcendent world that proclaims we're more than this evil, despite its power." When I'm genuinely victimized by racism in my daily life, I want to be able to name it, to name that it hurts me, to say that I'm victimized by it. Yet it is crucial that I never see that as all that I am.

Yes, exploitation occurs, but something else occurs at the same time. Yes, racism occurs, but something else occurs at the same time. How can we get in touch with all of these different things? People *are* genuinely exploited. That reality doesn't take away from the many instances where people give up their own agency and, in so doing, help sustain the context of exploitation. Only by holding on to the sense that we can never be completely dehumanized by "others" can we create a redemptive model. If you're attached to being a victim, there is no hope. One has to identify points of blockage, or victimage, to agency, and from there build a collective process that can change an institution, that can transform culture and society.

A culture of domination like ours says to people: There is nothing in you that is of value; everything of value is outside you and must be acquired. This is the message of devaluation. Low self-esteem is a national epidemic and victimization is the flip side of domination. While revolution must begin with the self, the inner work must be united with a broader social vision. Many people are deeply engaged in complicity with the very structures of domination they critique. Without critical vigilance there is no way to correct this mistake.

Theory-making, certain forms of critical thinking are essential to a process of change. We have been led to believe that we can have change without contemplation. Militant resistance cannot be effective if we do not first enter silence and contemplation to discover—to have a vision—of right action. The point is not to give up rage, rather that we use it to deepen the contemplation to illuminate compassion and struggle. What might people have thought if rather than people exploding in violent rage about the Rodney King incident, there had been a week of silence? Something like that would have completely unsettled our cultural stereotypes about black people—people of color—of resistance.

It serves the interest of domination if the only way we respond to being victimized is by unleashing uncontrollable rage. Then we really are just mirroring the very conditions that brought us into victimization—violence, the conquering of other people's territory. If we talk about burning down other people's property as a "takeover," is this any different from what the United States did in Grenada or Iraq? This is not stepping outside the program, it's mirroring it. The other side of total victimage is rage. Women in the early feminist movement who saw themselves as complete victims were often overwhelmed by blinding rage—the two things go together. They become a dangerous force intimately wedded to the psychology of domination.

A fundamental shift in consciousness is the only way to transform a culture of domination and oppression into one of love. Contemplation is the key to this shift. There is no change without contemplation. The image of Buddha under the Bodhi tree illustrates this—here is an action taking place that may not *appear* to be a meaningful action. Yet it transforms.

1. Joanna Macy, *World As Lover, World As Self* (Berkeley, California: Parallax Press, 1991).
2. Gloria Steinem, *Revolution from Within: A Book of Self-Esteem* (Boston: Little, Brown and Co., 1992).

Pema Chodron

No Right, No Wrong

I CONSIDER IT my good fortune that I was thrown into a way of under-standing Buddhism which in the Zen tradition is called "don't know mind." Don't know: don't know "right," don't know "wrong." As far as I'm concerned, if you're going to try and make things right and wrong you can never even talk about fulfilling your bodhisattva vows.

The bodhisattva vow has something to do with going naked into whatever situation presents itself to you, and seeing how you hate certain people, how people trigger you in every single way, how you want to hold on, how you want to get into bed and pull the covers over your head. Seeing all of this just increases your compassion for the human situation. We're all up against not finding ourselves per-fect, and still wanting to be open and be there for others. My sense of what it means to be a bodhisattva on the path, a student-warrior-bodhisattva, is that you are constantly caught with "don't know." Can't say yes, can't say no. Can't say right, can't say wrong. My undying devotion to Trungpa Rinpoche comes from his teaching me in every way he could that you can never make things right or wrong.

Trungpa Rinpoche was a provocative person. In *Cutting Through Spiritual Materialism,*[1] he says that the job of the spiritual friend is to insult the student, and that's the kind of teacher he was. If things

This essay is adapted from "No Right, No Wrong: An Interview with Pema Chodron," conducted by Helen Tworkov for *Tricycle: The Buddhist Review,* Vol. III, No. 1, Fall 1993, pp. 16–24. Reprinted by permission.

got too smooth, he'd create chaos. I needed that. I didn't like being churned up and provoked, but it was what I needed. It showed me how I was stuck in habitual patterns. The closer I got to him, the more my trust in him grew. It wasn't trust that he would be predictable or follow some kind of reliable code. It was trust that his only motivation was to help people. His whole teaching was about leading people away from holding on to some kind of security. And I wanted my foundations rocked. I wanted to actually be free of habitual patterns which keep the ground under my feet and maintain that false security which denies death. Things are not permanent, they don't last, there is no final security.

Trungpa Rinpoche was always trying to teach us to relax into the insecurity, into the groundlessness. He taught me about how to live. So I am grateful to him, no matter what. He upset me a lot. I couldn't con him, and that was uncomfortable. But it was exactly what I needed. Sometimes, in certain situations, I can see how I'm a con artist, and I can see how I'm just trying to make everything pretty and smooth, and all I have to do is think of Rinpoche and I get honest. He has the effect on me of relentlessly—in a dedicated way—keeping me honest. And that's not always comfortable.

Rinpoche encouraged me to be very strict with my vows. He used to say, "You know, people will be watching you, people will watch how you walk, how you move, and you should really represent this tradition well." In terms of how to be a nun or monk, his teachings were always very straight, very pure. But he needled me about other things. I remember one time saying something to him about feeling that I was a nice person. I used the word "nice," and I remember the look that crossed his face—it was as if he had just eaten something that tasted really bad. And he would also do this thing, which many students have talked to me about, where you'd be talking on and on in your most earnest style and he'd just yawn and look out the window.

As the years went on, I felt everything he did was to help others. But I would also say now that maybe my understanding has gone even deeper, and it feels more to the point to say I don't know. I don't know what he was doing. I know he changed my life. I know I love him. But I don't know who he was. And maybe he wasn't doing things to help everyone, but he sure helped me. I learned something from him. But who was that masked man?

Rinpoche loved women. He was very passionate and had a lot of relationships with women. In retrospect, I would have said to other women students that that might be a part of it if you get involved with him. You should read all his books, go to all his talks, and actually see if you can get close to him. And you should do that knowing that you might get an invitation to sleep with him, so don't be naive about that, and don't think you have to do it or don't have to do it. But you have to decide for yourself who you think this guy is.

The other students were often the ones who made people feel like they were square and uptight if they didn't want to sleep with Rinpoche, but Rinpoche's teaching was to throw out the party line. However, we're always up against human nature. The teacher says something, then everybody does it. There was a time when he smoked cigarettes and everyone started smoking. Then he stopped and they stopped and it was ridiculous. But we're just people with human habitual patterns, and you can count on the fact that the students are going to make everything into a party line, and we did. The one predictable thing about him was that he would continually pull the rug out no matter what. That's how he was.

I was very slow to feel real devotion toward Trungpa Rinpoche. For ten or fifteen years I felt that I was lacking in devotion, but then about four years before his death, that changed. I tell this to newer students who are having the same problem. I tell them: Just hang in there and be true to what you think you're being taught. Groundlessness is the name of the game, it's not about attachment. If devotion sets in right away, it could be from a sense that now you have a new mommy or daddy and there's this cozy feeling to it. But by becoming Buddhists, we don't get a new family. Becoming a Buddhist is about becoming homeless.

When devotion finally did come, it was extremely strong and I was grateful. You feel such gratitude that somebody pointed out the nature of your mind and gave you instructions that actually encouraged you to be brave and compassionate and to let go of old ways of thinking and old securities. But I would say now that my devotion to Trungpa Rinpoche has gone further since his death. I'm really willing to entertain the idea that maybe he wasn't perfect, maybe everything he did wasn't to benefit people. In other words, my sense of not having to make it all right or all wrong is stronger now. I can actually hold my devotion purely and fully in my heart and still say: Maybe he was a madman. And it doesn't change my devotion because he taught me something about not saying "yes" or "no" but resting in groundlessness. And that's more profound than my saying, Oh, no, he never did anything to hurt anybody—because what do I know? That's just my projection. And making him wrong—that's someone's projection, too.

I call myself a student-teacher because it's very threatening to actually think of being a teacher. Of course, there are people who consider me that and so I have to take responsibility. But you get pride in being a teacher and a kind of false humility can set in. So somehow you're caught in the groundlessness of the confidence in the Dharma, which has nothing to do with you but which can come out of your mouth and which will benefit sentient beings. Confidence that the more you get out of the way, the more you can provide the truth. And at the same time, there is this humbling experience of being exactly where you are and knowing what some of your limitations are. That tension between confidence and humility is what you get if you are going to relate to reality honestly. You don't get that security of one hundred percent confidence, which turns into pride, and you don't get the converse feeling that you are just nothing. You're big and small at the same time.

Trungpa Rinpoche used to say that the first step in the training of the warrior, which is to say, one who is cultivating their courage, is to place them in a cradle of loving-kindness. And this is really true. In the Buddhist teachings we talk about cultivation of maitri, or loving-kindness, toward oneself. This does seem necessary in order to have the willingness to work with all the messy and delightful parts of yourself. Real safety is your willingness to not run away from yourself. In terms of creating a safe environment, you want to create a space in which people can look at themselves and it's going to be safe to do that. No one is going to laugh at them for crying or falling apart. Now that's the first stage, because what you're really talking about is how to live in this world where people do ridicule and laugh at you. And so we don't just want to create a lot of practitioners who can only exist in a "safe" situation where there is no insult, where there's no roughness. The cradle of loving-kindness is not about getting stroked. It's more about developing a friendship with yourself in a very complete way. The real sense of safety that people need is that things aren't going to be hidden. It's important to create a situation where people aren't lying.

Certain practices dislodge a lot of emotional material—for instance, *tonglen.* Tonglen is a practice where you work with your breath. You breathe in suffering and connect with it fully—yours and other peoples'. It's a willingness to feel what hurts, not to shy away, not to reject it. You're willing to take on suffering and develop compassion for it and even relax with it. And when you breathe out, you give away joy, a sense of inspiration, delight. So you get used to sharing and giving what you're usually attached to and want to keep for yourself. It's very advanced practice when you start working with other people because it shows you every place that you shut down, hold back—every single place where you close your heart. If you're a practitioner of the Dharma, you want to see that and make friends with it. I think if you really want to become enlightened, somehow you've got to put yourself on the line. If you're already a student and want to wake up fully, then you're going to get the tests and challenges you need, and they're all going to come from working with other people. Safety becomes wanting to avoid all that.

The concern here is obviously one of not wanting to see students get hurt. Once you become a teacher—just as if you become a monk or a nun—you can't blindly keep doing what you always did. You have to be more mindful about how your behavior affects others. But it's important for students to see that Dharma teachers have tempers or aggression or passion. Buddhism isn't about seeing a world all cleaned up or thinking that the world can be all cleaned up. My whole training in Buddhism has been that there is no way to tie up all the loose ends. And that comes from my teachers and from the teachings. You're never going to erase the groundlessness. You're never going to have a neat, sweet little picture with no messiness, no matter how many rules you make. It's important to have all the different positions expressed, from the left to the right, from the most liberal to the most uptight.

I wouldn't want to see a list of "bad" teachers or "good" ones— here are the saints and here are the sinners. For so many of us that's our heritage, to make things one hundred percent right or one hundred percent wrong. It has been a big relief to me to slowly relax into the courage of living in the ambiguity. You can't make it right, can't make it wrong. I've never met anybody who was completely right or completely wrong. A lot of people see me as very trustworthy, and that gives me a lot of insight, because I know who I really am. Maybe on a scale of one to ten I'm pretty respectable, but still, it confirms that there is no all "right." And what does that mean anyway? My heroes are Gurdjieff and Chogyam Trungpa Rinpoche and Machig Labdron, the mad yogi of Bhutan. I like the wild ones. I'm the kind of person who only learns when I get thrown overboard and the sharks are coming after me.

As a woman I don't like that many male teachers misuse their positions and come on to women students. But I'm tempted to say that when a teacher is very realized it *is* actually different than when they're not. But who is to decide? Nobody can decide except the student who is in a relationship with that teacher. That's an unconditional relationship. You vow to stick by each other no matter what. And that teaches something about unconditionally sticking with your own life. When things revolt you and scare you, those things point out those parts of yourself that you are rejecting.

My personal teacher did not keep ethical norms and my devotion to him is unshakable. So I'm left with a big koan. But there are predictions from the time of the Buddha that say that when the rules and regulations become emphasized over liberation or realization it is the sign of the decline of Buddhism. Historically, there is always tension between things getting too tight and then too loose. From my view, it doesn't matter what is happening as long as it is all out in the open and we are not feeding into the fundamental source of suffering, which is ignorance. As long as there is a lot of dialogue and all the different feelings and views are being presented and are in debate, then it doesn't become some sort of McCarthyism where you have to hold a particular point of view—or watch out. It would be very unfortunate to think that we can smooth out all the rough edges. It would kill the spirit of Buddhism if it became uncomfortable or dangerous for people to hold opposing views.

I have arguments with friends who feel that keeping the five monastic precepts defines being a Buddhist. There are many different views, such as if you don't keep those precepts you cannot call yourself a Buddhist, or that if you eat meat you are not a Buddhist. I don't hold these views myself but I enjoy a good lively debate with people who do. I don't care what the views are as much as I care that people are out there debating them.

As a nun, it's not as if I don't like the precepts. The precepts represent no exit, "the wisdom of no escape." And they represent that there is no way to get away from yourself—ways that you usually use to build up your ego structure or that distract you from the groundlessness. They give you a clear mirror for seeing how you try to get ground under your feet and how we scramble to not feel that groundlessness. I live by those precepts and I live with people who live by those precepts, and I have seen them benefit people tremendously. But the argument I have sometimes with other monastic friends is whether every Buddhist should be strictly following those precepts. Precepts don't work if they're imposed from the outside like a straitjacket. You have to want to set the boundaries that tightly for them to be of benefit. If you force someone to keep the precepts when they do not want to or are not ready to, then it's like they're in prison.

A lot of people think that because I keep these precepts, I'm somehow above politics and scandal. So I can see that students want these clean role models. But clean role models were never that useful for me. My models were the people who stepped outside of conventional mind and who could actually stop my mind and completely open it up and free it, even for a moment, from a conventional, habitual way of looking at things. And so people look for different things. But to look for "safety" in a role model, someone that will never hurt you and always confirm you, is very dubious. If you are really preparing for groundlessness, preparing for the reality of human existence, you are living on the razor's edge, and you must become used to the fact that things shift and change. Things are not certain and they do not last and you do not know what is going to happen. My teachers have always pushed me over the cliff, and that is what has awakened my compassion for what human beings are up against. I am afraid that because of where we come from as Westerners, with our Judeo-Christian heritage, that if you get too focused on doctrine, on codifying, or ethics as a major emphasis, it just turns into harsh judgment. And then there is no genuine compassion.

Genuine compassion comes from the fact that you see your own limitations: you wish to be kind and you find that you aren't kind. Then, instead of beating yourself up, you see that that's what all human beings are up against and you begin to have some kind of genuine compassion for the human condition. And you see how challenging it is to be a human being. You try to be peaceful and never raise your voice and you find out that you have a lot of rage. The Dharma is about making friends with the groundlessness and discomfort of those feelings. It is not about making rules so that those emotions never arise. Compassion doesn't come from trying to clean up the whole act.

What we might call Big Mind, or Wisdom Mind, or Enlightenment, or Sacred Outlook, is the main thing. It actually doesn't have anything to do with religion or philosophy. People have human habitual patterns and are caught in a very small view of reality. It's not quite as small as that of a mouse or a flea, but it's really limited. And there is another whole way of perceiving that could be experienced by anybody. In my own sangha what was not emphasized early on and what is being emphasized now—or what people are ready for now—is compassion, the importance of our interconnectedness with each other. That would take care of all these rules. People need to see that if you hurt another person, you hurt yourself, and if you hurt yourself, you're hurting another person. And then to begin to see that we are not in this alone. We are in this together. For me, that's where the true morality comes from. That morality is based on much more profound seeing. That other morality is all about protecting "me." That is not the real intention of the precepts, but they can so easily be misused as a safety zone. To codify things on a grand scale is too moralistic, too based on right and wrong, and too based on fear and on wanting to get ground under your feet.

The best approach is to have a lot of different ways that suit different students. But if we lose sight of what we're really doing, then we have a problem. If we lose sight of the fact that it's all about relaxing into the fundamental groundlessness, the fundamental nonsubstantial nature, then that would be a problem. But let's just say that different students need different things in order to enter into that. If you're already a student and want to wake up fully, you're going to get the tests and challenges you need, and they're all going to come working with other people. And safety becomes wanting to avoid all that. I don't go out looking for trouble, but the big joke is trouble always comes knocking on your door. If you start to have a direct, honest relationship with reality, you know you're asking for trouble because it's not always going to congratulate you, it's not going to be convenient. And in the process you learn how life itself pulls out the rug.

Trungpa Rinpoche showed me that life wakes you up. It's tricky because the ego is so slippery. And my ego is still very slippery, but he got that message into me so that subsequently other people and other situations can show me where I am stuck and holding back and what my blind spots are. I'm haunted by the fact that I don't always see them.

Psychotherapy has a lot to offer Buddhism in terms of its language and because it really deals with people's suffering. And unfortunately, people can misuse Buddhism to try to just get comfortable. The teachings on the nature of emptiness can be misused to numb yourself out and circumvent real issues. But actually Buddhism is about diving into your real issues and fearlessly befriending the difficult and blocked areas and deep-seated habitual patterns that keep us stuck in ignorance and confusion. I feel that Buddhism can work together with psychotherapy. Buddhism can definitely work with people's real issues, it can be an enormously powerful tool and maybe work in balance with psychotherapy. But if it comes to making Buddhism into psychotherapy, then we risk losing a sense of vast mind and timelessness, the sense of magic, of having your whole conventional mind just dropped and seeing things in a fresh way, of making the mind available to insights that just completely cut the root of confusion. And psychotherapy doesn't do that. So the real challenge to my generation of teachers is to not water down Buddhism.

We need to ask, How many of the present generation of teachers actually have realized that Big Mind?

I think it's something that each teacher needs to be haunted by continually. Because we are in a prison of our own conception, a prison with a very tiny view. When you go to certain places in the world, places that some traditions call power spots, or you enter certain buildings or meet with certain people, you get popped out of your own mindset and realize you've been in prison. Then you see that you don't ever want to be in prison again. You don't want to go back to the narrow perspective of this habitual mind. But you also realize that the narrow perspective gives you a lot of security. You know it's false security, a lie, but starting to wake up is a lot like giving up an addiction. You're going to go through withdrawal symptoms, weaning yourself from this addiction to habitual, small-minded patterns of perception. You could say enlightenment is no more addiction. You're just fully awake, fully on the spot, without having to hide out.

This is the major challenge for teachers today—that we don't get stuck in mundane mind, in problem resolution, in concretizing, trying to put ground under our feet, and that we're willing to die over and over. Otherwise, we will never show that empty mind to our students.

I hold as a view that what I see in others is a reflection of me. I only know about myself. When I hear people judging very harshly, I feel I'm hearing as much about their hang-ups as I am about the issue. I'm hearing about the places in themselves that they can't relate to. No matter how much of an atrocity it is, if it's pushing your buttons so that it is causing great confusion in you, then you have got to look into your bewilderment in order to be able to communicate with the ugliness of that situation. Nothing ever changes in this world through hating the enemy. Nothing ever changes through aggression and hatred. So if it's pushing your buttons, whether it's Hitler or an abusive parent or an immoral war—Hitler was wrong, a parent who abuses a child is wrong—but you have got to keep working with your own negativity, with those feelings that keep coming up inside you. Because we have also had the experience of seeing wrong being done when there is no confusion and no bewilderment and we just say, Stop it!

No buttons have been pushed. It's just wrong, unaccompanied by righteous indignation. When I feel righteous indignation, I know that it has something to do with me. In order to be effective in stopping brutality on this planet you have to work with your own aggressions, with what has been triggered in you, so that you can communicate from the heart with the rapist, the abuser, the murderer.

When women come to me with feelings of anger and betrayal and complaints about male teachers, I never say, Oh, there's no harm being done, this is just your trip. I ask, Do you really want things to heal? Or do you just want to make someone wrong? Do you just want to get revenge on someone who hurt you or do you want things to heal? That's the question. Revenge never heals anything. And blaming others never heals anything. But what happens when someone speaks to you from the heart? Everyone responds to some kind of kindness, some kind of openness, some kind of curiosity, better than they do to hatred.

In this life we are not going to solve all the problems. But if you yourself are working with non-aggression and honesty, that can change the balance of aggression in the world. The bottom line for Dharma practitioners is not to get so involved with somebody being the enemy out there. That just adds more aggression. It is not Dharma to make the teacher that you feel is doing harm your enemy. You have to find a way to relate to the feelings that that teacher brings up in you and to communicate from the heart with that teacher. If another person is not healed, then you are not healed, and if you aren't, they aren't. The habitual human pattern is to try to get rid of our own suffering by blaming it on someone else, or by blaming it on oneself. In either case you make somebody wrong.

The Dharma is about stepping into the groundlessness of neither right nor wrong. Or not having the security of either right or wrong—that's the major challenge, to think bigger than just in terms of problem-solving. The Dharma is not about curing. It's about healing. The word that Trungpa Rinpoche used was "workable." All situations are workable. That's the nature of reality—it's workable.

1. Chogyam Trungpa, *Cutting Through Spiritual Materialism* (Boston: Shambhala Publications, 1973).

Glossary

Definitions for these terms are derived from several sources, primarily *The Encyclopedia of Eastern Philosophy and Religion* (Boston, Shambhala Publications, 1994), with additional glosses and interpretation. Terms used rarely and/or otherwise defined in the text are not repeated here.

Arahat (Pali): "worthy one"; a practitioner who has attained complete freedom from the origins of greed, hatred, and delusion and who, on passing away, enters nibbana. The spiritual ideal of Hinayana/Theravada Buddhism

Bhikkuni (Pali); **Bhikshuni** (Sanskrit): Buddhist nun. The terms for a Buddhist monk are Bhikku (Pali); Bhikshu (Sanskrit).

Bodhisattva (Sanskrit): "awakened being"; an enlightened being who vows to help liberate all other sentient beings before entering nirvana. The Mahayana spiritual ideal.

Dakini (Sanskrit): "sky-goer"; a Tibetan Buddhist term for a female personification of enlightened consciousness.

Dana (Pali): gift, alms, donation; an important Buddhist virtue, one of the six perfections *(paramita)*. In a broader sense, the spirit of generosity.

Dharma (Sanskrit): truth, law, doctrine; the Buddhist teachings. The lower-case term dharma(s) refers to fundamental phenomena.

Heart Sutra: a primary text of Mahayana Buddhism, distilled from the body of texts called the *Prajnaparamita* ("Perfection of Wisdom").

Hinayana (Sanskrit): "Small Vehicle"; a term applied by the later Mahayana Buddhist schools to the early Buddhist schools which stressed the arahat ideal (*see also* **Theravada**).

Karma (Sanskrit): "action"; a mental or physical action and the consequences of that action; the sum of all one's actions in present and previous lives; the chain of cause-and-effect.

Koan (Japanese): a conundrum or question used as an object of meditation in some forms of Zen practice, designed to subvert or exhaust the conventional, logical processes of mind. Used in a broader sense, any situation or quandary that challenges a practitioner to delve deeply into conscious awareness underlying a merely intellectual understanding.

Lama (Tibetan): a Tibetan Buddhist religious master or guru.

Mahayana (Sanskrit): "Great Vehicle"; a later development of Buddhism that emphasizes the bodhisattva ideal. Includes the Northern Buddhist schools (China, Japan, Korea, and some schools of Vietnamese Buddhism).

Mandala (Sanskrit): a symbolic representation of cosmic forces in two- or three-dimensional form, important in Tantric Buddhist philosophy and practice; understood as both "center and periphery" and a symbolic representation of the field of influence of a particular diety.

Metta (Pali); **Maitri** (Sanskrit): "loving-kindness"; a primary Buddhist virtue.

Metta Sutta (Pali): a primary Theravada text aimed at cultivating the quality of loving-kindness.

Mokugyo (Japanese): in the Zen tradition, a carved wooden drum used for sounding out the beat during chanting.

Nirvana (Sanskrit); **Nibbana** (Pali): the state of liberation from samsara; ultimate reality.

Prajna (Sanskrit): "wisdom"; transcendental wisdom or insight into ultimate reality.

Puja (Sanskrit): worship, ceremony, religious service.

Rakusu (Japanese): in the Zen tradition, a rectangular piece of fabric composed of sewn-together pieces, worn around the neck, which symbolizes the Buddha's robe.

Roshi (Japanese): "old master"; a Zen master.

Rinpoche (Tibetan): "precious one"; honorific term for an accomplished lama.

Sadhana (Sanskrit): in Vajrayana Buddhism, a term for a particular type of text and the meditation and visualization practices presented in it.

Samsara (Sanskrit): the cycle of existences in the world, characterized by suffering.

Sangha (Sanskrit): the community of ordained monks and nuns; in a broader sense, the community of Buddhist practitioners.

Satipatthana (Pali): a fundamental Hinayana meditational practice, focusing on mindfulness of body, feeling, and mind.

Satori (Japanese): a term for the experience of awakening.

Sensei (Japanese): teacher.

Sesshin (Japanese): in the Zen tradition, a period of intensive meditation practice.

Shunyata (Sanskrit): "emptiness"; ultimate reality; the lack of inherent, independent existence of persons or things.

Sutra (Sanskrit); **Sutta** (Pali): discourses and teachings attributed to the Buddha.

Tantra (Sanskrit): in Buddhism, a term for various kinds of texts, or a general term for the activity and practices of Vajrayana Buddhism, focusing on the human capacity for transformation utilizing all aspects of experience, positive and negative.

Theravada (Pali): "Way of the Elders"; Southern Buddhist school (Sri Lanka and the Buddhist countries of Southeast Asia) deriving its lineage from the earliest schools of Buddhism (*see also* Hinayana). Its principle texts, gathered in the *Tipitaka* (Sanskrit: *Tripitaka*),

"Three Baskets," which includes the *Sutta-pitaka,* the *Vinaya-pitaka* (the monastic code), and the *Abhidhamma-pitaka* (Sanskrit: *Abhidharma*), are collectively known as the Pali Canon.

Three Jewels (also **Triple Gem, Triple Treasure**): the Buddha, Dharma, and Sangha.

Upaya (Sanskrit): "skillful means"; the ability of a bodhisattva to guide beings to enlightenment using any efficacious method.

Vipassana (Pali); **Vipashyana** (Sanskrit): "penetrating insight"; a form of meditative practice that cultivates intuitive insight.

Vajrayana (Sanskrit): "Diamond Vehicle"; a school of Mahayana Buddhism that reached its full development in Tibet and the Himalayan region, which incorporates elements of ritual and visualization; commonly used as a synonym for Tibetan Buddhism or Tantric Buddhism.

Zafu (Japanese): round meditation cushion.

Zazen (Japanese): sitting meditation.

Zen (Japanese): Japanese rendering of the Chinese *Ch'an,* a transliteration of the Sanskrit *dhyana,* "meditation." A school of Mahayana Buddhism.

Zendo (Japanese): meditation hall.

Note on foreign terms: Many Japanese, Pali, Sanskrit, and Tibetan terms require the use of diacritical marks to render them phonetically correct; usages in this book appear in transliterated form (e.g. *sh* in shunyata; *ch* in bhavachakka) to approximate their pronunciation in English.

Selected Bibliography

This selection of recent works (published in the past decade) is a representative sampling of studies on women and Buddhism, works by and profiles of women Dharma teachers, and spiritual autobiographies and biographies. More comprehensive, scholarly, or topic-specific bibliographies can be found in many of the books cited here. For a good general bibliography including books and articles from the mid-1980s and earlier, see Sandy Boucher's *Turning the Wheel*.

Allione, Tsultrim. *Women of Wisdom.* London: Routledge & Kegan Paul, 1984; New York: Penguin/Arkana, 1986 (reprint).

Batchelor, Martine. *Walking on Lotus Flowers: Buddhist Women Living, Loving and Meditating.* London: Thorsons, 1996.

Beck, Joko. *Everyday Zen: Love and Work.* San Francisco: Harper & Row, 1989.
_____. *Nothing Special: Living Zen.* San Francisco: HarperSan Francisco, 1993.

Boorstein, Sylvia. *Don't Just Do Something, Sit There: A Mindfulness Retreat with Sylvia Boorstein.* San Francisco: HarperSan Francisco, 1996.
_____. *It's Easier Than You Think: The Buddhist Way to Happiness.* San Francisco: HarperSan Francisco, 1995.

Boucher, Sandy. *Opening the Lotus: What Women Want to Know About Buddhism.* Boston: Beacon Press, 1997.
_____. *Turning the Wheel: American Women Creating the New Buddhism.* Boston: Beacon Press, 1993 (revised edition).

Cabezón, José Ignacio, editor. *Buddhism, Sexuality, and Gender.* Albany, New York: State University of New York Press, 1992.

Chodron, Pema. *Start Where You Are: A Guide to Compassionate Living*. Boston: Shambhala Publications, 1994.

_____. *When Things Fall Apart: Heart Advice for Difficult Times*. Boston: Shambhala Publications, 1996.

_____. *The Wisdom of No Escape and the Path of Loving-Kindness*. Boston: Shambhala Publications, 1991.

Chodron, Thubten. *Open Heart, Clear Mind*. Ithaca, New York: Snow Lion Publications, 1990.

DuPrau, Jeanne. *The Earth House*. New York: Fawcett Columbine, 1992.

Feldman, Christina. *Quest of the Woman Warrior*. London: Aquarius, 1994.

_____. *Woman Awake: A Celebration of Women's Wisdom*. London: Penguin/Arkana, 1990.

Friedman, Lenore. *Meetings with Remarkable Women: Buddhist Teachers in America*. Boston: Shambhala Publications, 1987.

Galland, China. *Longing for Darkness: Tara and the Black Madonna*. New York: Penguin Books, 1990.

Gross, Rita M. *Buddhism After Patriarchy: A Feminist History, Analysis, and Reconstruction of Buddhism*. Albany, New York: State University of New York Press, 1992.

Halifax, Joan. *The Fruitful Darkness: Reconnecting with the Body of the Earth*. San Francisco: HarperSan Francisco, 1993.

Hirshfield, Jane, editor. *Women in Praise of the Sacred: 43 Centuries of Sacred Poetry*. San Francisco: HarperCollins, 1994.

Hopkinson, Deborah, Michele Hill, and Eileen Kiera, editors. *Not Mixing Up Buddhism: Essays on Women and Buddhist Practice*. Fredonia, New York: White Pine Press, 1986.

Huber, Cheri. *The Depression Book: Depression as an Opportunity for Spiritual Practice*. Mountain View, California: Keep it Simple (P.O. Box 91, Mountain View, California 94042), 1991.

_____. *The Fear Book: Facing Fear Once and For All*. Mountain View, California: Keep it Simple, 1995.

_____. *The Perils and Pitfalls of Practice: Responses to Questions About Meditation.* Mountain View, California: Keep it Simple, 1995.

_____. *That Which You Are Seeking Is Causing You To Seek.* Mountain View, California: Keep it Simple, 1990.

_____. *There is Nothing Wrong with You: Going Beyond Self-Hate.* Mountain View, California: Keep it Simple, 1993.

_____. *Trying to be Human: Zen Talks from Cheri Huber.* Mountain View, California: Keep it Simple, 1995.

_____. *Turning Toward Happiness: Conversations with A Zen Teacher and Her Students.* Mountain View, California: Keep it Simple, 1991.

Goldberg, Natalie. *Long Quiet Highway: Waking Up in America.* New York: Bantam Books, 1993.

Kabilsingh, Chatsumarn. *Thai Women in Buddhism.* Berkeley, California: Parallax Press, 1991.

Kaza, Stephanie. *The Attentive Heart: Conversations with Trees.* New York: Fawcett Columbine, 1993.

Khema, Ayya. *Being Nobody, Going Nowhere.* Boston: Wisdom Publications, 1987.

_____. *When the Iron Eagle Flies: Buddhism for the West.* London: Penguin/Arkana, 1991.

King, Sallie B., translator and annotator. *Journey in Search of the Way: The Spiritual Autobiography of Satomi Myodo.* Albany, New York: State University of New York Press, 1993 (reprint).

Klein, Anne Carolyn. *Meeting the Great Bliss Queen: Buddhists, Feminists, and the Art of the Self.* New York: Beacon Press, 1995.

Macy, Joanna. *World As Lover, World As Self.* Berkeley, California: Parallax Press, 1991.

McDonald, Kathleen. *How to Meditate: A Practical Guide.* Boston: Wisdom Publications, 1994 (revised edition).

Moon, Susan. *The Life and Letters of Tofu Roshi.* Boston: Shambhala Publications, 1988.

Murcott, Susan. *The First Buddhist Women: Translations and Commentaries on the Therigatha.* Berkeley, California: Parallax Press, 1991.

O'Halloran, Maura. *Pure Heart, Enlightened Mind: The Zen Journal and Letters of Maura "Soshin" O'Halloran.* New York: Riverhead Books, 1995 (reprint).

Packer, Toni. *The Work of this Moment.* Rutland, Vermont: Charles E. Tuttle & Co., 1995 (reprint).

Salzberg, Sharon. *Loving-Kindness: The Revolutionary Art of Happiness.* Boston: Shambhala Publications, 1995.

Shaw, Miranda. *Passionate Enlightenment: Women in Tantric Buddhism.* Princeton, New Jersey: Princeton University Press, 1995.

Shin, Nan. *Diary of a Zen Nun.* New York: Dutton, 1986.

Sidor, Ellen, editor. *A Gathering of Spirit: Women Teaching in American Buddhism.* Providence, Rhode Island: Primary Point Press, Kwan Um Zen School, 1987.

Suzuki, Mitsu. *Temple Dusk: Zen Haiku.* Translated by Kazuaki Tanahashi and Gregory Wood. Berkeley, California: Parallax Press, 1992.

Teich, Anne, editor. *Blooming in the Desert: Favorite Teachings of the Wildflower Monk Taungpulu Sayadaw.* Berkeley, California: North Atlantic Books, 1996.

Tsomo, Karma Lekshe, editor. *Buddhism Through American Women's Eyes.* Boston: Shambhala Publications, 1995.
_____. *Sakyadhita: Daughters of the Buddha.* Ithaca, New York: Snow Lion Publications, 1988.

Tworkov, Helen. *Zen in America: Profiles of Five Teachers and the Search for an American Buddhism.* Tokyo and New York: Kodansha, 1994 (revised edition).

Waldman, Anne, and Andrew Schelling, editors and translators. *Songs of the Sons and Daughters of the Buddha.* Boston: Shambhala Publications, 1996.

Willis, Jan, editor. *Feminine Ground: Essays on Women and Tibet.* Ithaca, New York: Snow Lion Publications, 1989 (reprint 1995).

Young, Serinity, editor. *An Anthology of Sacred Texts By and About Women.* New York: Crossroad Publishing Co., 1993.

Journals

The following publications are excellent resources for interviews and articles of interest to women Buddhist practitioners.

Common Boundary. Published bimonthly by Common Boundary, Inc., 5272 River Road, Suite 560, Bethesda, Maryland 20816.

Inquiring Mind. Published biannually by the Dharma Foundation, P.O. Box 9999, North Berkeley Station, Berkeley, California 94709.

Shambhala Sun. Published bimonthly by Shambhala Sun, 1345 Spruce Street, Boulder, Colorado 80302-4886.

Tricycle: The Buddhist Review. Published quarterly by The Buddhist Ray, Inc., 92 Vandam Street, New York, New York 10013.

Turning Wheel: The Journal of the Buddhist Peace Fellowship. Published quarterly by the Buddhist Peace Fellowship, P.O. Box 4650, Berkeley, California 94704.

Yoga Journal. Published bimonthly by the California Yoga Teachers Association, 2054 University Avenue, Berkeley, California 94704.

About the Contributors

Tsultrim Allione, M.A., is the founder and spiritual director of Tara Mandala, a retreat center in Southern Colorado, and the author of *Women of Wisdom.* In the late 1960s she traveled and studied in India and Nepal and in 1970 became the first American woman to be ordained as a nun by His Holiness the Karmapa. She lived as a nun for several years, during which time she received teachings from Apho Rinpoche, Dudjom Rinpoche, Dilgo Khyentse Rinpoche, Sapchu Rinpoche, Trungpa Rinpoche, and Khamtrul Rinpoche. Since 1980, she has been a student of Dzogchen master Namkhai Norbu Rinpoche and teaches under his guidance. Tsultrim teaches internationally and during the summer months leads retreats at Tara Mandala. For more information, contact Tara Mandala Retreat Center, P.O. Box 3040, Pagosa Springs, Colorado 81147; Tel: (970) 264-6177; Fax: (970) 264-6169.

Shosan Victoria Austin has practiced Zen for twenty-five years, twenty of them at San Francisco Zen Center. She was ordained as a priest by Zentatsu Richard Baker and as head monk at Tassajara Zen Mountain Monastery by Sojun Mel Weitsman. Besides Suzuki Sensei, other teachers who helped form her practice are Tenshin Reb Anderson, Shri B. K. S. Iyengar, and Shrimatra Geeta Iyengar. She is currently the Director of Zen Center, where she teaches yoga for sitters and sews Buddha's robe.

Anita Barrows, Ph.D, is Associate Institute Professor of Psychology at the Wright Institute and maintains a private practice in Berkeley, California. She has published two books of poetry and individual poems in numerous journals and anthologies, including *No More Masks, Rising Tides,* and *Voices from the Ark,* and she has received several awards and fellowships, including a National Endowment for the Arts grant and a Quarterly Review of Literature Award. With friends and colleagues, she is working to integrate psychological theory with deep ecology and Buddhist spirituality. She has been practicing vipassana for many years and lives in Berkeley with her two children and many animals.

Michele Benzamin-Masuda is resident co-teacher with her husband Christopher Reed at Ordinary Dharma in Santa Monica, California, and co-founder of Manzanita Village Retreat Center in Warner Springs, California. She holds lay ordination in Vietnamese Zen master Thich Nhat Hanh's Order of Interbeing. She is a fourth-degree black belt in aikido, holds third-degree rank in iaido (sword fighting), and has been teaching both martial art forms for thirteen years.

Erin Blackwell is a writer living in San Francisco, like her father before her. She is arts critic for the *Bay Area Reporter,* and served as Arts Editor for the lesbian monthly *Dykespeak* before it changed its name to *Icon.* At the Headlands Center for the Arts, she claims to be writing a novel. Special thanks to Lilith, a black cat who flew all the way from France to sit with her.

Sandy Boucher writes and teaches in Oakland, California. She is the author of *Turning the Wheel: American Women Creating the New Buddhism.* Her new book is *Opening the Lotus: What Women Want to Know About Buddhism.*

Alta Brown, Ph.D., is an Adjunct Professor at The Institute of Buddhist Studies/The Graduate Theological Union, Berkeley, California and The Immaculate Heart College Center's M.A. Program in Feminist Spirituality, Los Angeles, California. She has been a student of Vajrayana Buddhism for twenty-five years and is being trained to be a Khenpo (Master of Studies) in that tradition. Her specialty is Buddhist ethics, particularly the practice of compassion in contemporary American society. She is the mother of six children and lives in Boulder, Colorado.

Pema Chodron is an American nun in the Kagyu lineage of Tibetan Buddhism, and Director of Gampo Abbey in Cape Breton, Nova Scotia. She was a student of the late Chogyam Trungpa Rinpoche and in 1974 received the novice ordination from His Holiness Gyalwa Karmapa. She took the full nun's ordination in 1981. She is the author of *The Wisdom of No Escape and the Path of Loving-Kindness*, *Start Where You Are: A Guide to Compassionate Living*, and *When Things Fall Apart: Heart Advice for Difficult Times*.

Thubten Chodron has been a Buddhist nun since 1977. She currently lives and teaches in Seattle with the Dharma Friendship Foundation and travels internationally to lead retreats. Her books include *Open Heart, Clear Mind* and *What Color Is Your Mind?* She helped organize "Life As a Western Buddhist Nun," the first training program for Western Buddhist nuns of the Tibetan tradition held in Bodh Gaya, India in spring 1996.

Ji Ko Linda Ruth Cutts is a Zen Priest with the San Francisco Zen Center where she has practiced since 1971. She is currently Tanto, Head of Practice, at Green Gulch Farm, where she teaches and lives with her husband and their two children.

Nina Egert is an ethnomusicologist, performance artist, photographer, and videographer, and is currently a doctoral candidate in anthropology at the University of California, Berkeley. She has been a Buddhist practitioner for over twenty years in the Nyingma sect of Himalayan Buddhism. She recently concluded her field research on the performative aspects of Buddhist ritual practices in India and the United States.

Melody Ermachild Chavis is a private investigator, a mother, and a grandmother. She studies with Sojun Mel Weitsman at the Berkeley Zen Center.

Barbara Gates is a writer living in Berkeley, California, with her husband Patrick and her seven-year-old daughter Caitlin. She has been practicing vipassana meditation since 1975. As co-editor of the journal *Inquiring Mind,* she explores Buddhism through writing about daily life.

Rita M. Gross is professor of Comparative Studies on Religion at the University of Wisconsin, Eau Claire, and a longtime student of Chogyam Trungpa Rinpoche. She is the author of *Buddhism After Patriarchy: A Feminist History, Analysis, and Reconstruction of Buddhism* and *Feminism and Religion: An Introduction.*

Jane Hirshfield is the author of three collections of poetry, most recently *The October Palace.* She has edited *Women in Praise of the Sacred: Forty-Three Centuries of Spiritual Poetry by Women* and *The Ink Dark Moon: Poems by Komachi and Shikibu, Women of the Ancient Court of Japan.* Her honors include fellowships from the Guggenheim and Rockefeller Foundations, as well as the Poetry Center Book Award, Bay Area Book Reviewers Award, and Commonwealth Club Poetry Medal. She practiced at San Francisco Zen Center, Tassajara Zen Mountain Monastery, and Green Gulch Farm between 1974 and 1982, and received lay ordination in 1979.

bell hooks is the author of several books, including *Ain't I A Woman? Black Women and Feminism, Talking Back: Thinking Feminist, Thinking Black, Black Looks: Race and Representation, Outlaw Culture: Resisting Representations, Art on My Mind,* and *Killing Rage: Ending Racism.* She is Distinguished Professor of English at City College, New York.

Anne Carolyn Klein is Professor and Chair of the Department of Religious Studies, Rice University, and a meditation instructor. Her most recent books are *Meeting the Great Bliss Queen: Buddhists, Feminists, and the Art of the Self* and *Oral Madhyamika in Tibet.* Since 1970 she has studied Buddhist thought and practice in the academy and with traditional teachers in the United States and Asia. Her primary teaching authorization is from the Nyingma Dzogchen Lama Khetsun Sangpo Rinpoche of Kathmandu, Nepal. She is co-director of Dawn Mountain, a Tibetan temple, community center, and research institute in Houston, Texas.

Susan Moon is a writer and Zen practitioner living in Berkeley, California. She is the author of a book of humorous fiction, *The Life* *and Letters of Tofu Roshi,* and the editor of *Turning Wheel: The Journal of the Buddhist Peace Fellowship.*

Kate O'Neill, M.Ed., has been a woman all her life—except when she was a girl. She has been practicing vipassana and Zen meditation since 1986, and was ordained into Thich Nhat Hanh's Tiep Hien Order (Order of Interbeing) in 1992. She lives in northern New Mexico, where she counsels, teaches, paints, writes, and meditates.

Lori Pierce, Master's of Theological Studies, Harvard Divinity School, 1990, is currently a doctoral candidate in American Studies at the University of Hawai'i, Manoa. Her dissertation focuses on Buddhism in America from 1945 to the present. She lives in Honolulu with her husband Marty Heitz and their daughter, Kaily.

Maylie Scott is a priest at the Berkeley Zen Center, where she has practiced for twenty-five years. She teaches and practices every other month with the Arcata Zen Group in Northern California, and works closely with the Buddhist Peace Fellowship, especially as a mentor for the BASE (Buddhist Alliance for Social Engagement) Program. She is involved in a variety of social activism and service projects.

Marilyn Senf is a psychologist who works as a psychotherapist in community mental health and in private practice in Oakland, California. She also teaches psychology at JFK University in Orinda, California. She trained in intersubjective and psychodynamic therapies in London and received her doctorate in psychology from the Wright Institute in Berkeley, California, with a dissertation on the revalorization of the feminine in psychoanalytic therapy. She has been practicing vipassana meditation since 1983.

Miranda Shaw, Ph.D., Harvard University, is the author of *Passionate Enlightenment: Women in Tantric Buddhism.* She currently teaches Buddhism and goddess traditions in the Department of Religion at the University of Richmond, Virginia and travels frequently to the Himalayas researching sacred dance, goddesses, and the survival of women's ancient spiritual traditions there.

Judith Simmer-Brown is chair of the Religious Studies department at The Naropa Institute in Boulder, Colorado. She was trained in South Asian religions and Sanskrit at Columbia University, the University of British Columbia, and Waldon University, and taught previously at Fordham University and Western Washington University. She has practiced Buddhism for twenty-five years, and is a student of Chogyam Trungpa Rinpoche. She is a board member of the Society of Buddhist-Christian Studies and of Shambhala International, and is currently writing a book on the feminine principle in Tibetan Buddhism.

Anne Teich has been a student of Buddhism since 1975, and is a founding member of Taungpulu Kaba-Aye Monastery in Boulder Creek, California. She received her doctorate in Buddhist Studies from the California Institute of Integral Studies in 1990. She is the editor of *Blooming in the Desert: Favorite Teachings of the Wildflower Monk Taungpulu Sayadaw*.

Sallie Jiko Tisdale is a Consulting Editor to *Tricycle: The Buddhist Review*, a Contributing Editor to *Harper's*, and the author of several books. She is a lay disciple of Kyogen Carlson Sensei at Dharma Rain Zen Center in Portland, Oregon.

Anne Waldman is the author of over thirty books of poetry, including most recently *Kill or Cure, IOVIS: All is Full of Jove, Books I and II, Fast Speaking Woman* (Twentieth Anniversary Edition), and translations with Andrew Schelling, *Songs of the Sons and Daughters of the Buddha*. She is the editor of *The Beat Book* and co-editor of *Disembodied Poetics: Annals of the Jack Kerouac School*. She co-founded the Kerouac School at The Naropa Institute in Boulder, Colorado with Allen Ginsberg in 1974. She is a renowned performer of her own work and has performed extensively in the United States and abroad.

Celeste West is director of the San Francisco Zen Center library and bookstore, Dharma dojo for tantrics who love to use words to go beyond words. Celeste met her first Zenoids in a Portland, Oregon beatnik coffeehouse in the early 1960s, and instantly loved Zen minimalism, iconoclasm, humor, and paradox. In 1989, she took the Precepts from Abbot and Laughing Buddha Issan Dorsey at the Hartford Street Zen Center in San Francisco, and is gradually learning the Way of Zen Freelance. She is the author of six books, most recently *Lesbian Polyfidelity: A Pleasure Guide for All Women Whose Hearts Are Open to Multiple Sensualoves, or How to Keep Nonmonogamy Safe, Sane, Honest & Laughing, You Rogue.*

Kate Wheeler, a Contributing Editor to *Tricycle: The Buddhist Review,* is a Buddhist practitioner. She is the author of a collection of stories, *Not Where I Started From,* and edited *In This Very Life* by Sayadaw U Pandita. She has won many prizes and awards for her fiction, and was recently nominated by *Granta* as one of the twenty best novelists under forty in the United States.

Jan Willis is Professor of Religion and Walter A. Crowell Professor of the Social Sciences at Wesleyan University, Middletown, Connecticut. She has studied with Tibetan Buddhists in India, Nepal, Switzerland, and the United States for almost three decades, and has taught for twenty-two years. She is the author of *The Diamond Light: An Introduction to Tibetan Buddhism, On Knowing Reality: The Tattvartha Chapter of Asanga's Bodhisattvabhumi,* and *Enlightened Beings: Life Stories from the Ganden Oral Tradition;* and the editor of *Feminine Ground: Essays on Women and Tibet.* She has published numerous essays and articles on Buddhist meditation, hagiography, and women and Buddhism.